Praise for *The Court v. The Voters*

"Are you worried about American democracy? Are you hoping the Supreme Court will save us? Well, for the last five decades, in cases from *Bush v. Gore* to *Citizens United v. FEC*, the right-leaning Court has regularly sided with democracy's enemies. In this incisive, eloquent, and important book, Joshua Douglas has the receipts—and a warning about what the Court might do to us next."

—Adam Cohen, author of *Supreme Inequality:*
The Supreme Court's Fifty-Year Battle for a More Unjust America

"In evaluating election rules, the Supreme Court now deemphasizes harm to voters and defers to state lawmakers. But this distressing story doesn't end here, as Douglas shares his judicious strategies for shoring up our democracy."

—Jennifer Frost, author of *"Let Us Vote!":*
Youth Voting Rights and the 26th Amendment

"Josh Douglas reminds us in *The Court v. The Voters* of Alexander Hamilton's prediction that of the branches of government, the judiciary 'will always be the least dangerous to the political rights of the Constitution.' Not anymore, he argues eloquently in this passionate book that briskly but thoughtfully analyzes nine key Supreme Court cases. One of the country's leading election law experts, Douglas shows how the Supreme Court has become 'the most dangerous branch' when it comes to voting rights and the power of political money. An important guide for all who want to protect and advance American democracy."

—E. J. Dionne Jr., author of *Why Americans Hate Politics*
and coauthor of *100% Democracy: The Case for Universal Voting*

"Joshua Douglas has written another required read for those interested in the complicated history of voting rights in the United States. These cases are necessary for understanding where we are, and Douglas has offered clarifying explanations of their continued relevance to our country's modern struggles."

—Jessica Huseman, editorial director of Votebeat

"Professor Douglas persuasively shows how the Supreme Court has profoundly undermined American democracy. He tells the story of nine cases, beginning in 1974, that individually and together have done great damage to the election system in the United States. Saving our democracy requires taking the lessons of this book, and its recommendations, very seriously."

—Erwin Chemerinsky, dean and Jesse H. Choper Distinguished
Professor of Law, University of California, Berkeley School of Law

"In this smart and important book, Joshua Douglas expertly explains and demystifies urgent topics all Americans need to know and understand: how the Supreme Court spent decades chipping away at voting rights, and what our country can do now to repair the damage."

—Erin Geiger Smith, author of *Thank You for Voting*

"Josh Douglas's detailed examination of how key U.S. Supreme Court cases have harmed the interests of voters is incredibly useful—and disturbing! Professor Douglas provides the correct diagnosis: a series of compounding rulings have severely undermined the fundamental right of voters to participate meaningfully in our democracy."

—Trevor Potter, president, Campaign Legal Center

"Progressive voters are angry at the Supreme Court for failing to protect voting rights, but many do not understand exactly what the Court did or the stories behind the cases. Joshua Douglas offers a readable field guide to *Citizens United*, *Bush v. Gore*, and other notorious election cases that is sure to edify and disturb the curious reader."

—Richard L. Hasen, author of *A Real Right to Vote*

"*The Court v. The Voters* is required reading for anyone concerned about the future of American democracy. Douglas removes legalese, uses compelling and accessible human stories, and connects the dots to show how an activist U.S. Supreme Court is complicit in dismantling democracy by making up new rules that allow politicians to entrench themselves and suppress the voices of voters."

—Spencer Overton, author of *Stealing Democracy: The New Politics of Voter Suppression*

"Citizens who want to understand the constitutional rules around voting often feel like people entering a play halfway through—the main players throw around case names and doctrines that are unfamiliar and confusing, and ordinary readers get the message that they are outsiders at their own elections. Joshua Douglas, who has devoted his career to understanding election law—and reforming it so that all Americans can vote—here untangles the plot of the play and explains in clear, nontechnical language how we got to the present mess and how We the People can get out of it."

—Garrett Epps, author of *American Epic: Reading the U.S. Constitution*

"This book empowers Americans to understand the downfall of our democracy—and to do something about it. From decreasing voter turnout among minorities and the poor to setting the stage for the January 6th insurrection, Douglas explains how Supreme Court rulings have brought our political system to its knees. In addition to exposing the causes of our electoral crisis and recommending promising solutions, this book will resonate with citizens on a personal level. Douglas's earnest and accessible text stands as a rare feat of critical legal scholarship for the people."

—Timothy K. Kuhner, author of *Tyranny of Greed* and *Capitalism v. Democracy*

THE
COURT
v. THE
VOTERS

JOSHUA A. DOUGLAS

THE COURT v. THE VOTERS

THE TROUBLING STORY OF HOW THE SUPREME COURT HAS UNDERMINED VOTING RIGHTS

BEACON PRESS · BOSTON

BEACON PRESS
Boston, Massachusetts
www.beacon.org

Beacon Press books
are published under the auspices of
the Unitarian Universalist Association of Congregations.

27 26 25 24   8 7 6 5 4 3 2 1

This book is printed on acid-free paper that meets the uncoated paper
ANSI/NISO specifications for permanence as revised in 1992.

Text design and composition by Kim Arney

Library of Congress Cataloging-in-Publication Data
Names: Douglas, Joshua A., author.
Title: The Court v. the voters : the troubling story of how the Supreme
Court has undermined voting rights / Joshua A. Douglas.
Other titles: Court vs. the voters
Description: Boston : Beacon Press, 2024. | Includes bibliographical
references and index. | Summary: "An urgent and gripping look at the
erosion of voting rights and its implications for democracy, told
through the stories of 9 Supreme Court decisions-and the
next looming case" —Provided by publisher.
Identifiers: LCCN 2023051015 | ISBN 9780807010938 (hardcover) |
ISBN 9780807010945 (ebook)
Subjects: LCSH: Voting—United States. | Suffrage—United States. |
United States. Supreme Court—Decision making.
Classification: LCC KF4891 .D68 2024 | DDC 342.73/072—dc23/eng/20231204
LC record available at https://lccn.loc.gov/2023051015

To Caitlyn and Harrison:

One day, when you read this book, I hope you will be proud of your dad's efforts to explain these important issues of American democracy to all who care about its strength and endurance.

And I hope you grow up to do your own small part to sustain that democracy for yourselves and for future generations.

Elections belong to the people.

—ABRAHAM LINCOLN

CONTENTS

INTRODUCTION

I couldn't believe my eyes. Was this really the America I knew? Was this truly the country celebrated around the world for its freedom? Was this the democracy I had pledged my life's work to study, with the hope of protecting and expanding the constitutional right to vote—the most fundamental right in our society—for everyone?

My phone was ablaze with calls and text messages. "What is happening?" a friend wrote. "This isn't America," another said. Journalists were calling to ask me to explain what was going on. I had no answers. I checked in with loved ones who lived in the nation's capital, making sure they were OK. I wanted to stop watching, but just like with a horrible car accident on the side of the road, no one could avert their eyes. I couldn't eat. I couldn't sleep.

Certain dates have special significance to our collective conscious. December 7, 1941, will always be a "day that lives in infamy" because of the attack on Pearl Harbor.[1] My parents can tell you about the exact moment they learned JFK had been assassinated on November 22, 1963. I remember September 11, 2001—I was in college in D.C. and could see the smoke from the plane that flew into the Pentagon—like it was yesterday.

January 6, 2021, will be etched in my mind forever.

I will never forget the unprecedented, abhorrent violence that unfolded at the U.S. Capitol that day, as Donald Trump's supporters stormed the Capitol to disrupt Congress as it tallied the Electoral College votes from the 2020 presidential election, which Joe Biden had decisively and fairly won. I'm an election law scholar, so (quite geekily) I had that date marked on my calendar for months, knowing that it would be a key moment for formally electing the president. The process on January 6 is normally boring and sleepy as members of Congress go through the ritual of declaring the winner of the presidential election. But instead of a routine matter, we all watched in shock as an insurrection exploded at the U.S. Capitol. I had expected some verbal fireworks on the floor of the House of Representatives that year given the volatile politics of the time, but I couldn't believe that armed insurrectionists had breached the Capitol itself. I gasped in horror at the ways they were defacing the halls of Congress and desecrating its grounds. I remember telling my kids to stop watching the TV because of the violent images.

January 6 revealed the fragility of our democratic institutions in a way that sickened so many of us. The presidency had fallen into the hands of an egotistical individual concerned only with himself and his unrelenting desire to stay in power. Donald Trump never promoted democracy. Much of Congress, too, had fallen under his grip: 147 Republicans voted to overturn election results in key states in an effort to subvert the will of the people—even after the violence had subsided and order was restored.[2]

While anti-democracy, power-hungry politicians had infiltrated the presidency and Congress, the third branch of government—the courts—served as a bulwark to these forces in the aftermath of the 2020 election. The Supreme Court rejected several frivolous lawsuits that sought to call the legitimacy of the election into question. In that sense, the Court stood for democracy—it refused to intervene to throw the election to the losing candidate. The Court very well could have offered a forum for Trump and his followers, but that would have been an obvious power grab that would have led to even further calamities.

But the Supreme Court is not blameless for what happened that day. The Court's rulings over the past fifty years have actively undermined voting rights, showing that judicial decisions can impact election outcomes. Trump and his supporters latched on to the wild idea that certain state legislatures could overturn the election results by awarding him their Electoral College votes or that courts would do his bidding. Too many people thought it was possible for state legislatures to simply overturn the vote totals based on the notion that state legislatures have unfettered power in this area and that the constitutional right to vote is secondary. Many of the Supreme Court's decisions over the past five decades have promulgated this crabbed view of voters' rights.

To understand the current crisis in American democracy, we need to focus on the Supreme Court. Its decisions laid the foundation for Donald Trump and his supporters in Congress to call the 2020 presidential election into question despite a total lack of evidence that the outcome was in doubt. Perhaps even more concerning, the Court has also given the green light to state legislatures to enact rules that severely restrict the right to vote by deferring to state election laws, even when those rules harm certain voters.

CAN WE TRUST THE SUPREME COURT TO PROTECT DEMOCRACY?

The Supreme Court of the United States is anti-democracy and anti-voter—and has been for far longer than you might think.

That's a bold claim, at least when considering prior public opinion surveys about the Court. An ABC survey from January 2021, soon after the January 6 insurrection at the U.S. Capitol, asked respondents whether they thought the Supreme Court would "protect democracy in the United States." Almost 60 percent of respondents said they trusted the Court to protect American democracy—15 percent said they trusted the Court "a great deal" and 44 percent said "a good amount."[3] The Court ranked higher on this question than Donald Trump, Joe Biden, Mike Pence, Republicans or Democrats in Congress, Nancy Pelosi, Ted Cruz, Mitt Romney, and Mitch McConnell.[4] Another poll, this one from October 2022 by the *New York Times* and Siena College, found that, of those who believed American democracy was under threat, 36 percent said the Supreme Court was "not a threat to democracy" and only 27 percent said it was a "major threat to democracy."[5] That said, overall trust in the Supreme Court decreased significantly in 2022 after the Court overturned *Roe v. Wade*.[6]

A close analysis of the Supreme Court's rulings reveals that—in a project that has spanned decades—the Court has contributed to the rise of anti-democracy forces animating our elections. Its decisions unduly defer to state legislators to craft election rules that help politicians stay in power while failing to protect voters. The Declaration of Independence says that a government's legitimacy derives from the consent of the governed, yet the Court's decisions have allowed entrenched politicians to suppress the votes of people who might vote against them.

This is not just a problem from *Bush v. Gore*, which essentially ended the 2000 presidential election dispute and led to George W. Bush winning Florida, and therefore the presidency, even though he had not received the most votes nationwide. It also doesn't stem only from *Citizens United*, the 2010 case about corporations and unions spending big money in campaigns. To be sure, these cases have been terrible for voting rights, but they were terrible in part because of the cases that preceded them, when the Court's rulings laid the groundwork for many of today's electoral dilemmas. A robust analysis of the continuing validity of American democracy requires a full reckoning with the Supreme Court's nefarious role in undermining it.

VOTING WRONGS INSTEAD OF VOTING RIGHTS

As a nation, we have a sorry history when it comes to the right to vote. In many states at the founding, only white, male property owners could cast a ballot. As historian Alexander Keyssar noted, "By 1790, according to most estimates, roughly 60–70 percent of adult white men (and very few others) could vote."[7] Slowly the franchise has expanded, most notably due to the Nineteenth Amendment, which gave women the right to vote, and the Voting Rights Act of 1965, a watershed law that broke down barriers to racial minority participation and representation. The Supreme Court issued rulings on several cases in the 1960s that robustly protected individual voters.[8] We were, at least in theory, steadily marching toward the ideal of greater inclusion that epitomizes a "more perfect union."

Unfortunately, in many states the legal rules on voting have backtracked since then. Instead of serving as a fail-safe protector of voters, the Court has approved the denial of voting rights to individuals convicted of felonies, endorsed strict voter ID laws, sanctioned gerrymandering, and dismantled the Voting Rights Act—one of the most important civil rights laws ever enacted. The Court hasn't advertised its move toward deference to states, with its accompanying harm to voters. It rules in incremental ways—chipping away a little here, a little there—until what's left is a legal doctrine that gives entrenched politicians wide leeway to enact self-serving rules that help them remain in power.

Numerous cases from the past five decades have fundamentally changed the way we run our elections—and, as a result, our entire society. The Supreme Court's rulings have skewed election laws, which in turn can affect who wins (and who decides to run in the first place). We often think of the Court as an independent actor that will stand up for constitutional ideals, including the right to vote. But the reality is that the Court's recent history has eroded voting rights and fair representation. All too often people view cases involving voting rights as the product of arcane legalese rather than a sustained attack on democracy. This book aims to change that narrative.

How did I decide which Supreme Court cases to profile? Anyone can quibble with a "top ten" (or "bottom ten") list of bad decisions, and there were certainly several awful rulings that didn't make the cut. There are, of course, much older cases that harmed the cause of democracy, but thankfully, most of those cases have been overruled. I wanted to explore the cases that still impact current law to this day.[9]

I started with the biggies. A book about the Supreme Court and voting rights must include *Bush v. Gore*, which opened the door to many other election law claims. Another obvious choice was the campaign finance case of *Citizens United*, which has contributed to skewed representation—but perhaps not in the way you might think. *Shelby County v. Holder*, the 2013 case that gutted the vital protections of the Voting Rights Act, was another important inflection point.

But I wanted to dig deeper to understand how and why the Court has moved away from the democracy-protective institution it once purported to be. The Warren Court of the 1960s (named after Chief Justice Earl Warren, who led the Court during this time) issued numerous rulings that upheld the right to vote and demanded a fair and equal democracy. Then, several cases in the 1970s, 1980s, and 1990s pulled back on the constitutional protection for voters, laying the groundwork for the Court's current jurisprudence. These older cases gave cover for newer conservative justices to write even more restrictive rulings. It's vital to understand these cases so that we can begin to unravel the Court's anti-democracy forces. Simply put, merely overruling *Bush v. Gore* or *Citizens United* won't fix our electoral woes. We need to go back to these earlier cases to understand why the Court blesses restrictive state voting rules without much oversight and places a heavy burden on voters who seek to exercise their fundamental rights.

There are tangible, real-world effects from the Court's voting rights decisions. After strong voter turnout in the January 2021 Georgia runoff election for the U.S. Senate, with two Democrats winning, the Republican-controlled state legislature immediately passed a law limiting the number of drop boxes available for people to deliver their ballots, among other restrictions.[10] Soon after the *Shelby County* case that immobilized the Voting Rights Act, North Carolina passed a massive voter suppression law that harmed voters by restricting voter registration opportunities and early voting.[11] Texas enacted a strict voter ID requirement, where your gun license—but not your state-issued student ID—counts for casting your ballot.[12] These state legislatures knew, because of the Court's rulings, that they were on solid constitutional footing in promulgating these laws, which erect significant barriers to the ballot box for already-marginalized communities. These examples barely scratch the surface of the multilayered attempt to skew representation through restrictive voting rules.

This book tells the story of the Supreme Court's hard turn toward anti-democracy and unequal voting rights in the last fifty years, with a conclusion that offers a path forward during these perilous times. A series of Supreme Court cases has helped to create an election system that is fundamentally unfair. Each case profiled in this book might seem straightforward by itself: one involves a state's ban on write-in voting, another is about a strict voter ID law, and yet another dives into felon disenfranchisement. There are cases that interpret the U.S. Constitution and others on the Voting Rights Act. In isolation, each individual case might not seem that bad. We still have elections and the declared winners still take office. But the cases are interconnected in a way that paints a broad—and dangerous—picture: at every turn, politicians have won and individual voters have lost. The decisions have built on each other to make it almost impossible to challenge a restriction on the right to vote, an unfair gerrymandered map, or a limit on the overwhelming amount of money spent in campaigns. Politicians can pass election rules that will help them win the next election and stay in office. We can no longer count on the Supreme Court to protect an equal right to vote for all. Voters are left with nowhere to turn to vindicate their rights.

Many people may think that legal issues are too arcane for them to follow or that complex Supreme Court decisions don't have much of a real-world impact on their everyday lives. Sometimes it might seem easier simply to ignore what is happening in the halls of government. But that would be a big mistake. Judicial decisions, especially those about democracy, have a major influence on self-governance, which is the very ideal on which our country was founded. Our constitutional rights are only as strong as our ability to exercise them meaningfully. Elected officials make countless decisions—on tax policy, educational quality, reproductive autonomy, climate change, immigration, public safety, and scores of other issues—that impact all of us. Who serves in these offices matters a lot. We the People should decide—in a free, fair, and equal process—who that is. Sure, many voters might not face obstacles when casting a ballot, but tons of voters do—and those individuals are often members of marginalized communities already.

Voters are the lifeblood of our democracy—and are also the focus of this book. Supreme Court cases always have real people behind them, from the Hawaiian activist who didn't like the listed candidates on the ballot and sought to write in someone else, to one of the longest-serving Black state lawmakers in the country, to a courageous voting rights lawyer-turned-state-supreme-court-justice who fought for fair representation, to everyday people who stood up for the right to vote. The book tells the stories of these amazing individuals to drive home the real-world impact of the Supreme Court's decisions. The stories within the cases help to make the legal concepts accessible; the lessons of the cases should concern anyone who cares about the strength and endurance of our democracy.

In law school I took a course on voting rights law. That class opened my eyes to how law and democracy intertwine to create a system that is subject to manipulation as politicians seek power. While many of my friends entered corporate law, I took a different path and focused on election law, which many people back then thought was a niche field. The presidential election occurs only once every four years, so was this work even relevant most of the time? Of course, these days election law has become an all-the-time concern, even in years without a national election. As a law professor, I see it as my job to shed a light on the ways in which our democracy isn't working as it should, with all of us having an equal say in whom we elect so we can collectively determine the best policies for society as a whole. I wrote this book to explain to voters, who are the most important actors within our system, just how much the decks are stacked against us.

Numerous Supreme Court cases, one building on the next, have produced a broken electoral system. We can—and should—lament the democracy that might have been. And then, we can—and should—double down in our efforts to protect the right to vote, the most fundamental and vital right in our democracy.

CHAPTER 1

THE 1980 ELECTION AND THE BEGINNING OF THE END

Anderson v. Celebrezze (1983)

	JUSTICE	APPOINTED BY
MAJORITY	Stevens, John Paul (*authored majority opinion*)	Ford, Gerald (R)
	Burger, Warren (chief justice)	Eisenhower, Dwight D. (R)
	Brennan, William J., Jr.	Eisenhower, Dwight D. (R)
	Marshall, Thurgood	Johnson, Lyndon B. (D)
	Blackmun, Harry A.	Nixon, Richard (R)
DISSENT	Rehnquist, William H. (*authored dissent*)	Nixon, Richard (R)
	White, Byron	Kennedy, John F. (D)
	Powell, Lewis F., Jr.	Nixon, Richard (R)
	O'Connor, Sandra Day	Reagan, Ronald (R)

It might seem strange to begin our exploration of how the Supreme Court has broken the right to vote with the 1980 presidential election. The result was a landslide, with Republican Ronald Reagan crushing the incumbent, Democratic president Jimmy Carter by a 489 to 49 vote in the Electoral College.[1] Reagan received almost 44 million popular votes compared to Carter's 35 million.[2] Reagan won forty-four states to Carter's six (Georgia, Hawaii, Maryland, Minnesota, Rhode Island, and West Virginia), plus Washington, D.C.[3] The election was a total rebuke of Carter, stemming from disapproval surrounding his handling of the Iran hostage crisis and a stagnant economy. Republicans also won control of the U.S. Senate for the first time since 1954.

What was so special about the 1980 election for the constitutional right to vote? The answer comes from the independent run for president by John Anderson, a significant political figure in 1980—at least for a few months, while his candidacy was hot! Anderson's legacy may be lost on most of us now, but his influence on the world of voting rights—through the Supreme Court case that bears his name—lives on.

WHO WAS JOHN ANDERSON?

John B. Anderson was born in 1922 in Rockford, Illinois—the same Rockford featured in the movie *A League of Their Own* based on the city's all-female baseball team, the Rockford Peaches. The son of Swedish immigrants, he worked at his family's grocery store when he was young. He was his high school's valedictorian before heading off to college at the University of Illinois, and then on to law school. When World War II interrupted his legal studies, he served in the U.S. Army and received four battle service stars before returning home to re-enroll in law school, earning a juris doctor degree from the University of Illinois College of Law in 1946.[4]

Anderson met his wife, Keke, after she took his passport picture; he proposed via telegram three months later and they were married for sixty-four years.[5] After working as a lawyer in Rockford, earning a master of law from Harvard, and serving in the U.S. Foreign Service in Berlin, he entered political life in 1956, winning the race for state's attorney in Winnebago County, Illinois. Four years later, when the incumbent Republican member of Congress announced his retirement, Anderson decided to enter the race. The district was decidedly Republican, so whoever won the five-person primary would likely also win the general election. Anderson came out on top in the primary and then won the seat that November. He would serve in Congress for twenty years, entering the presidential race during his tenth term.[6]

Anderson's initial years in Congress were marked by staunchly conservative viewpoints—at least, conservative for the time. He earned a "zero" rating from the liberal group Americans for Democratic Action. His Republican colleagues elected him as chair of the House Republican

Conference in 1969, the party's third-ranking position. But his views began to moderate in the late 1960s and '70s. He championed the Fair Housing Act in 1968 and spoke out against Richard Nixon regarding the Watergate scandal. Though he remained a conservative, Anderson's daughter recalled that he "evolved both personally and professionally on social issues" throughout his career.[7] NPR host Scott Simon recalled Anderson's early embrace of gay rights, "or—what he called in his Illinois prairie twang—affectional preference."[8] Rob Richie, who knew him through the organization FairVote, described Anderson as "unassuming," "someone people wanted to listen to and appreciate," and an "indefatigable optimist about what our democracy can be."[9]

In 1978 Anderson faced his first major congressional primary challenge from the right when Don Lyon, a conservative minister, ran against him. Lyon attacked Anderson relentlessly for not being conservative enough. Anderson won the primary, but that experience left him disillusioned. "It drove home to me in a very personal way the almost violent way in which the conservative wing of the Republican Party would seek to deal with someone whom they felt was beyond the pale," he said.[10]

That bruising election made him take stock: he was growing tired of his congressional work and wanted to pursue something else. Jim Mason, who wrote a book extensively detailing Anderson's presidential run, told me that Anderson "did not like his leadership post being challenged, did not like toiling away in a minority party, did not like the inability of the Congress to pass meaningful legislation, and wanted to get out and do other things with his life."[11] Anderson also didn't want to go through another tough campaign just to retain his congressional seat in 1980. So he set his sights on the White House.

On June 8, 1979, Anderson announced his candidacy to be the Republican nominee for president. But he faced formidable odds against Ronald Reagan, the popular actor and former governor of California, and George H. W. Bush, the former director of the CIA. Anderson appeared on the Republican primary ballot in twenty-one states, receiving 37 percent of the vote in his home state of Illinois (the highest percentage he earned in any primary) and 31 percent in Massachusetts—but he did not win any of the primaries, placing second in nine of them.[12]

The reality was that Anderson had become less conservative over time and less conservative than the Republican base. For instance, during one debate in New Hampshire, he declared his support for gun licenses: "When in this country we license people to drive automobiles, what is so wrong about proposing that we license guns to make sure that felons and mental incompetents don't get ahold of them?" The audience booed.[13]

The writing was on the wall: Ronald Reagan, who was more conservative than Anderson, would become the Republican nominee for president in 1980, with George Bush as his running mate. Anderson therefore decided to seek the presidency as an independent. Part of his motivation was a desire to run a different type of campaign that would respond to the new challenges that America faced, especially after the Watergate scandal, which was still fresh on voters' minds. As Jim Mason explained, "He felt that candidates ought to run with complete honesty, they ought to be painfully specific in their recommendations while seeking office, and they ought to show responsibility in the way they campaigned."[14] On April 24, 1980, Anderson formally announced his independent campaign.

But the path to the general election ballot was much harder for independent candidates than it was for a political party's nominee. Most states give automatic ballot placement in November to a party's nominee, who is formally determined during the big nominating convention in the summer of an election year. Independent candidates, on the other hand, are required to gather a bunch of signatures and submit them, along with other filing papers, by a certain date. Candidates must complete this task for every state where they wish to appear on the ballot, with each state having different rules on who can gather signatures, what information must be on the petitions, the deadline, and a host of other details. Anderson had significant support—in June 1980 he was polling at 24 to 26 percent nationwide—but this process still required a lot of coordination.[15]

Ohio's signature requirement—to gather 5,000 signatures on a petition to put a candidate's name on the ballot—was not particularly onerous. The state's filing deadline was the problem: to be on the general election ballot in November, independent candidates for president had to file their ballot access petitions at least seventy-five days before the Ohio primary—even though these candidates weren't even appearing on the Ohio primary ballot. Ohio's primary was on June 3, so the deadline to submit the documents to run as an independent was March 20, but Anderson hadn't declared his candidacy as an independent until April 24, almost a month after the deadline.[16]

Anderson had no problem gathering the requisite number of signatures in Ohio or in the other states with early filing deadlines. In Ohio he submitted around 14,500 signatures, well over the 5,000 that state law required.[17] The problem was that he was too late. On May 16, 1980, he submitted his petition and the signatures to Ohio secretary of state Anthony J. Celebrezze Jr., the state's chief election official. Celebrezze promptly rejected the petition because it arrived after Ohio's filing deadline for independent candidates.[18]

Anderson had expected Ohio election officials to reject his petition. When he developed the plan to leave the Republican Party and run as an independent in the spring of 1980, he knew that it was late in the game, especially as the primary season was already underway. As part of his political strategy, he retained a law firm to challenge state laws that would prohibit him from appearing on the general election ballot. Ballot access was key: his campaign wanted him to appear as an independent on all fifty-one ballots (the fifty states and the District of Columbia) so that he could demonstrate he was a national candidate who had a real shot at winning. Therefore, the rejection of his nominating petition in Ohio and four other states with early filing deadlines (Kentucky, Maine, Maryland, and New Mexico) posed a real problem. In a preview of a strategy that would dominate elections in future years, he sued. Indeed, a 1982 article noted, "The 1980 presidential candidates placed unprecedented reliance on litigation as a means to achieve political goals."[19] Anderson asked a federal court to declare the Ohio law unconstitutional because it abridged his rights as a candidate and the rights of individuals who wanted to vote for him.[20]

THE LAWSUIT

Anderson's litigation strategy was important to the overall message his lawyers sought to convey. Instead of just suing on behalf of himself based on the denial of ballot access, he also included a few of his supporters as plaintiffs. One plaintiff, George H. Hetrick, was an Ohio resident who had agreed to serve as a presidential elector pledged to Anderson, should he win the state. Leslie Laufman, MD, was another Anderson supporter in Ohio. And Gerald M. Eisenstat, an Anderson supporter from New Jersey, demonstrated the nationwide impact of keeping Anderson off the Ohio ballot: Anderson, Eisenstat's preferred candidate, would be much less likely to win a majority of Electoral College votes if he had no chance of winning Ohio's electors, a major prize in the Electoral College calculation.[21]

These individual plaintiffs, however, had little to do with the case beyond having their names on the court documents. Anderson's primary lawyer, George Frampton, does not recall ever interacting with them. They were simply Anderson supporters who had agreed to lend their names to the lawsuit and sign affidavits attesting to their interest in voting for Anderson if he were on the ballot. Anderson, too, did not have much of a hand in the litigation. He was more focused on the campaign itself. As Frampton put it, "Anderson was gallivanting around. He'd been a congressman who was kind of going to disappear, and then a Republican candidate who wasn't getting anywhere and all of a sudden, he was, you know, the cat's pajamas, so he was just delighted" at the enthusiasm surrounding his campaign as an independent.[22] Gaining ballot access was vital to Anderson's nascent effort. He left it to his lawyers, including Frampton, to drive the litigation against the laws that held him back—Ohio being the key focus.

Before this case, Frampton had already engaged in high-profile work as an assistant special prosecutor for Archibald Cox in the Watergate investigation and prosecution. He cowrote a book about the experience.[23] After Watergate, Frampton rented office space with the public interest law firm Rogovin, Stern, and Huge. Frampton did not intend to be part of the law firm; he had simply contacted Harry Huge about renting an office so he could have a place to write or pursue other matters. Huge not only provided the space but also started giving Frampton some legal work, which eventually led to Frampton joining the firm as a junior partner. The firm had won a big verdict against a West Virginian coal mine after a coal slurry impoundment dam broke, later immortalized in the book *The Buffalo Creek Disaster*, by Gerald Stern, who was one of the firm's lawyers. Frampton worked on a similar case for the firm involving a methane explosion, suing on behalf of the widows of mine workers. The *Anderson* case landed on Frampton's desk after John Anderson hired Mitch Rogovin, one of the firm's partners, to be the general counsel of his campaign as an independent presidential candidate. Rogovin asked Frampton to be the main litigator, knowing that he needed help. They would have to challenge state laws in a handful of places that set an early filing deadline for independent candidates so that Anderson would appear on the ballot.[24]

The legal argument was fairly straightforward: denying Anderson a spot on the ballot violated his and his supporters' First Amendment rights to associate and express their views, because it would prevent anyone in Ohio from voting for Anderson. As the district court judge who initially heard the lawsuit put it, citing prior Supreme Court cases, the Ohio law "implicates an individual's important interest in the continued availability of political opportunity and his right to associate for the advancement of political beliefs."[25] In addition, Ohio's practices treated independent candidates differently from political party nominees, raising equal protection concerns. The state automatically put the Democratic and Republican Party nominees, as well as minor party candidates, on the general election ballot in November. The parties selected their nominees at national conventions held over the summer. Therefore, a candidate could choose not to even run in Ohio's primary and they would still appear on the ballot in November if they secured their party's nomination at the convention. An independent candidate, by contrast, had to file by March 20 to appear on the November 4, 1980, general election ballot in Ohio. This scheme, Anderson argued, treated independent candidates differently from the nominees of the two major political parties and therefore violated the Equal Protection Clause of the Fourteenth Amendment to the U.S. Constitution.

THE CIVIL RIGHTS REVOLUTION OF THE 1960S

Although Anderson's lawyers envisioned the case as being about candidate access to the ballot, it also made sense for them to rely on robust theories of the right to vote under the First and Fourteenth Amendments to the U.S. Constitution. Only a decade and a half earlier, the Supreme Court had declared that the right to vote was among the most fundamental rights, such that states had to provide specific justifications for any laws that burdened the ability to cast a ballot or enjoy equal representation.

The 1960s represented a watershed time for the right to vote at the Supreme Court. In a series of cases, the Court elevated the importance of voting as foundational to our democracy. The U.S. Constitution does not explicitly confer the right to vote (it says only that states cannot deny voting rights based on certain characteristics such as race or sex), but surely the right to vote is a core component of a constitutional democracy. It was up to the Court to recognize constitutional protection for this fundamental principle. The first case that truly opened the Court's doors to election law claims was *Baker v. Carr* in 1962, in which the Court declared, "A citizen's right to a vote free of arbitrary impairment by state action has been judicially recognized as a right secured by the Constitution."[26] Justice William O. Douglas, in a separate concurring opinion, noted that "the right to vote is inherent in the republican form of government."[27] The Court followed up these statements in another case by explaining that "the right to vote freely for the candidate of one's choice is of the essence of a democratic society, and any restrictions on that right strike at the heart of representative government."[28]

A few years later, the Court explicitly recognized the right to vote as a "fundamental right" when striking down Virginia's poll tax.[29] It also noted that voting protects all other rights: "Other rights, even the most basic, are illusory if the right to vote is undermined."[30] It is impossible to effectuate other rights—to influence policymakers and the laws they enact on behalf of their constituents—if the right to vote is impinged. Politicians are supposed to be accountable to the people through elections, so if the people cannot vote freely, then they cannot keep politicians in check regarding all other issues. To be sure, the Court as far back as 1886 declared that voting is a "fundamental political right, because preservative of all rights," but its case law until the 1960s did not actually offer robust protection.[31]

In the 1960s, however, the Court finally gave stronger scrutiny to state laws that burdened the right to vote. For instance, in 1969, in striking down a limit on who could vote in school board elections, the Court declared that it should *not* defer to states in dictating election rules:

> The presumption of constitutionality and the approval given "rational" classifications in other types of enactments are based on an assumption that the institutions of state government are structured so as to represent fairly all the people. However, when the challenge to the statute is in effect a challenge of this basic assumption, the assumption can no longer serve as the basis for presuming constitutionality.[32]

This passage essentially means that although courts usually defer to legislative judgments, states must provide stronger justifications for their rules when it comes to the right to vote. That's because voting laws that infringe on this fundamental right can skew democratic representation and have repercussions on policymaking. A major function of the judiciary is to protect political minorities, so courts should not just defer to states' election rules, especially if those rules unduly burden political minorities. Politicians have every incentive to craft voting laws that will help to keep themselves in power. Courts exist in part to protect this individual right against legislative encroachment.

The cases from the 1960s require states to satisfy what lawyers call "strict scrutiny." To justify a law that impacts a fundamental right such as voting, states must demonstrate that they have a "compelling interest" for the law and that the rule is "narrowly tailored" to achieve the state's goals. Essentially, a state must show that it has a really good justification for the election rules it passes and that there are not any better ways to run elections that do not cause as much harm to voters.

As the 1980 campaign began and Anderson considered state laws that prevented him from appearing on the general election ballot, Americans enjoyed robust legal protections for their ability to participate in the political process. States had to satisfy a high bar to justify laws that burdened a voter's ability to cast a ballot—including laws that would effectively prohibit someone from casting a vote for their preferred candidate by keeping that candidate off the ballot.

ANDERSON'S INITIAL WIN IN COURT

Anderson sued in Ohio and the other four states that had early filing deadlines. He won ballot access in all five. The Ohio case, because it is the one that eventually went to the Supreme Court, is the most important. It was the first of these decisions to come down in 1980, so other courts could point to it as persuasive. In it, District Judge Robert Duncan followed Supreme Court precedent by noting the importance of the rights at issue for Anderson and his supporters.[33] He found that Ohio's law "imposes a substantial burden on plaintiffs' fundamental rights and is not justified by any compelling state interest."[34] Invoking that "strict scrutiny" standard, he wrote, "When rights as fundamental as these are substantially abridged by legislative enactment, the First and Fourteenth Amendments command that the law may be justified only if it is necessary to achieve a compelling state interest."[35] And he rejected Ohio's argument that the early petition-filing deadline was necessary for administrative ease. Ultimately, Ohio did not have a good enough reason to harm Anderson's supporters and burden their right to vote by imposing such an early filing requirement on independent candidates, especially when the candidates of the two major parties did not face similar hurdles.

The state tried to appeal the case in the fall of 1980, to no avail. The Supreme Court denied an emergency hearing without issuing a written opinion, although three justices—Justices Byron White, William Rehnquist, and Potter Stewart—said they would have taken the case and set oral argument for early October, a month before the election.[36] The Supreme Court decides which cases it wishes to hear and will accept an appeal if four justices agree, so they were one vote shy of this threshold. But it was a close call: the archived papers of Justice Lewis Powell include a flurry of memos between the justices in mid-September 1980, and it appears that at one point there were enough votes for the Court to become involved—until Justice Powell changed his mind. As Powell wrote to his colleagues, "If the issue were not resolved authoritatively by this Court prior to the election, conceivably the outcome of the election might be left in doubt. My guess, however, is that the will of the people would be respected and there would be no post election litigation."[37] Justice Powell also indicated in this memo that he thought the district court was correct to order Ohio to put Anderson's name on the ballot. He would change his mind when the case returned to the Supreme Court in 1983. (Justices White, Rehnquist, Powell, and Sandra Day O'Connor ultimately dissented from the Court's 1983 decision in favor of Anderson.) The Court's refusal to take the case in 1980 meant that Anderson would appear on the Ohio ballot—and all other states' ballots—that November.

THE 1980 PRESIDENTIAL ELECTION

While John Anderson won his initial lawsuits in Ohio and all of the other states that had early filing deadlines, his campaign's progress was rocky throughout the summer and fall. Anderson enjoyed some success in the polls in June—the height of his campaign—with support from moderate-to-liberal Republicans, some Democrats, independents, professional workers, and college students. At one point polls showed that he was the first choice of about a quarter of the electorate, but a combination of mistakes and the difficulty of running against the two major parties proved fatal to his chances at victory.[38] As the *Washington Post* reported on the eve of Election Day, "Anderson's candidacy was improbable from the start, perhaps fatally so. Illusionary. Impossible. Unlikely, at best."[39]

Erudite, with dark, horn-rimmed glasses and a shock of white hair, Anderson sought to be the alternative in a race consisting of the unpopular Carter and brash Reagan. He called for a 50-cent gas tax, at a time when gas cost about $1.15 a gallon, to encourage energy conservation.[40] He traveled to the Middle East and Europe during the Republican National Convention to show off his presidential chops, but the trip failed to generate buzz, costing his campaign a lot of money while failing to create positive publicity. The Carter campaign attacked Anderson brutally, fearing that he was a major threat to Carter's chances of reelection.

Then there were tactical mistakes, such as when Anderson released a 317-page National Unity platform but forgot to bring any copies with him to give to reporters when he flew to the Midwest—exposing the differences of campaigning before the internet age![41] He showed up for a rally in Philadelphia to find the hall only one-eighth full, in part because his campaign had decided to charge a $3 entrance fee. As the *Washington Post* reported at the time, although Anderson had momentum in the summer of 1980, "Somehow, somewhere along the way, the magic slipped away from John Anderson. By his own admission he became a 'sidebar' in the presidential race."[42] He won zero states and received about 5.7 million votes, or about 6.6 percent of the nationwide total.

Anderson retired to Florida and largely stayed out of the public eye, teaching courses in politics and law and serving as a chair and advisor to FairVote, an organization that champions Ranked Choice Voting, a system that allows people to rank candidates in order of preference; Alaska, Maine, and numerous localities now use Ranked Choice Voting for their elections (with Nevada joining them if voters approve a second ballot proposition in 2024). But the case he started for the 1980 election continued to live on. Although Ohio had complied with the court order to place Anderson's name on the ballot, the state decided to appeal the ruling that had struck down its law so it could impose the filing deadline for independent candidates in future elections. George Frampton, Anderson's lawyer, recalled that the Ohio governor, a Republican, and the attorney general, a Democrat, were both "pissed off" about the lawsuit, especially after they lost at the district court. "This was an attack on a system that had been built up over decades," Frampton noted. Frampton recalls top Democrats saying to him and his fellow lawyers, "You're good Democrats. Why are you doing this?" Before the 1980 election, Ohio Democrats were concerned about Anderson siphoning away votes from Jimmy Carter. After, they were just upset that the lower court's decision might erode the dominance of the two-party system.[43]

The state initially found a favorable audience at the Sixth Circuit Court of Appeals.[44] That court reversed the lower court and upheld Ohio's ballot access scheme. In its decision, the court posited that the state could require an early filing deadline to give voters enough time to learn about the candidates. As the court put it, "Ohio may very reasonably conclude that requiring presidential candidates to be in the public eye for a significant time materially advances its interest in careful selection."[45] The court therefore deferred to Ohio's determination on how to run the election. It glossed over the problem for Anderson and especially his supporters: Ohio's rule made it impossible to cast a ballot for their preferred candidate.

Anderson was no longer running a campaign for president in November 1981 when the appeals court decision came down. Frampton recalled that Anderson did not even care at that point. "Anderson wanted to have nothing to do with it," Frampton told me. "He wasn't interested in us continuing to represent him to do anything, including defend the case." Frampton and his team had to talk Anderson into letting them appeal to the U.S. Supreme Court, mostly so they could try to recover attorney's fees. Frampton's law firm had taken on the case pro bono, so they had not received any compensation for their efforts. But they always thought they might be able to recover legal fees from the states they had sued. Given that they had lost at the Sixth Circuit Court of Appeals, taking the case to the U.S. Supreme Court (and winning) was the only route left to recover financially. Anderson eventually agreed to let them appeal the case. "He owed us," Frampton said, "after we helped put him on the ballot in so many places."[46] But otherwise, Anderson had nothing to do with the appeal.

The Supreme Court agreed to take the case, setting oral argument for December 6, 1982. During the argument, Frampton, Anderson's lawyer, highlighted the First Amendment right to associate that was at stake, as well as "an intertwined but somewhat separate right to vote which is not found as such in the Constitution, but I think this Court has recognized is fundamental to the democratic process."[47] That is, Frampton invoked the implicit constitutional right to vote as a key component of his argument. He also noted that Ohio did not need to have such an early deadline for independent candidates to file their petitions: the papers simply "sit in somebody's in-box, or hopefully a safe, gathering dust for three months."[48]

After the oral argument Frampton thought he had a decent chance of success, especially given his calculation that Justice Harry Blackmun, whom he knew well, was likely the swing vote. Frampton had clerked for Blackmun during the time of *Roe v. Wade* and they had developed a close relationship, often enjoying coffee together and visiting each other's families. Frampton says he never spoke with Blackmun about the *Anderson* case, but "it made me a little uncomfortable" to know that Blackmun's vote was so important. Frampton doesn't recall ever talking about the case with Blackmun, even after the decision came out. "It wasn't a case that was very interesting to him," Frampton surmised.[49]

The Supreme Court issued its decision in *Anderson v. Celebrezze* on April 19, 1983. The Court ruled in favor of Anderson and against the Ohio law by a 5–4 vote, with Blackmun joining the majority.

Frampton remembers being delighted at the win, especially because it meant that he and his firm could seek attorney's fees from the states they had sued. But he also recognizes that his side "barely squeaked through," in that the Court ruled in Anderson's favor but did not adopt the most stringent test for voting rights protection that was at the core of his argument.[50] That very deficiency would spell trouble for the future of the right to vote.

WHY IS THIS CASE SO IMPORTANT?

Far from being a minor dispute about whether a third-party candidate who ultimately received only 6 percent of the vote could appear on the ballot, the decision in *Anderson v. Celebrezze* has reverberated for decades. It has been cited in over 1,500 cases and scores of scholarly articles. It is the first case that makes up the prominent "*Anderson-Burdick*" test for burdens on the right to vote. (We'll talk about *Burdick* in the next chapter.)

Justice John Paul Stevens wrote the opinion for the 5–4 majority. The main point of his majority opinion was straightforward: the Ohio law that required independent candidates to file their papers to run for president well ahead of the general election was unconstitutional. Stevens began his analysis by explaining that the rights of candidates for office and the rights of voters are intertwined: "In approaching candidate restrictions, it is essential to examine in a realistic light the extent and nature of their impact on voters."[51] The Court then noted that the rights of voters to cast a ballot for a candidate of their choice is "fundamental" and a "basic constitutional right" implicating the freedom of association under the First Amendment.[52] Essentially, in echoing cases from the 1960s, the Court reaffirmed the importance of the constitutional right to vote. With respect to this Ohio law, Justice Stevens noted that "the March filing deadline places a particular burden on an identifiable segment of Ohio's independent-minded voters."[53]

But then Justice Stevens offered further guidance that opened the door to the lesser protection for voting rights we have today. He recognized that the state could have "important regulatory interests" that might justify election laws that impact voters—so long as those restrictions are "reasonable" and "nondiscriminatory."[54] The next analytical move was, in hindsight, the most devastating. Instead of invoking "strict scrutiny," the strongest level of judicial review, which epitomized the cases from the 1960s and which elevated the importance of the right to vote, Justice Stevens crafted a new, less-stringent balancing test for courts to employ:

> [A court] must first consider the character and magnitude of the asserted injury to the rights protected by the First and Fourteenth Amendments that the plaintiff seeks to vindicate. It then must identify and evaluate the precise interests put forward by the State as justifications for the burden imposed by its rule. In passing judgment, the Court must not only determine the legitimacy and strength of each of those interests; it also must consider the extent to which those interests make it necessary to burden the plaintiff's rights.[55]

This passage created a three-part test that courts still use today, in which they weigh the burdens on voters with the state's interests in regulating the election how it wants. A court must evaluate (1) the burden on voters, (2) the state's asserted need for its voting rules, and then (3) balance them against each other.

Why is this test so concerning? The answer will require us to explore some of the more recent cases in which the Court mangled the rule even further, but the basic reason is that it gives states stronger footing to justify their voting laws by citing general interests such as administrative efficiency or the desire to improve election integrity. Before, states had to explain, with specificity, why their rules were necessary to achieve their precise goals in how they run an election, as opposed to a better rule that would harm fewer voters. Now, instead, states can offer vague rationales for their voting laws, citing a broad notion of administrative efficiency or fraud prevention—without further detail—to justify the burdens they impose on voters. Essentially, although constitutional protection had previously placed a heavy thumb on the voters' side of the scale—befitting a fundamental right in our democracy—the Court was now giving states greater latitude to make it harder to vote.

The state ultimately lost this case. Justice Stevens soundly rejected Ohio's asserted interests in its early filing deadline, finding that the state had not sufficiently supported its law. This was a good outcome because it opened the door for third-party candidates and independents to appear on the ballot, rejecting formal, legal measures that cut them out of the process. Independent candidates offer more choices to voters who may be disaffected by the two major political parties.[56] But in reaching that result, Justice Stevens gave states too much leeway to justify their election rules.[57] Future cases latched on to this crack in the edifice of judicial protection for voting rights.

Justice Stevens probably did not intend to offer states greater freedom to burden voters. His test purports to require states to meaningfully justify their rules. The language from *Anderson* speaks of "precise interests put forward by the State" and whether those interests make it "necessary" to burden the right to vote. That language signals a heavy burden for states to shoulder as they craft their voting laws. As we will see, however, the Court in future cases largely ignored these crucial phrases, failing to require states to provide strong justifications for their election rules. *Anderson* therefore represented the opening salvo in the breakdown of the Court's previously robust protection for voting as a fundamental right. Instead of requiring states to satisfy the "strict scrutiny" standard from the 1960s, which is the highest measure that is most skeptical of state rules burdening the right to vote, the Court eventually used a watered-down interpretation of the *Anderson* test to give states more power to run their elections as they wish and to make it easier for them to defeat lawsuits challenging their voting processes.

The four-justice dissent in the case, written by Justice William H. Rehnquist (who would later go on to become chief justice), foreshadows this turn toward greater deference to states in their election laws. Instead of recognizing the fundamental nature of the right to vote and the burden Ohio's law placed on Anderson's supporters who wished to vote for him, Justice Rehnquist wrote that the law was perfectly constitutional so long as it was "rational" and allowed "reasonable access" to the ballot.[58] Compared to the language of strict scrutiny, those phrases signal that states need not offer much justification for their rules. States can win their cases by asserting more general platitudes about their need for sound election administration or the "stability of its political system."[59] Justice Rehnquist claimed that the Ohio law was merely a sore loser provision to prevent someone like Anderson from trying one path to the ballot, seeing the writing on the wall that he would lose, and switching in midstream. The problem for Rehnquist is that the state had conceded that the measure did *not* operate as a sore loser provision in this instance, given that Anderson never appeared on the Ohio primary ballot; he withdrew and became an independent before the primary took place. But that did not stop Rehnquist. He asserted that states don't have to defend their laws in court with precise rationales.[60] That's quite a different approach from the strict scrutiny test used in the 1960s cases, which had more rigorously protected the right to vote. Indeed, according to Justice Harry Blackmun's notes, Justice Rehnquist said during the justices' meeting about this case that "strict scrutiny is judicial puppetry," so it's unsurprising that he wanted to do away with that higher standard.[61]

There's plenty of room to argue that *Anderson* wasn't all bad: states must now have an easier path for independent candidates to appear on the ballot, and it is generally a good thing to open the system up beyond the Democratic and Republican nominees to give all voters an equal voice in who should win (though a system such as Ranked Choice Voting is preferable so that third-party candidates do not simply become "spoilers" by taking away votes from one of the major party candidates). People who prefer a third-party or independent candidate can more easily express their views at the ballot box thanks to this case. The *New York Times*, in its obituary for Anderson after he died in December 2017 at the age of ninety-five, noted, "The most enduring impact of his 1980 independent campaign came in the courts, where his victories enabled later third-party candidates like H. Ross Perot and [Ralph] Nader to get on the ballot."[62]

But that's not entirely correct. The most enduring impact of the *Anderson* case is more subtle and dangerous: it began the Supreme Court's descent into underprotecting the right to vote. It would take another case, this one about writing in a vote for "Donald Duck" for a seat in the Hawaii House of Representatives, to further the damage.

CHAPTER 2

A VOTE FOR DONALD DUCK

Burdick v. Takushi (1992)

	JUSTICE	APPOINTED BY
MAJORITY	White, Byron *(authored majority opinion)*	Kennedy, John F. (D)
	Rehnquist, William H. (chief justice)	Nixon, Richard (R) (associate justice) Reagan, Ronald (R) (chief justice)
	O'Connor, Sandra Day	Reagan, Ronald (R)
	Scalia, Antonin	Reagan, Ronald (R)
	Souter, David H.	Bush, George H. W. (R)
	Thomas, Clarence	Bush, George H. W. (R)
DISSENT	Kennedy, Anthony M. *(authored dissent)*	Reagan, Ronald (R)
	Blackmun, Harry A.	Nixon, Richard (R)
	Stevens, John Paul	Ford, Gerald (R)

Alan Burdick was in college in the mid-1960s when he voted for the first time. A student at Yale, he still voted in his hometown of Fair Lawn, New Jersey, and his unique votes for the three school board seats caused something of a stir in the New York City suburb. Burdick didn't like any of the candidates on the ballot, claiming they were all "crappy." He wrote in three people he thought would do a better job instead: his dad (who had been on the school board previously), his dad's prior campaign manager, and a friend who would eventually go on to become a political science professor. He sought to make a political statement that the candidates on the ballot were unacceptable and that there were other people in the community who would do a much better job.[1]

He never expected that the local newspaper would write a column about his ballot. As he told me, these write-in votes became the talk of the town for a few days—which ultimately had the intended effect: people were openly discussing the merits of those who had run for office. This was, he said, far more effective than voting for those he deemed to be mediocre candidates or leaving his ballot blank.[2]

Fast forward a few years, to when Burdick found himself living in Kailua, Hawaii. He had served in the Peace Corps in Micronesia, gone to law school in California, returned to Micronesia to do legal work, and then moved to Hawaii because, as he put it, he didn't want to wear a coat and tie every day. Coincidentally, his neighbor was Dan Foley, a fellow lawyer he had befriended while they were both in Micronesia. Their backyard conversations were often about the political and legal news of the day. One such conversation centered around a December 1985 California Supreme Court decision that had ruled San Diego's ban on write-in voting unconstitutional.[3] A few months later, across the fence they shared, he and Foley discussed whether they could use that case to challenge Hawaii's rules, which also prohibited write-in voting. Burdick had previously asked poll workers in Hawaii about the ability to cast a write-in vote, but they had all said it was not permitted. The poll workers claimed that the "machine" wouldn't allow it, and Burdick half-jokingly wondered if they meant the polling machines or the political machine that controlled Hawaii's government. This new California case might give him a way to challenge Hawaii's prevailing practice. Burdick and Foley, who worked as a lawyer for the ACLU in Hawaii, crafted a plan to push the state to change its rules.

Burdick first called the Hawaii Voter Education Desk, a hotline for voters to ask questions about the voting process. The person who answered referred him to Morris Takushi, the state's director of elections. In a phone call, Takushi said that he interpreted Hawaii laws to prohibit write-in voting, but he indicated that Burdick could make a further inquiry with Gerard Jervis, the director of research for the lieutenant governor's office, as Hawaii's lieutenant governor serves as the state's chief election officer. Burdick and Jervis spoke by telephone in June 1986, and Jervis asked Burdick to provide his thoughts on write-in voting in a letter. Burdick proceeded to write a seven-page memo in which he outlined why he thought the ban on write-in voting violated his constitutional rights.[4] Jervis passed along Burdick's letter to the state's attorney general's office, which provided its definitive interpretation of Hawaii law: despite the California case, there was no constitutional requirement to allow write-in voting.[5]

There was only one thing left for Burdick to do: sue the state.

Part of his motivation stemmed from his dissatisfaction with the ruling class of Hawaii's politics. Hawaii was then an overwhelmingly blue state, as it remains today. But, as Burdick put it, the "establishment Democrats" controlled the government, and he is anything but an establishment voter. He describes his politics as at the "left end of the political spectrum," and it's clear that he has no sympathy for most Democrats in office, considering them to be way too conservative. In 1986, when Burdick wanted to write in a different candidate for the state legislature, Democrats held over 90 percent of all seats in the state. The Democratic primary was the only game in town. But, strangely enough, the particular neighborhood where Burdick lived back then was a very Republican area. There was usually never any real contest, and Democrats often didn't even put up any candidates in this particularly red district, much less someone who would have a chance of winning. Instead, the Republican nominee would always go on to win in the general election. Burdick was fed up with heading to the polls only to see no one on the ballot who shared his ideals. Write-in voting could provide him, and other voters, a way to register dissent with the current political order, as well as offer a fail-safe mechanism if a major problem arose with a political party's nominee.[6]

Burdick, with Dan Foley's help, filed a lawsuit to challenge the Hawaii law. They thought they had a strong argument: the California Supreme Court had recently said that a ban on write-in voting violated the fundamental right to vote. But instead of achieving a quick resolution that would expand write-in voting and protect the constitutional right to vote, the case would drag on for six years, involve six different rulings, and take Alan Burdick to the Hawaii Supreme Court and all the way to the U.S. Supreme Court.

THE HISTORY OF THE PRINTED BALLOT

We have not always cast a state-created ballot that already lists the candidates' names. Back in the day, in many places you had to create your own ballot to bring to the polls. All voting was essentially write-in voting.

During the Colonial period in North America, elections in some states were held by voice vote or a showing of hands, while other jurisdictions used some form of a paper ballot. Anthony Gaughan, a law professor and historian, has explained that secrecy of the ballot was often a fiction even in the places that used paper ballots. "Factional leaders sometimes pre-printed ballots that they handed out to supporters. In such cases, it was obvious which candidate the voter supported when they handed the sheriff their ballot. Furthermore, episodes of election fraud prompted some colonies to require that voters write their name on their ballot before casting their vote."[7]

Within twenty years of the United States' founding, most states had moved away from voice voting and instead accepted paper ballots that voters would bring to the polls. Of course, creating one's own ballot is not the simplest task, so political parties became involved, producing their own ballots for voters to pick up and then drop in ballot boxes. The ballots listed only the party nominees and were often printed in bright colors or with distinctive logos. The reason: party bosses could pay for votes and then watch the voters drop the party's brightly colored ballots into the ballot box before giving them a few bucks or a fifth of whisky. As a result, this system was rife with bribery and intimidation.[8] A book on the history of the secret ballot, written in 1917, recounted this anecdote, reprinted in a Supreme Court opinion:

> This sounds like exaggeration, but it is truth; and these are facts so notorious that no one acquainted with the conduct of recent elections now attempts a denial—that the raising of colossal sums for the purpose of bribery had been rewarded by promotion to the highest offices in the government; that systematic organization for the purchase of votes, individually and in blocks, at the polls has become a recognized factor in the machinery of parties; that the number of voters who demand money compensation for their ballots has grown greater with each recurring election.[9]

As the Supreme Court wrote in a 1992 case that upheld a ban on campaigning right outside of polling places,

> Approaching the polling place under this system was akin to entering an open auction place. As the elector started his journey to the polls, he was met by various party ticket peddlers who were only too anxious to supply him with their party tickets. Often the competition became heated when several such peddlers found an uncommitted or wavering voter. Sham battles were frequently engaged in to keep away elderly and timid voters of the opposition.[10]

Other countries were facing the same problems of bribery or harassment during their voting processes. Several Australian provinces came up with a solution: the government would print ballots ahead of time, listing all of the candidates for office, and voters would fill out their ballots in a closed booth. That way, political parties or other untoward vote influencers—such as employers or business leaders—could not as easily pay for votes, as voters would cast their ballots in secret without anyone knowing their choices. Several European countries adopted the Australian secret ballot in the late 1800s. Its first use in the United States occurred during the 1888 election in the states of New York and Massachusetts, as well as in Louisville, Kentucky. The reform proved wildly popular, and by 1896, over 92 percent of the American electorate was voting by secret ballot.[11] Today, of course, every state prepares a ballot that lists the candidates running for office.

Having the state print the ballot, however, created a new problem: there needed to be a mechanism to determine which people qualified as candidates. The law of ballot access was born. In addition, what if a voter wanted to vote for someone who was not on the preprinted ballot? Were they out of luck?

Several state courts in the late 1800s and early 1900s affirmed that, with the shift to the Australian secret ballot, the state also needed to allow for write-in votes. For instance, Massachusetts' highest court noted that judges had upheld the adoption of the Australian ballot "provided the acts permit the voter to vote for such persons as he please, by leaving blank spaces on the official ballot, in which he may write . . . the names of such persons."[12] Similarly, in 1905, the Pennsylvania Supreme Court declared that if the preprinted ballot did not have a space for write-in votes, then the election for a voter who did not like any of the listed candidates would "not be equal, for he would not be able to express his own individual will in his own way."[13]

Several prominent candidates have won their seats through write-in voting. The most famous example in recent years is probably Lisa Murkowski, the incumbent senator of Alaska, who lost the Republican primary in 2010 but waged a vigorous write-in campaign in the general election that led her to victory.[14] Strom Thurmond, the former governor of South Carolina, also became a U.S. senator through a write-in campaign in 1954. The incumbent Democratic senator had died in September of that year, and instead of holding a special primary, the state Democratic Party anointed a new nominee, State Senator Edgar Brown. Decrying what he perceived as an unjustified power grab, Thurmond ran a write-in campaign and won with 63 percent of the vote.[15] Two years later he ran in the Democratic Party primary, which he also won. He changed his party affiliation to Republican in 1964 and served in the Senate for over forty-seven years, until January 3, 2003.[16]

The most interesting and scandalous example of a write-in candidacy occurred in a Tennessee state senate race. The long-time incumbent, Senator Tommy Burks, was killed in October 1988, shot at point-blank range while sitting in a pickup truck at his pumpkin patch as he was about to welcome a visiting school group. The prevailing theory was that his opponent in that election, Byron Looper—who had changed his middle name from Anthony to "Low Tax"—had killed him, ostensibly to eliminate his opponent in that year's election. Election officials removed Burks's name from the ballot, per state law, and his party was not allowed to nominate a replacement because his death had occurred within thirty days of the election. But since Looper had not yet been convicted of the killing, he remained on the ballot. This may have been his goal—if he could, well, "eliminate" his opponent, then he would win the seat by default as the only remaining candidate. The only options available for voters were either to vote for a likely murderer or write in someone else. Burks's widow, Charlotte, agreed to be a write-in candidate—though she didn't actually campaign at all. She won overwhelmingly, receiving about 30,000 votes to Looper's approximately 1,500 votes.[17] She went on to serve in the state legislature for sixteen years.[18] Looper was eventually convicted of the murder and sentenced to life imprisonment; he died in prison in 2013.

But not all states permit write-in voting. As of 1986, when Alan Burdick began his lawsuit, Hawaii, Indiana, Oklahoma, and Nevada all barred write-in votes in every election—though Nevada permitted a vote for "none of the above."[19] Other states allowed write-ins during a general election but not in a primary.[20] Burdick thought the absolute ban on write-in voting in Hawaii violated his fundamental constitutional right to vote.

THE LITIGATION BEGINS

Burdick filed suit in August 1986 with an eye to the September primary or the November general election that year. For himself personally, he knew that a Republican would almost definitely win his district for the state house and he wanted a mechanism to register a protest vote. More broadly, he sought to use the lawsuit to argue for a change in Hawaii election law so that it would more explicitly recognize the expressive value of the constitutional right to vote.

The federal district court judge who heard the case, Judge Harold Fong, was a Ronald Reagan appointee who served on the federal bench for only thirteen years, cut short by his untimely death at the age of fifty-six due to complications from heart surgery. Judge Fong's *New York Times* obituary notes that *Burdick* was one of his most notable decisions.[21]

Judge Fong issued his first ruling in the case on September 29, 1986, a little over a week after the primary election. Judge Fong began his opinion by noting, "The right to vote in this society is so fundamental as almost to dispense with the need for discussion."[22] He then explained that a ban on write-in voting "strikes directly at the right to vote."[23] He also rejected the state's assertion that the write-in ban was necessary to give the public enough time to evaluate candidates and to otherwise protect Hawaii's election process. He observed that write-in candidacies can help voters respond to late-changing events between the primary and general elections, speculating that even that year's gubernatorial election in Hawaii might involve changing political winds depending on the release of a confidential governmental report about a smear campaign waged during the primary. Judge Fong therefore ordered Hawaii to allow for write-in voting that November. The appeals court immediately put that decision on hold, however, meaning that Hawaii did not permit write-in voting that year.

The case then took a circuitous route before finally reaching the U.S. Supreme Court. First, in May 1988, the Ninth Circuit Court of Appeals vacated Judge Fong's ruling because it was unclear whether Hawaii law actually prohibited write-in votes.[24] The Hawaii attorney general had interpreted Hawaii laws as providing no mechanism for voters to write in a candidate not listed on the ballot, but the statute itself was not that direct. The Ninth Circuit therefore said that the Hawaii Supreme Court, the highest authority on the meaning of state law, should provide a definitive analysis of the Hawaii statutes.

The Hawaii Supreme Court then offered its interpretation of Hawaii's election laws: they did, in fact, prohibit voters from writing in a candidate not listed on the ballot and forbade the state from counting and publishing any write-in votes.[25]

With a definitive ruling on what Hawaii law said, the case went back to Judge Fong at the federal district court, three and a half years after he had initially ruled on the matter. Judge Fong reiterated his findings from the first time he heard the case. "The right to vote for the candidate of one's choice is a fundamental right," Judge Fong wrote. "If a citizen has the right to vote, a right which is guaranteed by the U.S. Constitution, then he should be allowed to vote for any candidate of his choice."[26] The opinion is infused with the desire to protect the right to vote. In so doing, Judge Fong walked a delicate line between using "strict scrutiny," the highest level of judicial review that is the least deferential to states and most protective of constitutional rights, and the more watered-down *Anderson v. Celebrezze* balancing test discussed in chapter 1. Recall that the *Anderson* test allows a state to justify a burden on the right to vote with a sufficiently weighty reason. Judge Fong recognized that the Supreme Court had crafted the *Anderson* test in 1983, but also that there was additional Supreme Court authority that "suggests a stricter standard of review may be appropriate."[27] The key determinant was that Hawaii's prohibition on write-in voting directly burdened the fundamental right to vote. "[T]he ban on write-in voting is not merely a restriction on speech," Judge Fong noted. "It constitutes a total ban on the right to vote for the candidate of one's choice if that candidate is not listed on the ballot."[28] The state didn't have great reasons to support this total ban. Hawaii said that its rule helped to avoid factionalism, as it would ensure that losers in the primary could not try again at the general election through a write-in campaign. The state also suggested that the write-in ban fostered a more informed electorate because it required voters to learn about the candidates listed on the ballot. But because the prohibition amounted to a total ban on the ability of voters to cast a ballot for the person they want, "None of the interests the State has asserted is sufficiently weighty to justify this enormous burden on plaintiff's constitutional rights."[29] Judge Fong did not simply defer to the state's justification for its voting rule. He did not credit the state's general assertions of its need to run its elections as it wished. Instead, he elevated the importance of the constitutional right to vote, which included the ability to cast a vote for whomever the voter wishes—even a candidate not already listed on the ballot.

But the Ninth Circuit Court of Appeals was skeptical of Judge Fong's approach once again. District judges often joke that the appeals courts grade their homework, and on this particular assignment, Judge Fong received a poor grade not once but twice. In this second iteration, the Ninth Circuit judges disagreed with Judge Fong's approach to the constitutional question. The appeals court judges said that Burdick's desire to cast a write-in protest vote did *not* amount to a fundamental right. "Although Burdick is guaranteed an equal voice in the election of those who govern, Burdick does not have an unlimited right to vote for any particular candidate."[30] Perhaps most tellingly, the Ninth Circuit also disputed Judge Fong's approach to the deference offered to the state's rule and the proper way to use the *Anderson* balancing test. "*Anderson* does not require a showing of compelling state interests or narrowly tailored laws," the Ninth Circuit wrote. "It requires that the State's interests justify the burden placed on the plaintiff's constitutional rights."[31] The appeals court was saying that the key Supreme Court precedent to use was *Anderson v. Celebrezze*—even though *Anderson* involved ballot access for a candidate and not a direct restriction on voters—and that *Anderson* lowered the protection afforded to the constitutional right to vote. The state simply had to provide some reason for the burdens it placed on voters. The appeals court, differing from Judge Fong's approach, credited Hawaii's asserted interests in "political stability, voter education, and protecting the internal structure of the State's election laws" to uphold the law.[32] These generalized state goals won the day.

At this point, the litigation had gone on for four years, with several elections occurring in the meantime. Although Burdick had won twice at the federal district court, he had not yet been able to cast a write-in vote in any of these elections because the courts had put the rulings on hold during the appeals process. But he ultimately lost at the Ninth Circuit Court of Appeals. The next—and final—stop was the U.S. Supreme Court.

———

A photo of Alan Burdick from a *New York Times* article in 1991 shows him sitting at a desk, sporting a dark, bushy moustache and wearing a short-sleeve button-down shirt, the top two buttons undone.[33] Today, he's visibly older, with thinning, slicked-back gray hair and a clean-shaven round face with bushy eyebrows. But he's no less passionate about our democracy and the importance of voters in directing the government. Before our interview, he sent me a one-page memo with some of his preliminary thoughts: "We the People, not the politicians. Voters are the sovereigns. Politicians are servants of the people. Elections are in service of the voters, not in service of the candidates. That's the way the situation inherently is supposed to be."[34]

Burdick wasn't the easiest person to track down. After some internet sleuthing, my research assistant found a reference to him on the Facebook page of a group called Americans for Democratic Action Hawaii, so he sent them a message. They forwarded his message to Burdick, who wrote back quickly to say that he was willing to talk about the case, even though "it stirs unhappy memories that are not soothed in the present political context."[35] It took us several weeks to coordinate a meeting, especially with the time difference between my home in Kentucky and Burdick's residence in Hawaii. We finally met via Zoom on a Sunday afternoon—Sunday morning for him. He wore a flowery purple shirt that showed he had fully embraced the Hawaiian sartorial style. Behind him were bookshelves full to the brim with books, and the table next to him held stacks of CDs. I could see a box set suggesting he listens to the classical music of Schubert. A neighbor's dog barked incessantly during our lengthy conversation, and Burdick kept apologizing even though there was obviously nothing he could do about it.

We launched into a conversation about his life and political activism. Burdick's answers to my questions were often terse, but at other times he became more animated, freely offering his thoughts on a range of topics and going off on tangents about the state of Hawaii politics, such as how he believes most Hawaiian politicians are "DINOs"—Democrats In Name Only—and that it's not actually a progressive state. He told me that his political activism came "from the cradle," because both of his parents emphasized to him the importance of voting and political participation. His mother was active with the League of Women Voters, served on the town council for eight years, and won three elections to be the mayor of Fair Lawn, New Jersey.[36]

Burdick went to law school, he said, because it "just made sense" for a progressive activist to become a lawyer in the late 1960s and early 1970s, especially when the progressive-driven Court during that time issued many rulings that expanded civil rights. His experience in the Peace Corps in Micronesia altered his path, leading him to Hawaii, where he could have a more relaxed lifestyle.

Burdick kept coming back to one key point during our conversation: write-in voting was a serious endeavor to send a message to the political establishment that the candidates they put up were unacceptable. It wasn't enough, he said, to simply not vote for them. That wouldn't have the same effect. He remembered fondly his experience in Fair Lawn, when he first cast write-in votes for school board, catching the attention of a local newspaper columnist. Write-in voting, he said, was an important expressive activity that sent a specific message to politicians and the public: the voters are paramount in our democracy. Elections are not to serve the candidates or to simply ratify their selection. They are for the voters. He recalled once when a poll worker asked him if he had voted in all of the races. "No!" he responded loudly, so others at the polling place could hear him. "Many races don't have any candidates worth voting for."[37]

I asked him why he didn't just run for office himself if he didn't like any of the available choices. For one, he said, he didn't have the time, as he was working for a law firm back then. Additionally, although most of the state is Democratic, he lived in a highly Republican pocket, so he doubted he had any chance of winning. He also didn't know enough people, being relatively new to Hawaii. In any event, this was beside the point. The write-in vote was not to try to win the office. It was a statement of protest.

DONALD DUCK APPEARS IN COURT

The Supreme Court has mentioned Donald Duck in a judicial opinion only once: in *Burdick v. Takushi*. The cartoon duck with the semi-intelligible voice, adored by children (and loathed by some adults!), was the subject of a spirited debate during the oral argument in this case and even made it into the opinion itself. (Donald Duck has had one other glorious moment at the Supreme Court, when he was mentioned—again in the context of voting—during the oral argument for a case about Guam's disputed 1998 gubernatorial election).[38]

During the oral argument, Burdick's lawyer for the Supreme Court appeal, Arthur Eisenberg, was making the point that the Constitution gives Burdick the free speech right to cast a protest vote. One justice (Eisenberg remembers it as Justice Antonin Scalia, but the recording isn't entirely clear) piped up: "Donald Duck? Donald Duck?"* Then Justice Sandra Day O'Connor cut in: "Mickey Mouse, Donald Duck, whatever, that is fine?" Eisenberg responded, "We are claiming that the individual has a right to vote for Mickey Mouse or Donald Duck." When Justice Scalia later quipped that he is "worried about Donald Duck," Eisenberg

---

*It's likely that the justices picked up on the Donald Duck example from Hawaii's written brief in *Burdick*, which mentioned Donald Duck once when citing a 1989 court of appeals decision that had struck down a Maryland law that required non-indigent write-in candidates to pay a $150 fee to have votes for them reported publicly. The appeals court ruled that the Maryland law was unconstitutional. As part of the decision, the court explained that the state,

> appear[s] particularly troubled by the notion that, among the write-in votes, there may be votes for fictitious personages, notably the cartoon character Donald Duck. Of course, plaintiffs seek to have reported votes not for Donald Duck, but for serious minor party candidates.
>
> Nonetheless, we believe that such a vote might, under appropriate circumstances, be meant as serious satirical criticism of the powers that be. As previously indicated, we incline to the view that a vote for a fictitious character would be entitled to constitutional protection. Even were this not the case, however, the specter of Donald Duck as successful vote-getter does not persuade us to disregard the significant violation of protected constitutional rights that we discern here. Correcting this problem through censorship of the vote is utterly inconsistent with the principles under which our form of government operates. Dixon v. Maryland State Admin. Bd. of Election L., 878 F.2d 776, 785 n.12 (4th Cir. 1989).

Presumably this discussion in the state's brief in *Burdick* piqued the justices' interest, leading them to use it as a hypothetical scenario during the oral argument.

responded, "The State may have some dignitary interest in not recording in its books the vote for Donald Duck, but it is our position that that vote should, at the very least[,] be recorded as a vote no."[39] Essentially, Eisenberg said a vote for Donald Duck is a strong indication of a protest vote. The Court's opinion reiterated this assertion: "At bottom, [Burdick] claims that he is entitled to cast and Hawaii required to count a 'protest vote' for Donald Duck, and that any impediment to this asserted 'right' is unconstitutional."[40]

Alan Burdick, for his part, hated this exchange and told me that he did not agree with his lawyer's statement on this point. Write-in voting, he said, is a serious activity. It's a fail-safe mechanism for a voter to express a protest vote or to respond to changing circumstances. He never would have voted for Donald Duck or any other fictitious character. To this day, he's clearly bothered by the notion that many believe he wanted to abuse the ballot in this way. He wasn't trying to play games.

Thirty years later, Eisenberg, a lawyer for the New York Civil Liberties Union (the New York branch of the ACLU), still vividly remembers this line of questioning from the oral argument. *Burdick* was the only case he ever argued at the Supreme Court. He's worked for the NYCLU for over forty years, focusing on issues of voting rights and free speech. *Burdick* was the perfect case to pursue these dual passions: here, Hawaii was depriving Burdick of his right to an effective vote by saying he could not speak as he wished through the ballot.

Eisenberg and I spoke via Zoom on a Friday afternoon in September. Wearing a navy sweater, with graying wavy hair, and against a background showing photos of boats, Eisenberg quickly launched into the intricacies of the lawsuit. He was not involved with the *Burdick* case from the beginning; instead, after the Ninth Circuit had ruled against Burdick (the second time, that is), the Hawaii affiliate of the ACLU contacted Eisenberg to ask for his opinion on whether to appeal the case to the U.S. Supreme Court. After reviewing the Ninth Circuit's opinion, he agreed that there was a good chance the Supreme Court would be interested in hearing the dispute and that they had a strong argument to reinstate Judge Fong's initial ruling against Hawaii. As Eisenberg had been focused on voting rights and free speech in his legal practice, they determined that he should take the lead in writing the briefs and arguing the case once the Court set it for oral argument.[41]

For Eisenberg, the case was about one simple thing: the importance of the right to vote, which should include the ability for a voter to cast a protest vote against the current choices on the ballot. He also thought he had a winning case. Just nine years earlier, in the *Anderson* case, the Court had said that a state must justify burdens on the right to vote with specificity and offer precise reasons for the way it regulates its election system. Eisenberg didn't think Hawaii had offered any good justifications for its write-in voting ban. And he believed his case was even stronger than *Anderson*, in which the Court had ruled against the Ohio law. *Anderson* involved a restriction on candidate access to the ballot, whereas *Burdick* was a direct regulation of voters. If Ohio had not offered a strong enough reason for making it harder for Anderson to appear on the ballot, then surely Hawaii's rationales for the write-in ban—which mostly had to do with Hawaii's fear of factionalism among the electorate and its desire to run its elections as it wished—were even less persuasive.

Eisenberg focused his argument on the infringement of Burdick's right to vote and his right to register his disagreement with the current choices through a protest vote. As he said to the justices, "When Hawaii says to Mr. Burdick, in the interest of promoting consensus, you can vote for only one candidate or not vote at all, consensus may be a very valuable interest, but consensus depends upon consent, and the State has an obligation as well to recognize the dissenting members of its society in the important aspect of voting."[42] Voting, after all, is intimately tied to the right to free speech, and Burdick wanted to use the ballot to express his views. Isn't that the whole point of voting?

THE COURT WEIGHS IN

The first sentence of the Supreme Court's analysis section, in its opinion rejecting Burdick's argument, disabuses the reader of any notion that the Court considered the right to vote as fundamental and deserving of the most robust judicial protection: Burdick "proceeds from the erroneous assumption that a law that imposes any burden upon the right to vote must be subject to strict scrutiny. Our cases do not so hold."[43] Strict scrutiny, you may recall, is the strongest test that the Court employs for burdens on the most important rights in our democracy, like free speech or the right to privacy. Under strict scrutiny, a state must justify any infringements

on the right by showing that its law is directly related to achieving an extremely important state goal. But the Court here was saying that the right
to vote does not deserve that same level of protection. The reason? The
test from *Anderson v. Celebrezze*, the case involving John Anderson's run
for president in 1980 as an independent. Although the Court in *Burdick*
acknowledged that the right to vote is a "fundamental right," it used the
Anderson case to lower judicial protection against state encroachments.
The Court credited the state's need to "assure that elections are operated
equitably and efficiently."[44] It highlighted Hawaii's "important regulatory
interests" to justify the restrictions on voters and cited an interest in stability. For instance, the majority explained that the write-in ban assists the
state by allowing an unopposed candidate at the primary to be deemed the
winner without the state having to run a general election for that office.
Burdick expressed bitterness at the origin of that rule: a recent 1988 state
constitutional amendment, which he thinks the state attorney general had
engineered in part to defeat his litigation.[45] Burdick had objected to that
rule as unfair to voters and as an example of how the state's election system is set up to help candidates, not voters, especially given the number of
uncontested races due to Hawaii's one-party dominance.

The Supreme Court's majority in this case also noted that it was fairly
easy for someone to appear on the ballot in Hawaii: they simply must
gather a handful of signatures—either fifteen or twenty-five, depending
on the office. Therefore, if Burdick really wanted to vote for someone, he
should have helped them gather that minimal number of signatures to
appear on the ballot.

But the Court did not address the real problem: what if Burdick does
not learn until after the filing deadline has passed that only one person—
whom he will not support—has decided to run? What if he simply wants
to register his displeasure with all of the available candidates? What if
the political winds change between the filing deadline and Election Day?
Under Hawaii's regime, Burdick is out of luck. He can cast a ballot, for
sure, but he has lost the ability to cast an *effective* vote that represents his
true feelings.

In rejecting Burdick's argument, the Court squarely indicated that
voter restrictions are permissible and that states need not offer specific
justifications to support their rules. They can simply cite the need for
administrative efficiency or the desire to maintain political stability, and

that's enough. As the majority wrote, in response to the contrary viewpoint, "The dissent's suggestion that voters are entitled to cast their ballots for unqualified candidates appears to be driven by the assumption that an election system that imposes any restraint on voter choice is unconstitutional. This is simply wrong."[46] The Court also never even mentioned the California Supreme Court case that had spurred Alan Burdick to take on this fight in the first place; it was more or less silently overruled, which Burdick found particularly unsatisfying.

Burdick at least took some solace that three justices sided with him in dissent. It's telling that Justice John Paul Stevens was one of the dissenters. Justice Stevens wrote the Court's majority opinion in the *Anderson* case. He was the justice who had created the new test for the right to vote in that decision. But now he was taking the opposite viewpoint, joining Justice Anthony Kennedy's dissenting opinion. Perhaps Justice Stevens did not realize that a future majority would distort the test to give states even broader leeway to enact voting laws without specific rationales. As the dissent says, "A State that bans write-in voting in some or all elections must justify the burden on individual voters by putting forth the precise interests that are served by the ban. A write-in prohibition should not be presumed valid in the absence of any proffered justification by the State. The standard the Court derives from *Anderson v. Celebrezze* means at least this."[47] The majority had not faithfully applied that rule. It instead feared that a more stringent standard would engage the judiciary in too much oversight of elections. It embellished the *Anderson* test to essentially say, "States, we trust you to do the right thing when it comes to the right to vote."

Of course, there was a good reason for Burdick and other Hawaii voters not to trust state legislators to do the right thing and protect everyone's voting rights. Hawaii is an overwhelmingly Democratic state. As noted before, the primary election is often the only game in town, as the Democratic nominee is almost certain to win the general election in November in most districts (as well as in statewide races). Democratic legislators had every incentive to craft voting rules that would help to keep themselves in power. A ban on write-in voting can tamp down insurgent candidates. The Democratic establishment selects the individuals they want to run and those people easily gain access to the ballot. A strong write-in candidate could mess up that plan. The write-in ban also ensures that the public is less aware of protest votes, as no one can cast a vote for someone other than the listed candidates.

Art Eisenberg, the lawyer who argued the case for Burdick at the Supreme Court, summarized the significance of the *Burdick* decision by noting that the Court adopted an "instrumental" view of the right to vote.[48] What he meant is that, instead of embracing voting as a fundamental right in our democracy, the Court saw the ballot as merely an instrument to elect someone to office—not a tool of expression. When understood through this narrow lens, the right to vote loses much of its significance, opening the door to additional regulation. After all, who really cares if Burdick can't register his protest vote when it's almost certain that his vote will have no effect on the outcome and that the same candidates will ultimately win? What's the big deal for the overall election system? This myopic view, however, cuts out the main actor in our democracy: the voter.

Notice the shift from *Anderson*, which—while not using the highest form of judicial review—still required states to offer "precise interests" for a voting law and explain why those interests made it "necessary to burden" voters' rights.[49] That sounds like a high standard for a state to meet, which is why Eisenberg, Burdick's lawyer, thought they would win their case. But the Court in *Burdick* did not properly use that test. The justices in the majority instead emphasized the "flexible" nature of the inquiry and said that a state could justify a less-than-severe burden on voters by citing "important regulatory interests."[50] In plain English: The state can win if it infringes on the right to vote only a little bit or harms only a few voters. The creeping change in the Court's jurisprudence is subtle, but no less damning: it went from highly valuing the fundamental right to vote in the 1960s, to softening that protection in the *Anderson* case, to even further deference to states in *Burdick*. Hardly anyone at the time took serious notice of this quiet but damaging shift.

BURDICK'S SAD LEGACY

Alan Burdick knew that the case was bad law, and he's "ashamed" that his name is associated with a ruling that harms voters. That's one of the first things he told me during our conversation: it's his "biggest regret." He noted that he filed the case at a time when the Supreme Court was more liberal, with noted civil rights champions William Brennan and Thurgood Marshall still on the Court. He decried the lengthy appeals process—especially the trip to the Hawaii Supreme Court in the interim, which slowed things down and delayed when the Supreme Court would ultimately hear the case. "If I had known that it was going to go that way, I never would have launched this exercise," he lamented. "I'm appalled that my name is down there for all this bad law."[51]

The pain was clear on Burdick's face. When I asked him what message he would give to my law students, he said, "Be careful before you file a lawsuit, because they can be full of adverse consequences." He recognized that the case stands for far more than the proposition that a state can ban write-in voting. Courts have used it to strip protection for the right to vote, something Burdick values so highly as the most important right in our democracy. He wanted to help voters, but he knows that the consequences of his lawsuit ultimately hurt them.

Burdick learned of the negative decision while he was back home in New Jersey visiting his mother. Someone—he doesn't remember who—called to tell him that he had lost at the highest court in the land. He was disappointed, but not surprised. He didn't have a great feeling about his chances when he appealed the Ninth Circuit Court of Appeals loss, but his lawyers wanted to take on the cause. He was disappointed about the focus on Donald Duck at the oral argument, feeling like the Court was missing his main point: that write-in voting is a serious mechanism for voters to express a true message about the available candidates. And, to this day, he regrets even starting the *Burdick v. Takushi* case because of its implications for the constitutional right to vote. He knows that many people have heard of the "*Anderson-Burdick*" standard and he feels badly about how courts have employed the test to curtail voting rights. He's ashamed that his name is the second part of that test.

Morris Takushi, for his part, doesn't remember the case at all. As the director of Hawaii elections back then, he was the officially named defendant, but he has no recollection of the decision. When I contacted him, he noted that he had only learned of the ruling years after it came down, when someone told him that he "had the distinction of having [his] name recorded in judicial history, as a defendant, in one of the historic cases that had been before the U.S. Supreme Court." He ended his email, "ALOHA ke AKUA ia 'oe!"[52]

———

The *Burdick* case devalued the constitutional right to vote in several ways. Most tellingly, it failed to recognize the importance of allowing a voter to express a preference—even if it is to show disagreement with all of the current choices—at the ballot box. It also gave states wide leeway to regulate their elections as they wish, with less meaningful judicial oversight. And it denied someone like Burdick the ability to cast a vote that would count in the way he wanted. No wonder Alan Burdick himself has become disillusioned with the current political climate and voters' ability to fix it.

The implications of the Supreme Court's decision in *Burdick* have reverberated for decades and have infected every aspect of our electoral system. It's not just that states can ban write-in voting. It's that the new standard for the right to vote, "*Anderson-Burdick*," offers strong deference to states in election administration, even if that means some voters are shut out.

This derogation of the constitutional right to vote has real-world effects. As we'll see in the next chapter, it's one of the main reasons states are allowed to enact strict voter ID laws—leading to unfair disenfranchisement.

CHAPTER 3

THE FIGHT OVER VOTER ID

Crawford v. Marion County Election Board (2008)

	JUSTICE	APPOINTED BY
MAJORITY	Stevens, John Paul *(authored plurality opinion)*	Ford, Gerald (R)
	Roberts, John G., Jr. (chief justice) *(joined Stevens's opinion)*	Bush, George W. (R)
	Kennedy, Anthony M. *(joined Stevens's opinion)*	Reagan, Ronald (R)
	Scalia, Antonin *(authored opinion concurring in judgment)*	Reagan, Ronald (R)
	Thomas, Clarence *(joined Scalia's opinion)*	Bush, George H. W. (R)
	Alito, Samuel A., Jr. *(joined Scalia's opinion)*	Bush, George W. (R)
DISSENT	Souter, David H. *(authored dissent)*	Bush, George H. W. (R)
	Breyer, Stephen G. *(authored dissent)*	Clinton, Bill (D)
	Ginsburg, Ruth Bader *(joined Breyer's dissent)*	Clinton, Bill (D)

In the aftermath of the 2016 election, reporter and author Ari Berman painted a stark picture of American democracy: Donald Trump might have won the presidency because of strict voter ID requirements in states like Wisconsin. Just look at the numbers, Berman said. Democratic Party nominee Hillary Clinton lost Wisconsin by about 23,000 votes, yet turnout was down substantially in 2016—especially in minority-heavy areas that tend to support Democrats, such as Milwaukee. Indeed, about 41,000 fewer people voted in Milwaukee in 2016 than in 2012. Much of that decline, Berman asserted, could be attributed to the state's new law requiring voters to show a photo ID at the polls.[1]

Berman profiled voters like Andrea Anthony, who had misplaced her driver's license only a few days before Election Day. Anthony took her expired Wisconsin state ID and a proof of residency with her to vote. The poll worker, however, was forced to give her a provisional ballot, which is essentially a separate ballot that is set aside and would not count unless Anthony obtained a new ID and presented it to the municipal clerk's office within ten days of the election. Because she did not have the time to jump through these procedural hoops, her vote did not count—the first time in her life that she had been effectively disenfranchised.[2] Neil Albrecht, the director of Milwaukee elections, said he would "estimate that 25 to 35 percent of the 41,000 decrease in voters, or somewhere between 10,000 and 15,000 voters, likely did not vote due to the photo ID requirement."[3] Barry Burden, a political science professor at the University of Wisconsin, noted that student turnout was also down in 2016 both because of the photo ID requirement and because the presidential candidates did not campaign much there.[4] Lower turnout among liberal-leaning voters, of course, might have contributed to Clinton's loss in the state.

We don't know if Hillary Clinton would have won Wisconsin in 2016 without the new photo ID law. Many analysts think she had flaws as a candidate, including her failure to campaign aggressively in the state. And whether the voter ID law changed the result is beside the point; it's undeniable that some voters had a harder time casting a ballot because of an unnecessary voting law. No one should suffer a pointless burden to exercise their fundamental right to vote.

Yet that is exactly what the Supreme Court's 2008 decision in *Crawford v. Marion County Election Board* has brought about. In that case, the Court refused to invalidate Indiana's new voter ID requirement, which at the time was the strictest in the nation. By "strict," I mean that voters had fewer options to comply and individuals who did not have an ID had to take tedious steps to have their votes count. For instance, the law required a voter without a valid, government-issued ID with one's name and photograph to fill out a provisional ballot and then travel to the municipal clerk's office after Election Day to show an ID or fill out an affidavit saying that they are indigent or have a religious objection to being photographed. Otherwise, election officials could not tally their vote.

Crawford is a logical outgrowth of the Court's decisions in *Anderson* and *Burdick*, which we have explored already. These three cases go together to form a trilogy—call it *Anderson-Burdick-Crawford*, or ABC—that gives states wide leeway to run their elections as they see fit, even if their rules lead to voter suppression. It is important to understand what the Court said in *Crawford*, how future legislatures have recognized that there are few constitutional limits on the restrictive election laws they can pass, and how courts have deferred to states' rules. For some people, voting today is harder than it was a decade or two ago, and *Crawford* is one of the main culprits.

The story of the *Crawford* litigation in and of itself isn't the most riveting. It doesn't involve an insurgent presidential candidate or an individual who now regrets his decision to file a lawsuit. There are no cartoon characters like Donald Duck. Our focus here will be on the message the justices sent to state legislatures and the way in which the Court furthered the rule from *Anderson* and *Burdick*—more or less giving states a free pass to enact laws that restrict the constitutional right to vote.

BILL CRAWFORD, A CIVIL RIGHTS CHAMPION

Bill Crawford identified the assassination of Martin Luther King Jr. as his political awakening. He was at a campaign stop for Robert Kennedy when Kennedy announced that King had been shot. "That was very traumatic for me," Crawford told the *Indianapolis Star*. "Here was a man I thought had given everything he could to his community, and I got to thinking that I had not done anything."[5] He ultimately decided to run for office, winning a seat in the Indiana House of Representatives in 1972 and serving for forty years, until his retirement in 2012. When he retired he was the longest-serving Black state lawmaker in Indiana's history.[6]

I had the great honor of interviewing Crawford in May 2015, shortly before his death a few months later. He was kind, soft spoken, and generous. Even over the phone, I felt like I was in the presence of true greatness.

Crawford recalled how he had been part of the legislative debate in 2005 when Republicans introduced the new voter ID law for Indiana's elections. He was quick to point out that, although Republicans in the state proposed the new restriction for what they claimed were innocuous reasons, "the implication fell heavily on African Americans."[7] During the floor debate on the proposed law, Crawford lamented that the idea was of the same ilk as poll taxes and literacy tests—just another way to depress Black voter turnout.[8] This sentiment echoes one of the guiding principles of Crawford's public service: ensuring equality for all and always fighting against measures that have a disproportionately negative impact on racial minorities. Others who were involved in the debate, such as the president of the local NAACP chapter, thought that race was a clear motivating factor given that the state had seen an increase in Black elected officials and that a strict voter ID requirement would make it harder for Black people to vote because they are statistically less likely to have an ID that satisfies the law.[9] As a judge on the court of appeals who heard the case put it plainly, "Let's not beat around the bush: The Indiana voter photo ID law is a not-too-thinly-veiled attempt to discourage election-day turnout by certain folks believed to skew Democratic."[10]

After the legislation passed, Crawford became the primary plaintiff in a lawsuit to challenge the new voting rule. Other organizations were also involved, including the NAACP and the Indiana Democratic Party. Using Crawford as the first-named plaintiff made political sense: he was well-known in the community and could represent the harms this voter ID law would create. For his part, Crawford simply said, "I was willing and involved in the debate in the [Indiana] House. So I was simply the right person at the time."[11] As Joe Simpson, who was involved in the litigation as the then treasurer of the local NAACP, put it, "He had no fear of speaking up for those who could not speak for themselves."[12]

Although Crawford was the primary plaintiff and his name is associated with the case, the lawsuit was really a battle of lawyers. Both sides had good ones. In the plaintiff's corner, Bill Groth, a well-known attorney in Indiana, took on the cause to challenge the law. When the case eventually reached the Supreme Court, the plaintiffs also hired Paul Smith, who had a lot of experience appearing before the justices. Smith argued the case, but that was partially by chance: he won a coin flip against another lawyer on the team. On Indiana's side was Tom Fisher, the state's top government lawyer.

STATES RIGHTS OVER VOTING RIGHTS

The litigation took the typical route through the federal judiciary, with an initial opinion at the trial court, an appeal to the U.S. Court of Appeals, and then a further appeal to the U.S. Supreme Court. The plaintiffs lost at every stage. But at least one prominent judge later regretted his decision. Judge Richard Posner of the Seventh Circuit Court of Appeals wrote that he had not fully grasped the harms the voter ID law would create. In 2013, Judge Posner wrote in a book, "I plead guilty to having written the majority opinion (affirmed by the Supreme Court) upholding Indiana's requirement that prospective voters prove their identity with a photo ID—a type of law now widely regarded as a means of voter suppression rather than of fraud prevention."[13] That sentiment encapsulates the key debate within this case: To what extent do voter ID laws actually root out fraud versus how much do they suppress the right to vote?

The courts squarely came down in favor of the state, though there were dissents throughout. For our purposes, what's most important—and most damning—is the approval that the Supreme Court gave to voting laws that will inevitably harm voters. The approach the Court took in the *Anderson* and *Burdick* cases are partly to blame.

Indiana offered three reasons for its new photo ID requirement for voting. First, the state said that the voter ID law was intended to modernize its election system. Second, the state claimed the law was necessary to root out the potential of voter fraud. And third, the state asserted that the new law would safeguard voter confidence in Indiana elections. Let's take each justification in turn to see how the Court's acceptance of these interests boiled down to one thing: allowing states to pass virtually whatever voting laws they want with only the flimsiest of supporting evidence.[14]

With respect to election modernization, the Court noted that "the integrity of elections is enhanced through improved technology" and that Congress had encouraged states to modernize their electoral systems.[15] That statement is unobjectionable as a general matter. The real question is whether the specific "improved technology" the state adopts actually improves anything. What, exactly, was the problem that Indiana needed to address with respect to its voting system? The state didn't really say. It instead relied on its next justification—the desire to root out voter fraud.

Here, we need to be very precise about what kind of fraud actually exists and what effect the photo ID requirement would have on that potential fraud. The opening sentences of this section of the Court's opinion provide a salient answer: "The only kind of voter fraud that [Indiana's new voter ID law] addresses is in-person voter impersonation at polling places. The record contains no evidence of any such fraud actually occurring in Indiana at any time in its history."[16] Yes, that's right. There was *no* evidence of such fraud. One would think that that statement would end the matter.

Indeed, the only kind of fraud that a voter ID law can prevent is in-person impersonation, where someone shows up to the polls pretending to be someone else. That kind of fraud simply does not happen to any significant or measurable degree. In part, that's because engaging in fraud of this type is really foolish. It would take a lot of people to be part of the jig to alter election results, and with more people involved, the chances of being caught are much higher. That is probably why we have never seen more than isolated, anecdotal evidence of in-person impersonation. Justin Levitt, a law professor at Loyola Law School, Los Angeles who has also worked on voting rights for the Department of Justice, studied every election between 2000 and 2014 to compile a list of credible allegations of in-person voter fraud. Can you guess how many incidents he found? Thirty-one. Out of over one billion ballots cast over those fourteen years, there were only thirty-one credible allegations of in-person impersonation in all general, primary, special, and municipal elections.[17] Keep in mind that some of those allegations were ultimately unfounded, often arising due to people having the same name. That's not to say that voter fraud doesn't exist, and of course even one instance of voter fraud is one too many. But when we balance the benefits of a rule with the harms it causes, we must be clear about the actual evidence of fraud that the law will prevent.

The Supreme Court did not grapple meaningfully with its acknowledgment that Indiana had presented zero evidence of the kind of fraud that the voter ID law would avert. Instead, the Court suggested that in-person voter fraud could still be a problem—a view based almost entirely on its occurrence over a century ago. In a footnote, the Court cited the late-nineteenth-century Tammany Hall political machine in New York City, which paid voters to go to the polls several times throughout the day, thwarting the watchful eye of poll workers by shaving off a little more of their beard each time.[18] That's right: to justify a law in the name of election "integrity" in 2008, the Court's best evidence was from the late 1800s. The justices also cited election fraud in 2003 in East Chicago, Indiana, but that 2003 incident involved absentee balloting, not in-person voting. The new voter ID rule would not have made a difference, as the Indiana law exempted absentee voters from presenting an ID—and the election system caught the fraud anyway. Essentially, to reject a challenge to the law, the Court rested on pure speculation that in-person voter fraud could theoretically happen. Put differently, Indiana was given a free pass to enact its voter ID requirement without having to provide any evidence that it had a problem with its elections that it needed to fix.

Finally, the Court credited Indiana's asserted interest "in protecting public confidence 'in the integrity and legitimacy of representative government.'"[19] That general interest, of course, could justify *any* voting rule. A state should be concerned about safeguarding voter confidence. That doesn't mean, however, that a state is free to make it harder for some people to vote. Moreover, a lack of confidence in the voting system is often the state's own fault. Indiana claimed it needed the voter ID law because it had failed to carefully clean up its voter rolls, and the Court credited this assertion. Although having inflated voter rolls does not inextricably lead to voter fraud, the Court agreed that the state's own incompetence gave it a good enough reason to enact a strict voter ID rule, thereby harming additional voters.

Professor Atiba Ellis of Case Western Reserve University refers to this ploy as the "meme of voter fraud." As he puts it, "The meme of voter fraud is the idea that unworthy voters are attacking the electoral system by voting fraudulently through impersonation or other bad acts. Although scholars of election law aptly demonstrate that the meme is a myth, the meme nonetheless endures as a rationale for the continued passage of heightened voter regulations like voter identification laws."[20] We saw this same phenomenon after the 2020 election. Former President Trump and many of his supporters relentlessly peddled falsehoods saying there were problems with the election. Not surprisingly, many people—especially conservatives—now think there are major integrity issues with our election administration. States like Georgia and Texas used that public sentiment to enact even stricter voting rules. It's a vicious cycle: politicians who will benefit from lower voter turnout convince the public, without any actual evidence, that the election system is broken; public opinion polls reflect the sentiment that election integrity is a major concern; those very same politicians use the public opinion that they themselves generated under false pretenses to enact even stricter voting laws. The Supreme Court bought this ploy in the *Crawford* case hook, line, and sinker.

On the other side of the scale are the burdens on voters. Here, the Court changed its tune. While it did not require Indiana to offer real examples of voter fraud, it faulted the plaintiffs for not bringing forth enough evidence of the burdens voters would face in complying with the ID requirement. The justices recognized that the law would likely make voting more difficult for some voters; it just didn't think the plaintiffs had either articulated those burdens well enough or provided sufficient evidence on the number of voters who might suffer disenfranchisement. The Court essentially said that it would not invalidate the law despite the well-founded worry that the ID requirement would make it harder for some people to vote—but it was completely fine with Indiana's evidence-free speculation that voter fraud might occur. This sentiment ignores the real problem: although most people may have no trouble complying with the new voter ID rule, some voters will be shut out of democratic participation entirely. The fact is that some people, such as poorer individuals who live in the inner city, do not have a driver's license and have no need for an ID in their everyday lives. Sure, they could go obtain one, but that requires time and resources, like taking off work to go to the department of motor vehicles office. And they might not have the required underlying documentation, such as a birth certificate, which requires money and time to obtain. Even a seemingly small expense of $25 or $50 to obtain a birth certificate can put a dent in the budget for someone living paycheck to paycheck. All to exercise the most fundamental right in our democracy.

Although there is no evidence that a photo ID requirement for voting deters any actual fraud, there is plenty of evidence that Indiana's law—like other similar laws passed in the wake of the *Crawford* decision—has harmed real voters. Studies have shown that a photo ID requirement can decrease turnout, with a disproportionate impact on racial minorities, indigent individuals, and older voters, all of whom are less likely to have the required ID.[21] It isn't hard to find real-world examples. As I was writing this chapter, I posted on Twitter that I was reading *Crawford* for probably the hundredth time and that the opinion still made me angry. Someone responded: "Infuriating. That law prevented my grandmother from voting in an election that year because her long-used photo ID 'wasn't good enough.' First time she missed an election since [the day I was born.]"[22]

Notice what's happened here. Back in the 1960s, the Court required states to justify any burdens on the fundamental right to vote with specificity. States had to satisfy a high bar to impose a voter restriction. In *Anderson*, the Court eased the test somewhat, saying that states must offer a "precise interest" for its rules and explain why it is "necessary to burden" voters' rights.[23] In *Burdick*, the Court approved Hawaii's generalized need to "assure that elections are operated equitably and efficiently" and failed to require the state to offer a precise justification for depriving Alan Burdick of his ability to write in a candidate of his choice.[24] And now, in *Crawford*, the Court was satisfied with Indiana's broad assertion of a desire to promote election integrity, while failing to credit the real, tangible burdens that voters would face.

DID THE COURT UPHOLD ALL VOTER ID LAWS? NOT EXACTLY

Many proponents of ID laws for voting like to point out that Justice John Paul Stevens, known as a liberal, wrote the Court's opinion in this case to uphold Indiana's voter ID requirement. But that broad assertion ignores some of the context behind the decision. Justice Stevens wrote what is known as a "plurality" opinion, meaning that the decision answered the question on whether the law was invalid, but it did not have the assent of at least five of the nine justices. Instead, fewer than five justices joined the main opinion and there was no majority viewpoint. One determines the winner of the lawsuit by adding the votes of those in the plurality with the votes of others who agreed with the result but not the reasoning of the main opinion. The opinion Justice Stevens wrote in this case was for only himself, Chief Justice Roberts, and Justice Kennedy. That opinion left the door open for future challenges to voter ID laws with better evidence of the burdens that voters would face.

Justice Scalia, a noted conservative, wrote a separate opinion, joined by Justices Thomas and Alito, in which he agreed not to strike down the Indiana law but also sought to declare that *all* voter ID requirements are perfectly constitutional. Requiring an ID to vote, he said, did not amount to much of a hurdle for voters: "The burden of acquiring, possessing, and showing a free photo identification is simply not severe, because it does not even represent a significant increase over the usual burdens of voting."[25] Justice Scalia also did not want to encourage future litigation: "This is an area where the dos and don'ts need to be known in advance of the election."[26] And he found the state's asserted reasons for the law "sufficient" to justify the "minimal" burden on voters.[27] In sum, Justice Scalia refused to consider how the voter ID requirement might harm any individual voter who would have difficulty obtaining an identification that would suffice. Instead, he believed that states should be free to impose essentially whatever election rules they want, except (presumably) an explicit, direct denial of the right to vote.

Three liberal justices—Ginsburg, Souter, and Breyer—dissented, emphasizing the harms that voters would face and the lack of evidence the state had presented to justify its law. As Justice Souter wrote, "[A] State may not burden the right to vote merely by invoking abstract interests, be they legitimate or even compelling, but must make a particular, factual showing that threats to its interests outweigh the particular impediments it has imposed."[28] The state had failed to do so here, resting on an abstract concern of election integrity instead of a specific problem it sought to address.

Therefore, *Crawford* was basically a 3–3–3 decision. Three justices (Stevens, Roberts, and Kennedy) signed on to the lead opinion that credited the state's generalized interests and said that the plaintiffs had not shown enough of a burden on voters, but they left the door open to future challenges with better evidence; three justices (Scalia, Thomas, and Alito) argued that all voter ID laws are perfectly acceptable; and three justices in dissent (Souter, Ginsburg, and Breyer) would have invalidated the law. It's incorrect to claim, as some proponents of ID laws have done, that the Supreme Court *upheld* all voter ID requirements. There was no majority opinion for that proposition. Justice Stevens's narrower opinion—which is considered the lead opinion given its more limited scope—refused to invalidate Indiana's law, but it said nothing about the constitutionality of voter ID laws as a general matter. That might sound like technical legalese, but it's an important distinction. The Court did not say that voter ID laws are always constitutional; it just thought that these plaintiffs hadn't made their case.

Of course, I have no doubt that the Court today would likely do exactly as Justice Scalia wanted and uphold all voter ID requirements. The

Court is much more conservative now and the trend to defer to a state's election rules has only increased since *Crawford*. But as a factual matter, *Crawford* did not explicitly approve of *all* voter ID requirements.

The history since *Crawford* has been extremely litigious, yet the message from *Crawford* has largely remained: states have wide leeway to enact whatever voting rules they want, even if those laws burden some voters.

———

I became aware of the *Crawford* litigation almost from its inception. In 2005 I was attending law school and was enrolled in a course on voting rights with Professor Spencer Overton at George Washington University Law School. That class put me on the path to become a voting rights scholar. At the time, Professor Overton was serving on the Carter-Baker Commission, a group chaired by former President Jimmy Carter, a Democrat, and former secretary of state James A. Baker, a Republican. The commission was considering ways to reform our elections in the wake of the 2000 election debacle in Florida and the close presidential election results in Ohio in 2004. Professor Overton came into class regaling us with stories from the commission's meetings. I was fascinated that my professor was part of an esteemed group looking at democratic reform and was sharing those same insights with our class.

The commission's final report recommended that states require voters to show an ID that complies with the REAL ID Act, a federal law that said states must verify a person's full legal name, date of birth, address, Social Security number, and U.S. citizenship before issuing a driver's license or other identification. The commission believed that this same requirement could apply to voting. Importantly, however, the commission said that states should ease in the requirement and not apply it for at least five years, until 2010, to ensure that voters had time to obtain a compliant ID.[29]

Professor Overton was not convinced. He debated with us in class whether, even in five years, a requirement to show an ID might harm certain voters, especially traditionally marginalized groups such as poor people and racial minorities. He told us that he had raised these objections but that the majority of the other commissioners had shot him down. He even drafted a dissent of about 500 words long—he shared it with the class to hear our thoughts—but the rest of the commissioners had rejected it for being too long, instead adopting a 250-word limitation on such a dissent. He posted his full dissent on a website. In it, he lamented that the "Commission's ID proposal would exclude Americans of all backgrounds, but the poor, the disabled, the elderly, students, and people of color would bear the greatest burden."[30]

The Carter-Baker Commission's proposal is particularly important, given that Justice Stevens relied on it in his opinion in *Crawford*, quoting from two paragraphs of the report to suggest that identification laws can help to inspire confidence in our voting system. He neglected to point out that the commission thought states should wait to implement any ID law until at least 2010—which was still two years away when *Crawford* came down—to give states time to ease in the requirement. Unfortunately, Justice Stevens also failed to mention Professor Overton's dissent or the dissents from other commissioners, such as former Senate Majority Leader Tom Daschle, to show that the commission's recommendations were not unanimous. Proponents of voter ID laws have improperly embellished the importance of the commission's report to suggest that even liberals (Justice Stevens and President Jimmy Carter) support the idea.

TODAY'S FIGHT OVER VOTER ID

Voter ID laws have become such a hot-button issue that I'm probably not going to convince any readers to change their views on whether they are good or bad. For me, the answer is clear. On the one hand, there is tons of evidence that strict voter ID laws have the potential to disenfranchise certain groups of voters, particularly poor people, younger voters and students, the elderly, and racial minorities. These voters are simply less likely to have an ID that will count. Consider an example of college students in Texas, where a state university photo ID—which a university will not issue without verifying one's identity—does not suffice for voting. A Texas gun license, however, is perfectly fine.[31] You may have a driver's license in your wallet, but lots of people do not. Although the percentage of individuals without a government-issued ID is relatively small—studies say that around 5 to 10 percent of people do not have a compliant ID—that still equates to millions of voters.[32] Given structural racism and demographic trends, people of color are disproportionately less likely to have an ID.[33] The bottom line is that these fellow citizens with fewer resources must jump through unnecessary hoops to participate in our democracy.

You might be wondering, "Don't you need an ID to board a plane or buy Sudafed?" Not really. We have workarounds that include additional screening if you show up to the airport without identification, and pharmacists can take down your information and sell you Sudafed without a photo ID.[34] Moreover, boarding a plane or buying cold medicine isn't the most fundamental right in our democracy. And those without an ID, who are disproportionately poorer, probably aren't flying much anyway.

On the other side of the debate is the amount of voter fraud that exists and the kind of fraud that a voter ID law might deter. Even though some politicians may wish to regale us with stories of massive problems with our voting system, the sheer fact is that voter fraud is virtually nonexistent. It's not zero—no one credibly argues that. But it is rare and hardly ever affects the outcome of an election. When it might, such as in a North Carolina congressional election in 2018 (which involved absentee ballot fraud by a Republican operative, not in-person voter fraud), election officials found it before officially certifying the results.[35] The system worked to detect fraud in that rare instance when it occurred at a pervasive enough level to call the outcome into doubt.

We therefore have the potential of meaningful voter suppression as a result of these laws, with few corresponding benefits. In fact, voter ID laws don't even make people feel better about the integrity of our election system. Researchers Nate Persily and Charles Stewart conducted a representative nationwide survey to determine people's views on the integrity of the election system in their state, and they found that the presence of a strict voter ID law had no impact on whether people felt more secure about their elections or whether they perceived that fraud is a problem.[36] The Court in *Crawford* was therefore wrong when citing a state's interest in safeguarding voter confidence: the laws don't even do that.

But most people still think voter ID laws are a good idea. Survey data suggests that up to 80 percent of voters support a photo ID requirement for voting, at least in the abstract.[37] Yet, 72 percent also think states should make in-person voting easier.[38] Of course, a strict photo ID law could make it harder for some people to vote in-person if they do not have the required identification. Moreover, photo ID laws come in all shapes and sizes. Some requirements are fairly lenient, with various fail-safe mechanisms for voters who do not have an ID. For instance, Kentucky's law, passed in 2020, lets voters fill out a form, under penalty of perjury, explaining why they do not have an ID, and then they can cast a regular ballot like anyone else. They can be prosecuted afterward (as they should be!) if they were actually voting fraudulently. That's quite different from Indiana's practice, which requires voters without an ID to fill out a provisional ballot, which will not count unless the voter travels to the county clerk's office within ten days to show an ID or fill out a form. (Some states have even shorter periods for voters to follow up with election officials.[39]) Few voters are likely to take these steps. One study showed that in the first Indiana election after the *Crawford* decision, in 2008, 1,039 individuals cast provisional ballots because they lacked an ID, yet only 137—just 13.2 percent—went to the county clerk's office to follow up with the required documentation.[40] The fact that only 1,039 people across the entire state had to take an additional step to have their ballot count may seem relatively small, except for two key facts: the number of fraudulent votes deterred was likely zero, and we have no idea how many voters didn't show up in the first place because of the hassle of the photo ID requirement.

Photo ID laws are not going away, thanks in part to the Supreme Court's tacit blessing of them. The *Crawford* decision came down in 2008, and between 2010 (when Republicans took over additional state houses) and 2012, lawmakers proposed strict photo ID bills in thirty-seven different states.[41] Ten states passed new laws in the four years after *Crawford*.[42] A subsequent investigation uncovered a remarkable nationwide campaign to push for the creation of these voter ID laws from the American Legislative Exchange Council (ALEC), a conservative organization that advises state lawmakers and receives a large chunk of its funding from conservative nonprofits and corporations. ALEC created model voter ID legislation, basing it on the Indiana law, and encouraged its members to introduce these bills in their states.[43] As an election policy analyst for the nonpartisan National Conference of State Legislatures explained in 2012, "I very rarely see a single issue taken up by as many states in such a short period of time as with voter ID. It's been a pretty remarkable spread."[44]

As of 2023, thirty-six states had a requirement that voters show identification at the polls.[45] According to the National Conference of State Legislatures, nine of these states—Arkansas, Georgia, Indiana, Kansas,

Mississippi, Missouri, Ohio, Tennessee, and Wisconsin—have ID laws of the "strict" variety, meaning that voters without a compliant ID must cast a provisional ballot and then take additional steps to have that ballot count.[46] North Carolina would also be on that list, except that its law has been enmeshed in litigation.[47] Texas, too, has been involved in litigation over its ID law, which became "non-strict" only as a result of those lawsuits.[48] Now, voters without an ID can fill out a Reasonable Impediment Declaration form and show a bank statement or utility bill as their proof of identity.[49] That process, however, hasn't prevented disenfranchisement. Sometimes, voter suppression is indirect, as voters aren't aware of the process or don't want to deal with the additional burdens. ABC News recounted the struggles of eighty-two-year-old Elmira Hicks, an African American woman living in rural Texas who could not renew her driver's license because she was not able to obtain her birth certificate—a common problem among older Black people in the South, who were often born at home and never even obtained an official birth certificate. She did not believe she would be able to vote without a compliant ID. Technically, once Texas tweaked its rule in response to the lawsuits, Hicks could bring her expired license and fill out the Reasonable Impediment Declaration—but why make someone like Hicks jump through those hoops? These stories demonstrate that our country's sorry history of racial discrimination in voting has not ended.[50]

There has also been an increase in litigation over voter ID requirements. Both sides have invoked Justice Stevens's opinion in *Crawford* to their advantage: states think the Court gave a green light to enact strict voter ID laws, while opponents note that Stevens did not say that voter ID laws are always constitutional. To be sure, opponents have enjoyed a few successes. In North Carolina, for instance, a federal appeals court struck down the state's ID law under the federal Voting Rights Act because it targeted minority voters "with almost surgical precision."[51] Pennsylvania state courts invalidated a strict ID law under the state constitution.[52] But these were fleeting victories. Most courts have upheld ID laws, using *Crawford* as the baseline for their decisions.

Photo ID requirements for voting probably don't change election outcomes. They also surely do not prevent fraud. They don't even increase the public's confidence in the integrity of the election system! But that's not the point. The Supreme Court's decision in *Crawford*, by essentially blessing these laws, allowed states to make it harder for people to vote for no good reason. The Court refused to scrutinize Indiana's generalized goal of improving election integrity. That approach gives states wide latitude: virtually any election rule might help election integrity in the abstract.

Many states heeded the call, knowing that the courts are likely to accept state voting laws under *Crawford*, even if those laws effectively disenfranchise some voters for no valid reason. What the Court started in *Anderson* and *Burdick*—greater deference to states—was more fully realized in *Crawford*. We no longer have a fundamental right to vote, at least not one that Supreme Court precedent will protect. Instead, states have the right to run their elections as they see fit.

CHAPTER 4

THE STIGMA OF
FELON DISENFRANCHISEMENT

Richardson v. Ramirez (1974)

	JUSTICE	APPOINTED BY
MAJORITY	Rehnquist, William H. *(authored majority opinion)*	Nixon, Richard (R)
	Burger, Warren (chief justice)	Eisenhower, Dwight D. (R)
	Stewart, Potter	Eisenhower, Dwight D. (R)
	White, Byron	Kennedy, John F. (D)
	Blackmun, Harry A.	Nixon, Richard (R)
	Powell, Lewis F., Jr.	Nixon, Richard (R)
DISSENT	Douglas, William O. *(authored dissent and joined Marshall's dissent in part)*	Roosevelt, Franklin D. (D)
	Marshall, Thurgood *(authored dissent)*	Johnson, Lyndon B. (D)
	Brennan, William J., Jr. *(joined Marshall's dissent)*	Eisenhower, Dwight D. (R)

Marty Glick was eager to chat, even if the topic was a lawsuit from almost five decades ago—and was a case he lost. Because, as he put it, he sort of won in the end. (Lawyers always think that!)

The year was 1974. *Richardson v. Ramirez*, which involved a challenge to the practice of felon disenfranchisement in California, had just reached the highest court in the land. The Supreme Court ultimately upheld the state's law that allowed counties to disenfranchise individuals with a felony conviction, even after they have served their time and completed all aspects of their probation and parole. The Court based its ruling on an obscure, mostly-forgotten three-word phrase, "or other crime," in the Fourteenth Amendment. In the process, the Court allowed for the continued disenfranchisement of millions of otherwise-eligible voters today.

I'm often asked why it's constitutional for states to disenfranchise anyone with a felony conviction on their record. The term "felony" encompasses a lot of crimes—typically those punishable by imprisonment for more than one year—so these measures take away the right to vote for millions of people. Isn't voting a fundamental right? Well, the answer is that the Supreme Court essentially blessed the practice five decades ago.

A FIGHT IN A RESTAURANT IN 1952

Abran Cruz Ramirez was twenty-two years old in 1952, living in Texas, when an argument at a restaurant changed his life. The record is not entirely clear on what happened that day, but the state charged him with "robbery by assault," a felony. He represented himself in the criminal proceedings and pleaded guilty, apparently influenced by the advice of the judge. Ramirez served three months in prison and then successfully finished his parole by 1962. That is, he had fully completed his sentence ten years prior to the start of the case that bears his name.[1]

Ramirez moved to California and settled in San Luis Obispo County, which is between Los Angeles and San Francisco. A farm worker, he was married and had five children.[2] In February 1972, when he was in his forties, Ramirez tried to register to vote in California, but the San Luis Obispo County clerk denied his registration on the basis of his Texas felony conviction from the early 1950s. At the time, California law allowed counties to disenfranchise any voter who had been convicted of an "infamous crime," and the county clerk determined that "robbery by assault" qualified as "infamous." As a result, Ramirez was denied the right to vote.[3] He died on March 16, 2014, at the age of eighty-five, so I was sadly unable to interview him for this book.[4] But his legacy lives on from the Supreme Court's decision in the case that bears his name.

Ramirez was not the only plaintiff. Albert Sang Lee, of Salinas, California, was married with four children and was fifty-four years old at the time of this case. Lee was convicted of possession of heroin in 1955. He served two years in prison before successfully completing his parole in 1959.[5] In 1972, seventeen years after his conviction and thirteen years after he had satisfied all terms of his sentence, the Monterey County clerk denied his voter registration application on the basis of his felony conviction.[6] The third plaintiff, Lawrence Gill, was living in Stanislaus County, California, just east of San Jose, with his wife and their four children. He had three felonies on his record: second-degree burglary in both 1952 and 1967, and forgery in 1957. He told the courts that his crimes all revolved around his desire to find money to support his narcotics addiction. Gill finished his prison sentences and parole, cleaned up his life, and was working at a local winery. His felony convictions, however, made him ineligible to vote in Stanislaus County.[7] Viola ("Vi") Richardson, the Mendocino County clerk who intervened in the case to defend the California law, was the named defendant.

Beyond having their names on the case, the plaintiffs didn't actually do much in this litigation. The main driver was an organization called California Rural Legal Assistance (CRLA). CRLA began the litigation, found the plaintiffs, and took the case all the way to the U.S. Supreme Court. Unlike *Burdick* (chapter 2)—which involved an individual who was upset at Hawaii's voting rules and decided to bring suit—the *Ramirez* case was an organizational effort that is an example of what civil rights lawyers call "cause" litigation or a "test case." Reform advocates saw a problem, created a legal strategy, and then identified affected people to be the plaintiffs. Marty Glick was one such advocate and served as the main lawyer.

Glick has spent his entire career fighting for civil rights. He's one of those lawyers whom you don't hear much about but who has been in the trenches supporting minority voting rights and other civil rights causes for decades. After graduating from Ohio State College of Law, he joined the Civil Rights Division of the Department of Justice, where he sued localities in the South that were denying Black people the right to vote. He then moved to California—mostly for the weather, he said—and joined CRLA.[8] Much of his work for CRLA involved helping migrant farmers secure the right to vote; in one case, he won a legal ruling to strike down California's English literacy test as a requirement for voting. He cowrote a book, *The Soledad Children*, that recounts a legal challenge he filed against California's discriminatory use of English-only IQ tests, which had resulted in the placement of thousands of Spanish-speaking children into classes for the "Educable Mentally Retarded."[9] The successful litigation undid this policy, leading to better education for thousands of children.[10]

CRLA provides free legal and lobbying services to low-income individuals in rural California.[11] Glick served as its litigation director and eventually became its executive director.[12] The *Ramirez* case came about through the work of CRLA field offices and the lawyers in the organization. Essentially, the group was thinking about ways to give a larger voice to California's marginalized communities. They realized that the state's felon disenfranchisement rule deprived many people of their power to affect change within the government. They also thought that California's practice—which allowed counties to decide for themselves which crimes were "infamous" and therefore qualified for disenfranchisement—was fundamentally unfair. A person convicted of a felony might be eligible to vote in one county but not in another, depending on the whims of the county clerks and their own definitions of what constituted an "infamous crime." The lawyers decided to challenge the law. Of course, they needed plaintiffs, so the field offices put the word out, especially in Spanish-speaking communities, seeking individuals who had been denied their right to vote. They were searching for a range of people—with long-ago and more recent convictions and from various parts of the state—all of whom had completed their sentences and successfully reentered society. Abran Ramirez, Albert Lee, and Lawrence Gill fit the bill perfectly.[13]

THE PERVASIVE IMPACT OF OUR CRIMINAL JUSTICE SYSTEM

I bet you know someone with a felony conviction—even if you don't realize it. I know several, including a few of my former students who were convicted of crimes before they came to law school. That fact doesn't prevent them from being great lawyers now. They made mistakes when they were younger but learned from them. People with a felony conviction are parents, siblings, family members, neighbors, coworkers, and friends. A conviction doesn't—or at least shouldn't—preclude them from becoming valued members of our society.

In fact, about 8 percent of the overall population—including 33 percent of the Black male population—has been convicted of a felony.[14]

That's a shocking number, when you think about it. You probably passed several individuals who have a felony conviction during your last trip to the grocery store.

Wealthier, disproportionately white elites who do not face the reality of our criminal justice system on a regular basis don't often discuss the overcriminalization of our society and its particularly harsh impact on Black and Brown people. Yet over two million people are incarcerated in the United States (though not all of them have been convicted, as some have just been arrested and others are awaiting trial). Drug offenses account for 20 percent of those incarcerations.[15]

THE DISPROPORTIONATE, DISCRIMINATORY EFFECTS OF FELON DISENFRANCHISEMENT

Felon disenfranchisement has a long pedigree. Those who violated the social contract in ancient Greece could be subject to a loss of most citizenship rights—essentially, banishment from society, termed *atimia*. Ancient Rome also had the practice of *infamia*, or a denial of public rights. Medieval times had the status of "civil death."[16] Some level of disenfranchisement for certain criminals is nothing new.

Importantly, however, few crimes—only the worst offenses—would qualify one for the loss of public rights. Kentucky was among the first states to provide for felon disenfranchisement. Its 1792 constitution declared, "Laws shall be made to exclude from office and from suffrage those who thereafter be convicted of bribery, perjury, forgery, or other high crimes and misdemeanors."[17] Notice how this list includes just a few crimes, though it does have the catch-all "other high crimes and misdemeanors." In the context of the U.S. Constitution, Alexander Hamilton (A. Ham. for you musical fans) explained that impeachable offenses for "high crimes and misdemeanors" were "those offenses which proceed from the misconduct of public men, or, in other words, from the abuse or violation of some public trust."[18]

Other states, such as Florida within its 1868 constitution, disenfranchised those who had committed an "infamous crime." Again, that phrase has a specific, limited meaning: it referred to "crimes that disqualify one from serving as a juror or testifying in court. These crimes include treason, felony, piracy, perjury, and forgery . . . as well as any crime that was punished by the pillory, whipping, or branding."[19]

But today's disenfranchisement is not your grandfather's—or even your great-great-grandfather's—disenfranchisement. Instead of a limited list of offenses against the public trust or "infamous" crimes, Florida's law includes hundreds of different felonies within its scope. As Professor Franita Tolson notes, "There is no reasonable interpretation of 'infamous crime' in the Florida Constitution of 1868—or any of the later iterations of that document—that could support Florida's current system, which disenfranchises individuals who commit any one of 533 different felonies, the overwhelming majority of which are not felonies at common law."[20] Professor Tolson argues that Florida has actually violated the terms of its readmission to the Union after the Civil War, because it currently disenfranchises individuals for many more crimes than the few that were felonies at common law at the time.[21]

Although the disenfranchised population has decreased in recent years, as states have reformed their laws, it's still shockingly high when compared to just a few decades ago. In the early 1970s, at the time of *Ramirez*, a little over a million people were disenfranchised.[22] That number ballooned in the late 1990s and into the 2000s, peaking at 6.1 million disenfranchised in 2016.[23] In the 2020 election, state laws disenfranchised about 5.17 million people.[24] That number represents one out of every 44 adults, or 2.27 percent of the total U.S. voting-eligible population.

Because our criminal legal system suffers from structural racism, these laws disproportionately harm racial minorities. Black people are disenfranchised at a rate that is 3.7 times higher than the rate for other groups.[25] We have a long, sorry history of racism, especially within our voting laws. Felon disenfranchisement perpetuates that discrimination.

The practice is also widespread throughout the country. Forty-eight states disenfranchise individuals convicted of a felony, at least while they serve their time. Only Maine, Vermont, and Washington, D.C., actually let incarcerated individuals vote (via absentee ballot) from prison. Instead of limiting disenfranchisement to a few kinds of crimes historically seen as the worst abuses against society, most states disenfranchise people for all sorts of offenses. The so-called war on drugs overcriminalized our society. Some states grant voting rights back after an individual has finished their sentence, but other states, such as Kentucky, disenfranchise these individuals for life, unless they can secure a restoration of rights from the governor. Mississippi sustained the legacy of Jim Crow by enacting

THE STIGMA OF FELON DISENFRANCHISEMENT • 59

felon disenfranchisement during the 1890 constitutional convention with the sole purpose, in the words of those who led the effort, "to exclude the Negro. Nothing short of this will answer."[26] The law remained on the books for decades and disenfranchised nearly 16 percent of the state's population.[27] In August 2023, the Fifth Circuit Court of Appeals, in a 2–1 vote, struck down the law as imposing cruel and unusual punishment, in violation of the Eighth Amendment.[28] The Supreme Court might have the final say on Mississippi's law.

The Supreme Court's decision in *Ramirez* approved of this skewed representation within our democracy. It said that the Constitution allows states to quite literally deprive those who are already marginalized in our society of their most fundamental civil right.

A COURT CHANGES ITS MIND

The California Supreme Court had actually faced the same issue—California's ban on those convicted of a felony from voting, even after they complete their sentence—seven years prior to its reconsideration of the question in *Ramirez* in 1973. The court's analysis of how voting rights law developed during those seven years is telling.

In 1966 in *Otsuka v. Hite*, the California court considered whether Los Angeles County could deny voter registration to an individual convicted of violating the Selective Service Act during World War II. Katsuki James Otsuka, a Quaker and a conscientious objector, had refused any military service. The court, in reviewing California law denying him the right to vote, highlighted the state's desire to "preserve the purity of the ballot box."[29] "The presumption is, that one rendered infamous by conviction of felony, or other base offense indicative of great moral turpitude, is unfit to exercise the privilege of suffrage, or to hold office, upon terms of equality with freemen who are clothed by the State with the toga of political citizenship."[30] In so holding, the court noted that although the U.S. Supreme Court had recognized voting as a "fundamental right," states could limit the franchise to prevent election malfeasance, with the theory that those convicted of crimes are more likely also to commit voter fraud. As the court opined, citing a case from 1884, "[T]he fact that such person committed a crime is evidence that he was morally 'corrupt' at the time he did so; if still morally corrupt when given the opportunity to vote in an

election, he might defile 'the purity of the ballot box' by selling or barter-
ing his vote or otherwise engaging in election fraud."[31]

But the California Supreme Court changed its tune just seven years
later, thanks to intervening U.S. Supreme Court decisions. In fact, the
same California justice who wrote *Otsuka*, Justice Stanley Mosk, also
wrote *Ramirez*. He explained that subsequent rulings from the U.S. Supreme Court had called into question the approach from *Otsuka*. Specifically, "In the seven years since *Otsuka* . . . , the test for judging the
constitutionality of a state-imposed limitation on the right to vote has
become substantially more strict."[32] In 1969, the U.S. Supreme Court decided a case called *Kramer v. Union School District*, in which it held that a
state must show that its voting laws are closely tied to its goal of running
a fair, smooth, and fraud-free election.[33] Morris Kramer challenged the
eligibility rules to vote for school board members in New York; only those
who owned or rented property or had school-age children could vote for
local school boards, ostensibly because they would care the most about
either local tax policy or school decision-making. The Supreme Court
struck down the eligibility rules, however, noting that the "fit" between
the state's goal of ensuring voters had a personal stake in the election and
the actual eligibility rules was not close enough. Some property owners
probably didn't pay any attention to the local schools, while some local
residents did not own property or have kids but cared a lot about living in
a community with high-quality education. Thus, the eligibility rules were
not closely tied to the state's specific goals. In legal terms, the law was not
"narrowly tailored," so it failed "strict scrutiny review."[34] As the California
Supreme Court recognized, *Kramer* solidified a strict test—obliquely set
out in an earlier case from 1966 striking down a poll tax, *Harper v. Virginia
State Board of Elections*, but made clearer in *Kramer* in 1969—for the right
to vote: a state has the burden of justifying voting restrictions with a specific, compelling state interest and must also show that the law is closely
aligned with achieving that interest. The test was more stringent than the
one the California Supreme Court had used seven years earlier in *Otsuka*.

Justice Mosk of the California Supreme Court expressly changed his
analysis of the constitutional right to vote after these U.S. Supreme Court
cases had affirmed the stronger protection for voting rights embedded
within the U.S. Constitution. That newer jurisprudence made the *Otsuka*
ruling untenable. It also meant that states had to use what is known as

the "least restrictive means" to achieve its goals. Essentially, if the state is concerned about election fraud, it must try to combat it in a way that is still most protective of voting rights. As the California Supreme Court put it in *Ramirez*, "We hold that the enforcement of modern statutes regulating the voting process and penalizing its misuse—rather than outright disfranchisement of persons convicted of crime—is today the method of preventing election fraud which is the least burdensome on the right of suffrage."[35] In other words, instead of disenfranchising those convicted of a felony, the best way to combat election fraud is to enforce voting rules and criminalize election malfeasance.

The California Supreme Court therefore struck down California's felon disenfranchisement law. The court explained that preventing voter fraud is still an important state interest, but that the better way to do it is to penalize misuse of the ballot instead of disenfranchising those with a felony conviction. Perhaps, the court noted, it was necessary to disenfranchise people who had committed an "infamous crime" early in the state's history, but with the adoption of the secret ballot and technological innovations in the voting process, there was no longer a need to curtail voter eligibility. "In sum, it may have been feasible in 1850 to influence the outcome of an election by rounding up the impecunious and the thirsty, furnishing them with free liquor, premarked ballots, and transportation to the polls; to do so in 1973, if possible at all, would require the coordinated skills of a vast squadron of computer technicians."[36]

There's one other aspect of the California Supreme Court's decision that is particularly important—what it did *not* say. While highlighting and elevating the constitutional right to vote, as implicitly protected within the Equal Protection Clause of Section 1 of the Fourteenth Amendment to the U.S. Constitution, the court said nothing about Section 2 of the Fourteenth Amendment. There was nary a mention of that provision. According to Marty Glick, Section 2 was not on anyone's mind when they litigated the case at the state court. But that would change, in a major way, when the case reached the U.S. Supreme Court.

SECTION 2 OF THE FOURTEENTH AMENDMENT

The U.S. Constitution does not explicitly confer voting rights. As discussed previously, there are several constitutional amendments that prohibit states from denying the right to vote on the basis of certain characteristics, such as race (Fifteenth Amendment), sex (Nineteenth Amendment), inability to pay a poll tax (Twenty-Fourth Amendment), or age over eighteen (Twenty-Sixth Amendment). In a series of cases in the 1960s, the Supreme Court recognized strong protection for the right to vote within the Equal Protection Clause of the Fourteenth Amendment.[37] The language itself is simple and broad: "No State shall . . . deny to any person within its jurisdiction the equal protection of the laws." The Court interpreted this provision as robustly protecting an equal right to vote for everyone.

But there's another provision within the Fourteenth Amendment that saw renewed relevance in the *Ramirez* case: Section 2. First, I'll just give you the relevant language so you can see how convoluted it is:

> But when the right to vote at any election for the choice of electors for President and Vice President of the United States, Representatives in Congress, the Executive and Judicial officers of a State, or the members of the Legislature thereof, is denied to any of the male inhabitants of such State, being twenty-one years of age, and citizens of the United States, or in any way abridged, except for participation in rebellion, or other crime, the basis of representation therein shall be reduced in the proportion which the number of such male citizens shall bear to the whole number of male citizens twenty-one years of age in such State.[38]

What does this language actually mean? It says that if a state denies the right to vote to anyone (well, at the time, only male citizens), then Congress can take away representatives from that state. Put differently: if a state denies the right to vote to some voters, then the state might lose members of Congress (Congress has never actually invoked this penalty). But there's a caveat within the language: "except for participation in rebellion, or other crime." That is, a state will *not* lose congressional representation if it denies someone the right to vote based on that person's "participation in rebellion, or other crime."

The interpretive question, then, is what is "participation in rebellion, or other crime"? The states ratified the Fourteenth Amendment in 1868, soon after the Civil War, as part of the efforts to secure equality for Black people under the law. An "originalist"—someone who thinks courts should construe constitutional language according to the meaning of the language at the time the text was written—would interpret the language "participation in rebellion, or other crime" in light of this post–Civil War time frame. The concern was that southern states might not enfranchise formerly enslaved people with full voting rights, so there needed to be a penalty if they took the path of continued discrimination. It also made sense to allow states to disenfranchise those who had rebelled against the Union. As Justice Thurgood Marshall put it in his dissent in *Richardson v. Ramirez*, the provision "put Southern States to a choice—enfranchise [Black] voters or lose congressional representation."[39]

Although the California Supreme Court had not considered the question at all, it became clear to Marty Glick that Section 2 of the Fourteenth Amendment would present a hurdle once the case made it to the U.S. Supreme Court. The government's written brief included a significant argument about it, and George Roth, California's lawyer who presented at the oral argument, mentioned the theory as well, suggesting that the language gives states the authority to disenfranchise anyone convicted of a felony.[40] The language, after all, exempts the penalty of reduced congressional representation if the state's disenfranchisement is based on the commission of an "other crime." So Glick took the argument head-on: "We would suggest that a reading of the legislative history first would lead to the conclusion that participation [in] rebellion or other crime is really meant [to] deal with the problem of the rebellion and not the problem of former conviction."[41] In the context of the words right around it, "other crime" should mean "other crimes related to the rebellion."[42]

As we will see, however, a majority of Supreme Court justices would disagree.

THE SUPREME COURT'S BROAD VIEW OF "OTHER CRIME"

Sometimes, bad lawyers still win their cases. Justice Lewis Powell took notes as he listened to the lawyers present their arguments to the Court; regarding the California county's lawyer, he jotted down, "Incompetent lawyer who didn't earn his transportation fare to attend their argument."[43] Ouch!

How did the state and county end up winning, with the Court upholding California's felon disenfranchisement provision?

There's an old adage that "hard cases make bad law." This case, however, should have been easy. On the one hand, the California Supreme

Court had noted that recent U.S. Supreme Court cases elevated the importance of the right to vote and required states to offer a precise justification for a law that impacts someone's exercise of the franchise. On the other hand, the state officials argued here that the opaque language of the Fourteenth Amendment's Section 2, which allows for disenfranchisement for "other crime," gives wide leeway for states to disenfranchise those convicted of a felony *for the rest of their lives*.

A narrow, originalist reading of the "participation in rebellion, or other crime" language would recognize that those who wrote that language were responding to the aftermath of the Civil War. To understand this constitutional text, the Court looked to the Reconstruction Acts, which were the federal statutes dictating the conditions under which the former Confederate states would be readmitted to the Union and again enjoy congressional representation.[44] Those laws provided that the Confederate states must adopt a state constitution that granted voting rights to "male citizens of said State, twenty-one years old and upward, of whatever race, color, or previous condition," but provided an important caveat: "except such as may be disfranchised for participation in the rebellion or for felony at common law."[45] Thus, "other crime" in the Fourteenth Amendment was tied to the rebellion and was understood in conjunction with "felony at common law" from the Reconstruction Acts. As Professor Tolson showed through her scholarship on the Fourteenth Amendment, however, the Court "ignored the [Reconstruction] Acts' textual limitation that disenfranchisement be only for felonies at common law." What was a "felony at common law"? Here's Professor Tolson again: "A felony at common law was a serious crime punishable, in some cases, by death. The nine traditional common law felonies under English law were murder, robbery, manslaughter, rape, sodomy, larceny, arson, mayhem, and burglary."[46]

Those who ratified the Fourteenth Amendment never intended it to serve as a blanket allowance for lifetime disenfranchisement for anyone convicted of any felony. They were instead focused on those who had rebelled against the Union and, perhaps, other serious criminals. The whole point of Section 2 of the Fourteenth Amendment wasn't to disenfranchise people; it was to secure voting rights for formerly enslaved individuals—to *enfranchise* Black people and make them full citizens. As Justice Marshall wrote in his dissent in *Ramirez*, "Section 2 provides a special remedy—reduced representation—to cure a particular form of electoral abuse—the disenfranchisement" of Black voters.[47] The Court's textual argument, to use the "other crime" language to uphold felon disenfranchisement, was therefore misplaced. The Court improperly construed Section 2 of the Fourteenth Amendment to allow states to disenfranchise anyone convicted of a felony. The right to vote, as protected within the Fourteenth Amendment's Equal Protection Clause of Section 1, now had a significant limitation from Section 2: a state can decide that felons are not lawful voters.

The Court also distinguished recent cases in which it had promoted the equality principle inherent in democratic participation: those cases didn't involve felons and were, therefore, apparently irrelevant. The Court essentially just ignored that case law. Instead, the Court said that "the exclusion of felons from the vote has an affirmative sanction in Section 2 of the Fourteenth Amendment."[48] The Constitution itself, the Court found, has a built-in allowance for felon disenfranchisement.

Fortunately, all was not lost on the issue. The Court explained that states themselves could repeal their felon disenfranchisement provisions. The Constitution permits felon disenfranchisement but does not require it. That's exactly what happened in California a few months after the Court decided *Ramirez*: the state's voters approved a state constitutional amendment to give back the right to vote to anyone who had completed their sentence.[49] In the end, Marty Glick said, they kind of won—at least for California voters. The lawsuit helped to push the issue of felon disenfranchisement to the forefront of the public's mind.

Of course, Glick still acknowledges that they lost in a big way. Instead of approaching the case with the fundamental right to vote at the forefront, the Court found a way "to dredge out" a phrase from century-old, never-before-used language to endorse the disenfranchisement of otherwise-eligible voters. It was an early indication that the Court was turning away from the primacy of voters in our democratic system and instead deferring to states in their election rules.

Imagine how different our politics might look had the Court come out the other way in *Ramirez* and limited felon disenfranchisement to only those convicted of "other crimes" that were related to rebellion or a serious violation of the public trust. For one, over 5 million more individuals would be allowed to vote. They would have a voice in our democracy. Some elections even might have turned out differently. Consider the razor-thin margin between George W. Bush and Al Gore in Florida's 2000 presidential election. Bush won by just 537 votes out of over 5.8 million cast, and with Florida came the presidency. That year, Florida disenfranchised around 827,000 individuals on the basis of a felony conviction.[50] Although people with felonies on their records are not monolithic and do not all vote the same way, it's at least plausible to think that more would have voted for Gore than for Bush. After all, felon disenfranchisement disproportionately harms racial minorities, who also tend to skew Democratic. Two political scientists calculated that if disenfranchised individuals had "participated in the election at our estimated rate of Florida turnout (27.2 percent) and Democratic preference (68.9 percent), Gore would have carried the state by more than 80,000 votes."[51] Bush's victory in 2000 had immeasurable consequences for our country, from the war in Iraq to education policy and the No Child Left Behind Act to a failure to address climate change. The point is not that Gore would have been a better president; who knows what travails his presidency would have faced. It's that Gore probably should have won the presidency—if all voters had been allowed to vote.

IT'S ALWAYS ABOUT FLORIDA

The fight over felon disenfranchisement continues to this day, although the question about its overall constitutionality appears to be settled thanks to the Supreme Court's decision in *Ramirez*. The debate has instead moved to state legislatures and the people themselves. Florida epitomizes the struggle.

In 2018, the state's voters approved Amendment 4 via a ballot initiative; the goal was to undo the state's practice of lifetime disenfranchisement for those convicted of a felony and give back the right to vote to 1.4 million Floridians. The initiative was the brainchild of Desmond Meade, an inspiring individual who himself had been convicted of various felonies, was addicted to drugs, and at one point had contemplated suicide, but who had then changed his life and gone to law school. He set his sights on easing the state's draconian felon disenfranchisement provision, becoming the head of the Florida Rights Restoration Coalition. In 2015, Meade began the campaign to convince the state's voters to change the state constitution, gathering almost 800,000 signatures to put the question on the ballot. The measure would restore voting rights to anyone convicted of a felony (except for murder or sexual offense) who had completed their sentence and parole. It passed in November 2018 with over 64 percent of the vote (as an amendment to the state constitution, it needed at least 60 percent to succeed).

The language of the new rule provided that an individual would regain the right to vote upon completion of "all terms of their sentence including parole or probation." In an effort to gut the impact of the amendment, the Republican-led Florida legislature passed a law in 2019 interpreting this provision to require anyone with a felony conviction to pay all court "fines and fees" associated with their sentence before the state would allow them to vote. The problem is that many people who have finished all other aspects of their sentence have no ability to pay these additional legal financial obligations. At least three-quarters of otherwise-eligible individuals still owe some court debt, and around 70 to 80 percent of those people are indigent and unable to pay.[52] Even if someone has the financial means, they often have no clue how much they owe—because the state won't tell them! Florida lacks a central database listing the amount of each person's unpaid fines and fees. Justin Levitt, a law professor and former Department of Justice voting rights attorney, compared the state's practice to "Lucy pulling the football away from Charlie Brown. And there's no law in Lucy pulling the football away. That's just cruelty."[53] Moreover, the state has assigned a lot of this debt to private collection agencies, which typically add exorbitant interest. The amount owed might increase exponentially, which essentially perpetuates the lifetime disenfranchisement of some of Florida's most vulnerable people. It's another echo of Jim Crow–era disenfranchisement, when white politicians more explicitly limited the voting opportunities of formerly enslaved people and their descendants to deny them full citizenship.[54]

Advocates filed lawsuits against this pay-to-vote requirement and the plaintiffs saw initial success. A federal judge struck down the law for those who are unable to pay—around 700,000 people, or half of the 1.4 million individuals the amendment was supposed to re-enfranchise.[55] But a federal appeals court reversed that decision. In a 6-4 ruling, with five Trump-appointed judges in the majority, the Eleventh Circuit Court of Appeals held that the Florida legislature's scheme to undo the effects of Amendment 4 was perfectly lawful.[56] The court rejected the claim that the law was effectively a poll tax or was otherwise unconstitutional. The majority wrote that requiring the repayment of all fines and fees "promotes full rehabilitation of returning citizens and ensures full satisfaction of the punishment imposed for the crimes by which felons forfeited the right to vote."[57] The court left unsaid how forcing poor people to pay a court fee—one that often balloons as a result of compounding interest—will help to "rehabilitate" them.

Ramirez undergirded the federal appeals courts' skepticism of the constitutional challenge to Florida's system. Early in its opinion, the court cited *Ramirez* when declaring, "The first question—is there a fundamental right involved—has been addressed already: felons who have been disenfranchised have no fundamental right to vote."[58] Let that sink in: Some American citizens simply have no fundamental right to vote under the Constitution. The court went on: "It is true, of course, that despite its fundamental status, the right to vote may be abridged or altogether withheld by the State. This is the holding of *Ramirez*."[59] The court was therefore skeptical of any claims against Florida's regime, in part because the Supreme Court had already approved of outright bans on voting for individuals convicted of a felony. If states can take away the right to vote for life, why can't they condition that right on paying all fines and fees— even if the state won't tell them how much they owe?

In other legal challenges to felon disenfranchisement, advocates have demonstrated that the practice disproportionately harms minority voters, which should constitute a violation of the Voting Rights Act.[60] But courts have rejected the argument that the Voting Rights Act prohibits felon disenfranchisement, though the cases have generated forceful dissents.[61] With *Ramirez* supplying the background concept that the Constitution protects felon disenfranchisement, courts have been unwilling to strike down the practice, essentially ignoring its obvious racial impact. It's the same kind of deference to state legislatures that we see from the other cases we have discussed, this time applied to the question of whether a member of our society can participate in voting at all.

To be fair, our electoral system has improved on this issue, at least when compared to the situation decades ago. Bipartisan majorities have approved the relaxation of felon disenfranchisement rules—though more Democrats than Republicans express support, probably because of the notion that those convicted of a felony might skew Democratic.[62] States that used to disenfranchise individuals for life, including Florida, Iowa, Kentucky, and Virginia, have eased their rules, sometimes through legislation or constitutional amendments and other times through executive orders from the governor—though future governors can reverse those decrees.[63] Other states, too, have moved toward the automatic restoration of voting rights.[64] Even Florida's story is not all bad, as more people can now vote than before.

It's odd, however, that we are still having this debate at all. Voting is a fundamental right. It's backward to read the Constitution, our founding document, as allowing states to take away that fundamental right. Democracy has not broken in D.C., Maine, or Vermont, where currently incarcerated individuals can vote from jail via absentee ballots. Of course, continued felon disenfranchisement has both political and racial ramifications, which is a primary reason it has endured. We shouldn't determine voting eligibility based on perceived politics and we must create a more inclusive democracy to evolve from the racial caste system that still pervades U.S. society today.

The bottom line is that, thanks to a Supreme Court decision from five decades ago, some people aren't allowed to vote because of a mistake they once made, perhaps years ago. They don't have the full rights of American citizenship. As we will see next, in many ways these individuals are treated worse than corporations—which (it should go without saying) aren't actually people at all.

CHAPTER 5

MONEY TALKS

Citizens United v. Federal Election Commission (2010)

	JUSTICE	APPOINTED BY
MAJORITY	Kennedy, Anthony M. *(wrote majority opinion)*	Reagan, Ronald (R)
	Roberts, John G., Jr. (chief justice)	Bush, George W. (R)
	Scalia, Antonin	Reagan, Ronald (R)
	Alito, Samuel A., Jr.	Bush, George W. (R)
	Thomas, Clarence	Bush, George H. W. (R)
	Roberts, Scalia, and Thomas each wrote concurring opinions to respond to the dissent; Thomas further disagreed with all other justices regarding the constitutionality of campaign finance disclosure.	
DISSENT	Stevens, John Paul *(dissented and concurred in part)*	Ford, Gerald (R)
	Ginsburg, Ruth Bader	Clinton, Bill (D)
	Breyer, Stephen G.	Clinton, Bill (D)
	Sotomayor, Sonia	Obama, Barack (D)

As we have seen so far, entrenched interests control access to the ballot and the ease of voting. The Supreme Court's decisions have devalued the constitutional right to vote and deferred to state politicians in their election rules. But another problem plagues our democracy as well: it's virtually impossible for a candidate to win a major election without significant funding. You cannot run a successful campaign—even for local offices in many places—without a lot of money. The reality is that wealthy people select and control candidates. The right to vote should include the right of the people to have meaningful choices. But too often, money, not the voters, essentially dictates the outcomes.

That message permeated a historic political campaign in 2010 when Murray Hill, Inc.—yes, a corporation—ran for Congress.

Murray Hill, Inc.'s campaign launch video opens to a beautiful orange sunrise over a city skyline. "It's a new day," a voice says. "Thanks to an enlightened Supreme Court, corporations now have the rights the Founding Fathers meant for us." As the video pans up to a tall corporate headquarters building with rows of reflective windows, the ad proclaims: "It's our democracy. We bought it, we paid for it, and we're going to keep it!" The ad ends, "I'm Eric Hensal, designated human for Murray Hill, Inc., and we approve this message."[1]

Murray Hill, Inc. is Eric Hensal's public relations firm. Hensal told me he came up with the idea to have Murray Hill, Inc. run for Congress in about ten minutes while driving to meet a friend at the Tastee Diner in Silver Spring, Maryland. He was listening to a radio program which was discussing the just-issued *Citizens United v. Federal Election Commission* decision when a thought struck him: if the Constitution gives corporations the right to spend money on campaigns, why can't they also run for office? He mentioned the idea to his friend over breakfast and they ran with it. They created the ad that weekend, primarily using stock footage, though they did pay for one clip of an American flag waving in the air because it was just "too perfect." The goal, he said, was to highlight the problems of the *Citizens United* decision and "take it to the absurd."[2] Their idea took off. Eric, as Murray Hill, Inc.'s designated human, was soon on the radio all over the world and even participated in a debate with Congressmember Chris Van Hollen of Maryland about money in politics. He also embraced the tongue-in-cheek humor surrounding Murray Hill, Inc.'s candidacy, joking that at least "there will be no sex scandals in a corporate Congress."[3]

As part of its historic bid, Murray Hill, Inc. sought to register to vote in Maryland. The Maryland State Board of Elections rejected its registration because it was "not a human being."[4] There was also a question about whether Murray Hill, Inc. was old enough to serve in Congress in 2010, given that it was incorporated in 2005 and the Constitution requires members of Congress to be at least twenty-five years old. Alas, although Murray Hill, Inc. made a big media splash, it never appeared on the ballot.

"END BUCKLEY"

To understand *Citizens United*, we must go back to a 1976 case called *Buckley v. Valeo*. Indeed, it is really *this* case, not *Citizens United*, that should raise the ire of anyone who laments the amount of money that floods our democracy. *Buckley* arose after Congress passed the Federal Election Campaign Act (FECA) in 1971 and amended it substantially in 1974 after the Watergate scandal, which involved the break-in of the Democratic National Committee headquarters in the Watergate Office Building—and the cover-up—which ultimately led to the resignation of President Richard Nixon.

FECA is complex and complicated, touching virtually every aspect of money in politics. For our purposes, three aspects are most important.

First, FECA limited the amount of money an individual or organization can give directly to a candidate for federal office (member of Congress or president). Such money is known as a *contribution*. The law said that there is a maximum amount someone may donate to a candidate for that candidate to then spend on their campaign. The initial contribution limit was $1,000 per candidate per election (with the primary and general elections counted separately), but it's been indexed to inflation, so the limit for the 2024 elections is $3,300—or $6,600 total to a candidate for both the primary and general elections.[5]

Second, FECA limited the amount someone could spend to create and disseminate a campaign ad in support of an individual running for federal office. That is known as an *independent expenditure*. Let's say I want to support my best friend, who is running for Congress. I can either give money directly to my friend's campaign (a contribution) and they can spend it how they want to help their candidacy. Or I can put up my own billboard without ever telling my friend what I'm doing. That's an independent expenditure. FECA set limits for both contributions and independent expenditures.

Finally, FECA included *disclosure* requirements. Regardless of how I spend my money, either the candidate or I must tell an agency, the Federal Election Commission (FEC), which will then publish the information. Check out FEC.gov and click on "campaign finance data." You can find out whether your neighbor, friend, or favorite celebrity has spent money on a candidate for federal office. This disclosure allows the public to know who is supporting a candidate and ensure that people are not violating the spending limits.

The *Buckley* decision considered the constitutionality of this behemoth of a law. The opinion is confusing, lengthy, and fractured, with many justices writing separate opinions. Essentially, the Supreme Court upheld the law's contribution limitations and disclosure requirements but struck down its independent expenditure restrictions. That is, the Court approved Congress's decision to limit how much money you can give directly to a candidate; held unconstitutional the law's restriction on how much money you can spend independently on your own electioneering to support or oppose a candidate's campaign; and said that Congress can require public disclosure from anyone spending money on federal campaigns.

The upshot of the *Buckley* decision was that Congress sought to regulate every aspect of money in politics, but the Court carved up the law, opening the door to unlimited independent expenditures in the process. Thus, there are no limits on an individual spending as much as they want on their own TV ads, billboards, or whatever to support or oppose a candidate's election. They can't talk to the candidate about their spending; it has to be fully independent and uncoordinated (at least in the formal sense) or it will count as a "contribution," which does have limits. But individuals can spend as much as they want on their own electioneering if they don't collaborate with the candidate. The split decision in *Buckley* created a problem—at least for candidates. As two scholars wrote, "In lifting the cap on individual expenditures while leaving in place the cap on contributions, the Supreme Court created a world in which politicians' appetite for money would be limitless but their ability to obtain it would not. [Other scholars] have analogized this to giving money-starved politicians access to an all-you-can-eat financial buffet but insisting they can only serve themselves with a teaspoon."[6]

The rationale behind *Buckley* reverberates to this day. *Citizens United* didn't really say that money equals speech—that was *Buckley*. The Court in *Citizens United* adopted the views of FECA's opponents from *Buckley*, that "virtually all meaningful political communications in the modern setting involve the expenditure of money."[7] The Court agreed that speech requires money, such that cutting off money inherently stifles speech. We can question that premise: I can speak as much as I want without spending a dime by going to the town square and standing on a soapbox (do soapboxes still exist?). I can post whatever screeds I want on social media. But disseminating my message widely is more difficult if there are limits on how much I am allowed to spend. In any event, if we truly want to unravel *Citizens United*, we have to overturn *Buckley* first.

Citizens United dealt only with the independent expenditure and disclosure requirements. In subsequent cases, the Court has continued to uphold a cap on direct contributions to candidates—so long as those limits are not so low as to make it really hard for a candidate to raise enough money to run an effective campaign.[8] But opponents of campaign finance regulations have set their sights on convincing the Court to strike those down as well. American democracy is already drowning in money, but some people apparently think more is needed.

WHAT DOES THE *CITIZENS UNITED* DECISION ACTUALLY SAY?

There's a lot of misinformation about the Court's decision in *Citizens United*. Bernie Sanders, at the Democratic National Convention in 2016, declared *Citizens United* to be "one of the worst Supreme Court decisions in the history of our country."[9] The case has generated proposed constitutional amendments, political movements, viral memes, and even rap songs, pervading the public consciousness.

Yet most people don't know what the case *actually* says. As legal scholars Heather Gerken and Erica Newland explain, "The most common tale told about *Citizens United* is that the Court treated corporations as if they were individuals for the first time. It thereby ushered in a new era of corporate spending. The story is that *Citizens United* has therefore caused a sea change in American politics. . . . All of that story is wrong, and some of it is nonsense."[10]

Here's what the decision *doesn't* say, at least explicitly: That corporations are people. That corporations can give as much money as they want to candidates. That money always equals speech. That corporations are going to flood the airwaves with political ads.

Here's what the decision *does* mean: wealthy interests, with their infinite financial resources, have new, innovative ways to skew our elections.

Let's step back a little. The *Citizens United* case stemmed from an organization called, well, Citizens United, a nonprofit group seeking to promote conservative viewpoints and candidates. The organization was founded in 1998 by Floyd Brown, whom a news report referred to as "among the nation's best-known conservative political knife throwers."[11]

He was behind the infamous "Willie Horton" political attack ad against Democratic nominee Michael Dukakis during the 1988 presidential election campaign, and in 1992, wrote a book titled *Slick Willie: Why America Cannot Trust Bill Clinton*. Clinton's press secretary once said that Brown was "personally responsible for some of the sleaziest politics this country has seen." Brown started Citizens United with the goal of "informing and educating the public on conservative ideas and positions on issues, including national defense, the free enterprise system, belief in God, and the family as the basic unit of society."[12] David Bossie, who served as Donald Trump's deputy campaign manager in 2016, worked as Citizens United's president for years. In the lead-up to the 2008 election, Brown and Bossie turned their sights on another Clinton—Hillary.

In 2007, most pundits assumed Hillary Clinton would win the Democratic nomination for president. Citizens United feared Clinton as president and produced a documentary, called *Hillary: The Movie*, to warn Americans of what it thought her presidency would look like. The trailer for the ninety-minute documentary features ominous music and clips of various politicians and commentators attacking Clinton as "deceitful," a "liar," "ruthless," and worse.[13] Citizens United released the movie in theaters and on DVD, and it also wanted to make the documentary available through video-on-demand services. But it had a legal problem: the Bipartisan Campaign Reform Act (BCRA) of 2002, which was Congress's update to the Federal Election Campaign Act, stood in the way. BCRA—also known as McCain-Feingold, after its two main sponsors, Republican Senator John McCain of Arizona and Democratic Senator Russ Feingold of Wisconsin—prohibited corporations (and unions) from spending money through their general treasuries on political ads within thirty days of a primary or sixty days of a general election. That is, the law limited corporate independent expenditures soon before an election. (Federal law also bans direct donations from corporations to candidates, but that provision was not the subject of this dispute.) Congress's goal in passing the law was to ensure that corporations, given their unique role in American society, would not unduly influence politicians through their advocacy. Corporations already have massive resources, so the concern was that they would use those resources to corrupt people running for office. Instead of being responsive to their constituents, politicians who benefited from corporate campaign expenditures would tailor their policies to benefit entities that were giving big bucks to their campaign.

Citizens United, as a nonprofit corporation funded by some for-profit entities, fell under this prohibition. Under the law, it couldn't spend money on advertising or disseminating *Hillary: The Movie* in the months just before the election. So, it sued. Its argument was that a limit on spending money on its own electioneering violated its right to free speech under the First Amendment.

As originally crafted, however, the lawsuit was just another attempt to chip away at campaign finance regulations. "Chip away" is the key phrase here: Citizens United made various technical legal arguments, and most Court observers did not think, at least at the outset, that the case would have monumental consequences. Even Ted Olson, Citizen United's lawyer, initially sought a narrow ruling saying that the McCain-Feingold law did not apply to documentaries distributed through video-on-demand.[14]

But once the lawyers stood up for oral argument at the Supreme Court, it became clear that the case was about much more than technical legalese surrounding limits on corporate independent expenditures. Justice Samuel Alito posed a devastating question to Malcolm Stewart, the government's lawyer: Could Congress ban a corporation from publishing a campaign book? Stewart hemmed and hawed over the hypothetical, so Chief Justice John Roberts took up the mantle: "If it's a 500-page book, and at the end it says, and so vote for X, the government could ban that?" Stewart's response: "We could prohibit the publication of the book using the corporate treasury funds."[15]

Uh-oh. The federal government had just claimed that under this campaign finance law, it could ban books. Could that really fly under the First Amendment?

The justices were concerned. After oral argument, the justices have a private conference where they discuss each case, and the initial vote at the conference was 5–4 in favor of Citizens United. Justice Anthony Kennedy planned to write a sweeping opinion for the majority that would rule unconstitutional *any* limit on a corporation spending money on its own campaign ads. That question wasn't squarely presented within the parties' written submissions to the Court; the briefs had focused more on Citizens United's technical arguments. As legal analyst Jeffrey Toobin wrote in the *New Yorker*, all of a sudden the conservative justices saw the dispute as a "vehicle for rewriting decades of constitutional law in a case where the lawyer had not even raised those issues."[16] Justice David Souter threatened to write a dissenting opinion that would "air . . . some of the Court's dirty laundry" and would claim that Chief Justice Roberts had "violat[ed] the Court's own procedures to engineer the result he wanted."[17] Ever the institutionalist, Roberts offered to punt the case until the next Supreme Court term and ask the lawyers on both sides to submit new briefs to address the broader First Amendment arguments.

Part of the problem was that the approach Roberts, Kennedy, and the other conservative justices espoused would require overturning prior cases that were only seven and twenty years old, respectively. The Supreme Court does not often overrule its own precedent—and hardly ever when the cases are so recent. The legitimacy of legal rules depends in part on what lawyers call *stare decisis*, which means "to stand by things decided." In other words, precedent should usually win out. In 2003, only seven years before the *Citizens United* decision, the Court had upheld the very federal law limiting corporate independent expenditures at issue in this case.[18] The Court's composition had changed significantly since then, though, with conservative Justice Samuel Alito replacing the more moderate Justice Sandra Day O'Connor. A 5–4 decision to uphold the federal regulation in 2003 was about to turn into a 5–4 ruling against the law only seven years later. Citizens United had initially brought a narrow challenge to the law as applied to its video-on-demand documentary instead of a broad constitutional attack, so Justice Souter thought that ruling the law unconstitutional and overturning recent precedent, without even giving the lawyers a chance to address these broader questions, was disingenuous, at best.

The Court set the case for an additional, special oral argument in September 2009, before it officially opened its new term in early October. The intervening summer saw several personnel changes: Justice Souter retired, Justice Sonia Sotomayor joined the Court, and Elena Kagan, the former dean of Harvard Law School, became the solicitor general, which is the government's top appellate lawyer. The solicitor general is sometimes referred to as the "tenth justice," given their influential role in arguing cases so frequently before the Court.

Citizens United was Justice Sotomayor's first case as a Supreme Court justice. It was also Kagan's very first argument as a lawyer—in any court.[19] A few years ago, Justice Kagan visited my law school and I had the privilege of sitting next to her during lunch. I told her that I teach the *Citizens United* opinion in my course on election law and asked her about the second oral argument in the case—her first argument as solicitor general. "What was the biggest hurdle you faced?" I wondered. The answer, she said, was obvious: "Can the federal government ban a book?"

Kagan gave the justices a deft response: "The government's answer has changed," she asserted.[20] The federal government would never try to limit the publication of a book, and even if it did, a court could rightly strike down that specific application of the law. But that didn't placate the conservative justices. The noted firebrand Justice Antonin Scalia said: "You're a lawyer advising somebody who is about to come up with a book and you say don't worry, the [federal government] has never tried to send somebody to prison for this. . . . That going to comfort your client? I don't think so."

The writing was on the wall: the Supreme Court would reject all limits on corporate electioneering.

"CORPORATIONS ARE PEOPLE, MY FRIEND"

Mitt Romney was campaigning for the Republican presidential nomination in August 2011 when he spoke at the Iowa State Fair. Wearing a short-sleeved navy polo shirt under a hot sun, he began talking about balancing the budget and tax policy. "Corporations!" a heckler cried out. Romney put on a wry smile and responded, "Corporations are people, my friend." After someone shouted back, "No, they're not!" Romney retorted: "Of course they are. Everything corporations earn ultimately goes to people. Where do you think it goes?"[21]

The message reverberated throughout the campaign. Stephen Colbert devoted an entire (hilarious) segment to it on his show, *The Colbert Report*, faux-praising Romney for being a pioneer in the fight for corporate equality. The verbal gaffe followed Romney, painting a distasteful picture for many voters of a person who cared more about corporations than about everyday Americans.

Yet *Citizens United* never actually declared corporations to be "people." That designation goes back centuries. In 1758, William Blackstone, an influential English legal thinker, referred to the corporation as an "artificial person" that had a separate legal identity.[22] In 1819, the Supreme Court, under Chief Justice John Marshall, agreed that corporations were private entities akin to individuals under the U.S. Constitution's Contracts Clause.[23] There is a long line of cases that confer various rights to corporations, such as a landmark decision from 1945 holding that the Fourteenth Amendment's Due Process Clause, which protects "persons," prevents corporations from being sued in faraway states unrelated to the suit.[24] The idea that corporations are fictional individuals has been part of the law for a long time. The practical reality is that the law must consider corporations to be "people," given the pervasive nature of corporations in our society. Otherwise, the Constitution would not protect people who organize together under a corporate form. The First Amendment, for example, says that "Congress shall make no law . . . abridging the freedom of speech, or of the press"; that protection surely must reach media corporations.

So what, precisely, did *Citizens United* hold? First, it acknowledged that many prior Court decisions had extended constitutional protections to corporations. Second, the Court cited a long line of cases saying that "the identity of the speaker is not decisive in determining whether speech is protected."[25] First Amendment rights do not depend on *who* is speaking. That makes sense: we would not want the government to suppress speech just because it doesn't like the speaker. Third, corporations unquestionably "speak" in some sense, in that they can disseminate information. Therefore, it follows that the government cannot fully restrict corporations from speaking on politics. In this way, corporations have the same First Amendment rights to engage in political advocacy as individuals.

No constitutional right, however, is absolute, as the government can limit the exercise of some rights if it has a good enough reason. Perhaps the best-known example is that you can't (falsely) yell "Fire!" in a crowded theater. (Some people leave out the crucial word "falsely" in that formulation; if you're in a theater and see a fire, by all means, yell "Fire!") The question is whether the government has a good enough reason to curtail those constitutional rights. That's the crux of the analysis in most constitutional cases: Has the government sufficiently justified a rule that infringes the exercise of a constitutional right?[26]

In both 1980 and 2003, the Supreme Court affirmed that the government has a strong rationale for limiting corporate political speech. For one, corporations might corrupt candidates by essentially bribing them to vote in certain ways in exchange for campaign spending. In addition, corporations have a unique ability to amass wealth, so its pervasive "speech"

might distort campaigns by making it seem as though the public supports
a particular policy when in fact it's the corporation rather than the public at large that would benefit. Further, corporate speech might drown
out individual speech, leading to inequities in the messages disseminated
during a campaign. The Court therefore upheld restrictions on corporations engaging in political campaigning in those prior cases because
the government had a really good reason for limiting corporate speech
rights—protecting the sanctity of the campaign itself.[27]

This inquiry is where *Citizens United* really broke new ground. The
Court ruled that the government cannot cite the potential of corruption
to justify a ban on corporations spending their own money on their own
campaign ads. The federal law at issue limited corporate independent
expenditures. Recall that these expenditures must be completely independent of a candidate. No coordination between the spender and the
candidate is allowed. A corporation's representatives can't talk with the
candidate about the content of the ad, when to run it, or where to disseminate it. Doing any of these things would make the ad a "contribution"
under the law, and corporations are banned from direct contributions
to candidates—a provision not at issue in this case. So the question was
whether these corporate independent expenditures, which are separate
from the candidate, can still lead to corruption.

Most people would agree that there's a potential for corruption here.
If you are a candidate and you know that a corporation or other outside
group is spending money to help your election, even if they don't coordinate with you, aren't you going to favor their interests when you're in
office? You want them to spend to help your reelection, after all. On a
big issue, aren't you more likely to side with those wealthy interests? Or
perhaps you have the power to kill a bill that would impose regulations
on businesses. Won't you consider how those who spent on your behalf
will view your vote—even if you've never spoken with them about their
ad? Catering to corporate interests instead of what's best for your constituents, all because you want to keep the corporation on your good side for
the next election, is surely a form of corruption. Policymakers are more
responsive to those who spend money, even if they don't directly coordinate with the spender.

That's how the Supreme Court saw things in both 1980 and 2003,
when it initially upheld government bans on corporate independent ex-

penditures. In 2003's *McConnell v. FEC*, the Court noted that corruption can include "undue influence on an officeholder's judgment, and the appearance of such influence" arising from campaign expenditures.[28] But things changed in *Citizens United*. Instead of acknowledging that campaign spending, in whatever form, can skew legislative decision-making, the majority of the Court found that "[t]he fact that speakers may have influence over or access to elected officials does not mean that these officials are corrupt."[29] By definition, according to the Court, independent expenditures cannot corrupt because the spender is not giving anything directly to the candidate. The Court narrowed the definition of corruption to include only quid pro quo exchanges: the donation of money to a campaign in exchange for specific legislative favors when the person is in office. Because independent expenditures are, well, independent of the candidate, the Court found that they simply cannot corrupt.

Of course, this crabbed view of corruption is divorced from reality. We all know that every major political candidate has "their" super PAC (Political Action Committee), an organization—typically created by their close advisors—that will spend gobs of money to help their election. Priorities USA is a major pro-Democratic super PAC that was formed in 2011 to support President Barack Obama's reelection campaign. Its founders? Former Obama campaign staffers. With a wink and a nod, campaigns can benefit from unlimited super PAC spending. That surreptitiousness, according to the Court, does not lead to corruption—nor even the appearance of corruption. Campaigns now put up stock footage of the candidate in the hope (and, let's be real, the expectation) that super PACs run by their friends will use it in campaign ads. When Pete Buttigieg ran in the Democratic primaries for president in 2020, a senior advisor noted on Twitter that it would be good for Nevada voters to see ads about Buttigieg's military service. Not surprisingly, VoteVets, a super PAC supporting Buttigieg's run, then spent $300,000 on ad buys in the state.[30] A wink and a nod, indeed, but one that is perfectly legal if there is no formal coordination between the candidate and the organization.

Speaking of money, the organization Citizens United spent about $1.25 million in legal fees in its bid to open up American politics to unlimited corporate spending.[31] That seems well worth it, for them, given the billions now spent on campaigns—billions that drown out the voices of the rest of us.

SHHH . . .

Trevor Potter was a Republican appointee to the Federal Election Commission, the federal agency that oversees campaign finance laws. He also served as John McCain's top campaign lawyer in both 2000 and 2008, when McCain ran for president. His Republican credentials—at least if you consider the Republican Party prior to Trump—are unimpeachable.

So perhaps it's surprising that Potter is one of the most outspoken critics of *Citizens United*. For a few months, this tall lawyer with sandy hair and an affable smile was also a TV star.

One day in 2011, Potter was sitting in his law firm office when he received a strange call. It was from a producer of the TV show *The Colbert Report*, which ran on Comedy Central late at night. What would happen, this producer asked, if a TV host decided to open a super PAC? These new organizations would allow individuals and corporations to spend unlimited money on campaigns so long as they were not coordinated with any candidates. Could Stephen Colbert raise and spend money through a super PAC? Colbert had floated the idea during a segment parodying Minnesota governor and presidential candidate Tim Pawlenty. Executives from Comedy Central's parent company contacted Colbert expressing concern as to whether he was serious about creating a political action committee. Colbert asked the producer to research the issue with a campaign finance lawyer.

Could Colbert actually do this?

Sure, Potter answered. There were forms to fill out and certain rules to follow, but it wouldn't be that difficult. "Could you explain this to Stephen?" the producer then asked. So Potter found himself on the phone with Stephen Colbert himself. Colbert was interested in the nuances of *Citizens United* and how he could exploit the ruling for comedic effect— while making a political point at the same time.

Colbert eventually asked Potter to appear on his show to walk through the details of creating a super PAC. The number one piece of advice the producers gave Potter before his first appearance was simple: "Don't try to be funny." That was Colbert's job, not the guests'. Potter went on and explained to Colbert how to create a super PAC. They filled out the necessary paperwork for a new super PAC named Americans for a Better Tomorrow, Tomorrow.

Super PACs such as Americans for a Better Tomorrow, Tomorrow must disclose their donors. Disclosure, the Supreme Court had said in *Citizens United*, is the answer to the concerns surrounding corporate political expenditures: the public can react accordingly by knowing who is spending money on certain campaigns. But what if a super PAC doesn't want to disclose its donors? Colbert playfully lamented that corporations were not donating to his super PAC because they were afraid of the public reaction if they did. Potter had a solution: Create another organization that doesn't have to disclose its donors, and then have *that* group donate to the super PAC. Under tax law, a social welfare organization need not reveal who donates to it. This makes sense; some people do not want to let others know about their charitable giving. But it also created a loophole in campaign finance law. Colbert could set up a social welfare organization—a not-for-profit, tax-exempt 501(c)(4) group—solicit contributions, and hide donors' names from public view. The 501(c)(4) just has to have as its "primary purpose" social welfare activities.

What does "primary purpose" mean under the tax law? "It's all a little gray," Potter said, to Colbert's faux delight. Colbert created a social welfare organization called SHH!. That 501(c)(4) group could then donate to the Colbert super PAC. And when the Colbert super PAC disclosed its donors, as required under the law, one of those donors was the not-for-profit SHH!. As Potter told Colbert, this was all perfectly legal. If the goal is to spend as much as you want without anyone knowing, you just needed to donate to a 501(c)(4) organization, which could then give all of that money to the super PAC. No one would ever find out. "How is this different from money laundering?" Colbert asked. "It's hard to say," Potter offered with a wry smile.[32]

In the end, the Colbert super PAC raised over $1.2 million.[33] Of course, that money was the product of a parody to demonstrate the perils of the Supreme Court's decision, and Colbert ultimately donated most of it to various causes. The real money raised via super PACs has not been though parodies but in actual elections, and the amounts have been staggering. Yet the predictions about *who* would spend that money were inaccurate. By and large, corporations have not invested significantly in political campaigns—at least not openly. Corporate money accounts for less than one-tenth of all independent spending by outside groups (that disclose their donors) in recent campaigns, probably because corporations do not want to alienate their customers through political advocacy.[34] Instead, the real rise in money has come from super PACs and other "outside" organizations. "Dark money" groups—those that don't reveal their donors—spent over $1 billion in the 2020 election, which is significantly more than in previous election cycles.[35] Though Republican interests initially benefitted the most from increased spending, Democrats later took the lead: the fifteen largest Democratic-leaning groups spent about $1.5 billion during the 2020 election, while the fifteen largest Republican-leaning groups spent around $900 million.[36] Much of this money comes from wealthy individuals. Just ten people and their spouses spent $1.2 billion in federal elections in the decade after *Citizens United*.[37] The top one hundred donors collectively gave $2 billion to super PACs or similar groups. Uber-rich people have had the most influence; Open-Secrets, which tracks campaign spending, has explained, "In an era where outside groups fill crucial roles, between functioning as arms of political parties or as extensions of political campaigns, wealthy donors are indispensable."[38] Power has shifted further away from the rank-and-file of the political parties to the wealthy backers of these "shadow parties."[39] Big political spenders are now as much of a candidate's constituents as are voters—if not more so. As two leading scholars put it, "This is a striking concept of 'constituents,'" especially for a democracy that prides itself on representation and political responsiveness.[40] We also have no idea how much foreign interests are spending on American elections through dark money groups.[41]

Money doesn't outright buy elections; the rich candidate or the one with the wealthiest backers doesn't always win. It's virtually impossible, however, to mount a viable campaign without significant funding. A candidate might raise those funds through small gifts, but a single donation from someone with deep pockets—say, Michael Bloomberg, with his $20 million donation to the Democratic-leaning Senate Majority PAC—"could effectively neutralize the efforts of thousands, even millions, of small donors."[42] This is not a Republican problem or a Democratic problem. It's a democracy problem.

Put it this way: Do you want to run for office? You better have *very* rich friends.

AN IDEOLOGY OF INEQUALITY

In 2014, Supreme Court Justice Ruth Bader Ginsberg was asked which opinion she would most like to overrule. "*Citizens United*," she said without missing a beat. "I think the notion that we have all the democracy that money can buy strays so far from what our democracy is supposed to be. So that's number one on my list."[43]

Citizens United has spawned an entire industry of policy thinkers, lawyers, and other experts trying to grapple with the intractable problem of money in politics. I asked many of them how the Supreme Court's decision impacts individual voters. Their answers were enlightening.

Jeff Clements runs an organization called American Promise that advocates for a constitutional amendment to reinvigorate the idea of "We the People" and reduce the role of money in politics.[44] He wrote a book in 2012, *Corporations Are Not People*, in which he lambasted *Citizens United*, and he has spent the past decade fighting the decision. As Clements put it (echoed by American Promise's top lawyer, Brian Boyle), our system of democracy rests on a principle of equality, but *Citizens United* rejects that formulation when it comes to political spending. The idea of one person, one vote means that everyone has an equal say in political representation, as everyone's vote is valued the same. But everyone's voice in a political campaign does not have the same value. *Citizens United*, Clements said, has created an "ideology of inequality." Sure, people can vote, but they have virtually no say in what issues are debated. The case therefore has created complications beyond campaign finance because it harms representation and responsiveness, both cornerstones of our democracy. In addition, our campaign finance regime shuts everyday people out of running for office because they know they have little shot at winning.[45]

Erin Chlopak litigates campaign finance cases for the Campaign Legal Center, a nonprofit litigation and advocacy firm that promotes democracy reform. During our conversation, she explained that *Citizens United* has had two significant impacts on democratic engagement. First, perhaps reflecting her frustration over the defeat of the Democrats' voting rights package in the Senate in early 2022, she noted that dark money can help fund campaigns against democracy enhancements, as dark money funders prefer a system they can influence behind the scenes. Second, the case perpetuates a legal regime favoring entrenched interests at the expense of voters. Professor Spencer Overton, my mentor in law school, called this idea the "participation interest" of democracy. Of course, participating in democracy entails voting, but it should also include so much more: volunteering for a candidate, contacting government officials, and contributing to a campaign. As Professor Overton writes, "Participation outside of the voting booth makes citizens producers of policy rather than just consumers."[46] Chlopak cited Professor Overton's formulation when lamenting the fact that today's campaign finance regime makes it harder for ordinary citizens to have much influence over policymakers.[47]

Adam Bozzi is the communications head of a group called End Citizens United, which works to promote policies to increase transparency in campaign finance and support enhanced voting mechanisms. I half joked with Bozzi that the organization really should be called "End Buckley" because the root of the issues stem from that 1976 case, and while he did not disagree, he noted that *Citizens United* had supercharged the problem of money in politics. Bozzi also pointed out an important impact of the influx of dark money: given the finite amount of advertising space available, voters often hear more from these shadow groups than they do directly from candidates. It's harder for voters to evaluate those dark money ads when they don't know who is speaking. This political environment reduces the direct connections between candidates and voters.[48]

We also cannot ignore the racial dimension of our campaign finance regime. As john a. powell, a law professor and civil rights champion, wrote over two decades ago in an article titled "Campaign Finance Reform Is a Voting Rights Issue," "Until we wholeheartedly acknowledge that wealth in this country is a racialized institution, effective participation by racial minorities in voting as well as in other important participatory arenas will be undermined."[49] He explained that the campaign finance system is "a form of vote dilution" because Black people cannot as easily participate due to wealth disparities, giving them less of a voice. This observation was in 2002, well before the *Citizens United* decision in 2010 and its pernicious, magnified effects on subsequent elections.

Citizens United also impacts who chooses to run for office. One study of female state legislators showed that the largest barrier to seeking higher office was raising enough money, but the concerns were not just about having to ask people for donations. Instead, the women interviewed cited an inability to tap into the right networks of big donors. Over 70 percent of the respondents pointed to the need to raise money as a significant barrier to running for higher office.[50] Another report showed that women are often excluded from the financial circles that include the wealthiest donors, as those networks tend to be part of male-dominated corporate America.[51] Although there have been great strides in recent years, women are still severely underrepresented in the halls of state legislatures and in Congress, and the campaign finance system is one reason why.

Notice the common threads among the reactions to *Citizens United* and our campaign finance system overall: representation, responsiveness, and equality. It's about letting the powerful continue to consolidate their power, leaving voters in the dust. There are scores of examples of industry execs influencing policy in a way regular voters could never do. Instead of "We the People" as sovereign, the system is set up to skew the debate and its outcomes.

These same perils infect the other areas of voting rights and election law we have already discussed. Whether it's in cases about the right to vote or rulings on how candidates conduct their campaigns, the Court abdicates its responsibility to ensure a fair system, offering unfettered trust to politicians and the rules they enact. Political equality and responsiveness fall by the wayside. Of course, supporters of *Citizens United* suggest that the opinion promotes "freedom" in that it allows for more speech by more entities. But they have a hard time answering the question: Freedom for whom? Not everyone, because not everyone has the means to have the same influence.

When we think of *Citizens United* as a case about *voters* in addition to campaign finance, we see how the ruling reinforces political inequality within our democracy. The Court implicitly rejected an equality principle in the right-to-vote cases we covered previously; it more explicitly rejected an equality rationale for campaign finance in *Citizens United*. The effect is skewed representation, distorted political debate, and unrepresentative outcomes.

The Court's underlying—if veiled—message: Voters take a backseat when it comes to rules about our democracy.

CHAPTER 6

AN "EMBARRASSING JUDICIAL FART"

Bush v. Gore (2000)

	JUSTICE	APPOINTED BY
MAJORITY	Rehnquist, William H. (chief justice) *(authored concurring opinion)*	Nixon, Richard (R) (associate justice) Reagan, Ronald (R) (chief justice)
	Scalia, Antonin *(joined Rehnquist's opinion)*	Reagan, Ronald (R)
	Thomas, Clarence *(joined Rehnquist's opinion)*	Bush, George H. W. (R)
	Kennedy, Anthony M.	Reagan, Ronald (R)
	O'Connor, Sandra Day	Reagan, Ronald (R)
	The majority issued a "per curiam" (unsigned) opinion for the five justices in the majority; Rehnquist also authored a separate concurrence.	
DISSENT	Stevens, John Paul	Ford, Gerald (R)
	Ginsburg, Ruth Bader	Clinton, Bill (D)
	Breyer, Stephen G.	Clinton, Bill (D)
	Souter, David H.	Bush, George H. W. (R)
	Each dissenting justice issued their own dissent and also joined the other dissents in whole or in part.	

T he story of *Bush v. Gore* is well known and well worn. You couldn't make it up if you tried. Because of the unique way we elect the president through the Electoral College—with each state having a certain number of Electoral College votes—the result of the 2000 presidential election comes down to one state, Florida, and just 537 votes in that state out of almost 6 million cast. The governor of that state, Jeb Bush, is the Republican presidential candidate's brother. The secretary of state, who administers the state's elections, is the co-chair of that candidate's Florida campaign. A faulty ballot design in one county, the "butterfly ballot," creates massive confusion, causing many Democrats to mistakenly cast their votes for the Reform Party candidate, Pat Buchanan, whom they abhor. Other people show up to vote only to find that the state has taken them off the rolls in an aggressive voter purge, even though most of these individuals are still eligible to vote. Any one of these issues could have changed the outcome of the election. A movie director would find such a plot too unbelievable.

Ultimately, the Supreme Court stepped in to halt the Florida recount on December 12, 2000, thirty-six days after Election Day. The Court's majority found that there was no longer enough time to conduct a proper recount, so it simply reverted to the prior certified results, which gave Republican George W. Bush a 537-vote lead in Florida and put him over the top in the Electoral College. The rest, as they say, is history. The Democratic nominee, Al Gore, conceded the next day—refusing to contest the result in Congress even though, or perhaps because, as vice president he would preside over Congress's tabulation of the Electoral College votes. George W. Bush was inaugurated on January 20, 2001, as the forty-third president.

There are scores of books, movies, and articles that explain those perilous thirty-six days between Election Day and the Supreme Court's decision in *Bush v. Gore*. The opinion was immediately and widely panned as unduly partisan and political, with little legal analysis. Over twenty years after it came out, two law professors noted that, at that time, no Supreme Court majority opinion had ever cited the case, suggesting that it "was viewed by polite society and by the justices themselves as an embarrassing judicial fart that we could all pretend not to hear or smell."[1]

This chapter will answer two fundamental questions about the case that bear upon the way the Supreme Court's voting rights jurisprudence has harmed American democracy: First, what did the Court *actually* say in *Bush v. Gore*? Second, what effect has the ruling had on today's law and politics? To use the colorful analogy from those law professors, will the smell from the "embarrassing judicial fart" ever go away?

FROM UNDERVOTES TO PREGNANT CHADS

The case (actually, there were multiple lawsuits) entailed a flurry of back-and-forth activity between state trial judges in Florida, the Florida Supreme Court, and the U.S. Supreme Court during those thirty-six days in 2000. The legal issues stemmed from a problem involving so-called undervotes on punch-card ballots. An undervote is a paper ballot that indicates votes for down-ballot races, such as Congress or state legislature, but not president. Did the voter decide not to vote for any presidential candidate, or was there a problem with the vote-counting machines? In 2000, many Florida voters cast their votes on paper punch-card ballots by pushing through the paper to create a small hole that corresponded to their preferred candidate's name. If you wanted to vote for George W. Bush, for example, you pushed out the small perforated portion of the paper—the chad—next to Bush's spot on the ballot. The election officials then sent the ballots through a machine that counted the votes based on the removed chads. The problem was that some voters did not push those little chads all the way through the paper. Sometimes the chads would be left partially attached—a hanging chad. Or the chad might be pushed in a little but not actually removed, known as a "dimpled" or "pregnant" chad. The machine would not register these ballots as a vote for any candidate. Yet a human review of those ballots might demonstrate that the voter did, in fact, intend to vote for a particular candidate.

On the evening of the election, network TV stations declared Bush the winner of Florida, then backpedaled and said Gore had won more votes, before then taking it back again and deeming the state too close to call. The election was so tight throughout the country that the winner of Florida's twenty-five Electoral College votes would win the presidency. Gore even called Bush that night to concede the election before calling him back to undo that concession. A concession, by the way, has absolutely zero legal effect on the election. It just contributes to the political storyline.

Gore's team quickly realized that the machines, particularly in Democratic-leaning counties, may not have counted all the votes properly if the voters had not fully dislodged the chads. Gore therefore asked for a manual recount in four counties: Miami-Dade, Broward, Palm Beach, and Volusia. Bush, seeking to preserve his slim lead, objected to the recount. Meanwhile, on November 26, Katherine Harris, Florida's secretary of state, certified Bush as the winner of Florida's Electoral College votes by a margin of 537 votes, even though not all counties had finished their recounts. Harris was also serving as the chair of Bush's election campaign in Florida, so she obviously had an interest in the outcome.

Gore was then forced to formally contest the result and seek a court-ordered hand recount of all ballots the machines had missed. He thought he could pick up enough votes in the Democratic-leaning counties to take the lead in the state. Florida law said that a vote should count if officials can discern the "intent of the voter."[2] Teams of election workers from each of the counties gathered to inspect ballots that the machines had not tallied because the machines had discerned no vote for president. Did these ballots show that the voters intended to choose a candidate? "Intent of the voter" is a pretty amorphous standard. Should a vote count if two corners on a rectangular chad are dislodged? What about three corners, so that the chad is hanging on by only one corner? Is that a legal vote? What about a so-called pregnant chad? Does the paper have to be pushed through entirely? There's a famous photo of an election worker holding a ballot up to the light and looking through a magnifying glass to determine if there was light coming through. Yes, the fate of the United States presidency was coming down to a magnifying glass.

There was also a timing concern. Federal law, through the convoluted Electoral Count Act of 1887 (which Professor Ned Foley called "one of the strangest pieces of statutory language ever enacted by Congress"), required states to have their electors meet on the same day throughout the country to cast their Electoral College votes.[3] In 2000, that day was December 18. Federal law also included what came to be known as the "safe harbor" deadline, which was December 12 that year. The safe harbor deadline basically said that if there's a dispute about which candidate won a state's Electoral College votes, Congress must count the ones certified six days before the electors met so long as the state had used a dispute resolution process that was set out before Election Day. It's a rule that helps Congress figure out which slate to count when there are competing submissions. Assume that Florida governor Jeb Bush sent Congress a slate of electors for Bush, but the Florida Supreme Court ordered a slate sent in for Gore. The safe harbor deadline said that Congress must count those Electoral College votes determined by December 12 so long as the procedure to decide who won them was established prior to Election Day. That is, if the Florida Supreme Court followed Florida law, as it existed prior to Election Day, and resolved the case by the safe harbor deadline, then Congress must count that slate and not the one from the governor (assuming he had not followed the procedures in Florida law). (Congress updated this law in 2022 after some Trump supporters exploited it to object to the 2020 election results.)

As mentioned earlier, the Florida Supreme Court issued several rulings in the case. The most important for the ultimate resolution came down on the afternoon of Friday, December 8, a 4–3 decision that ordered a manual recount of undervotes—ballots that didn't register a vote for president on the machine—across the entire state.[4] Gore had asked for a recount of only four counties, but the Florida Supreme Court expanded that recount to include all sixty-seven counties. A state trial judge, Terry Lewis, immediately implemented that order, issuing a ruling just before midnight to begin the recount.[5]

The very next day, Saturday, December 9, 2000, the U.S. Supreme Court put the Florida Supreme Court's decision on hold, by a 5–4 vote.[6] The effect of this order to "stay" the Florida Supreme Court's decision was to halt the statewide recount of undervotes that had just started. Counties had already begun to manually recount the paper ballots that the machines had read as having no vote for president, with the goal of finishing by December 12, the safe harbor deadline, but the Supreme Court's order required them to stop counting immediately. Typically, when the Court issues a preliminary order in a pending case, it does not offer its reasons for the decision. Because Justice Stevens wrote a dissent to the order, however, Justice Scalia issued his own opinion to explain the rationale for putting the Florida Supreme Court's decision on hold. Although nothing was final, Scalia claimed that Bush had an interest in preserving his lead: "Count first, and rule upon legality afterwards, is not a recipe for producing election results that have the public acceptance democratic stability requires," Scalia said.[7] The Supreme Court's order set an extremely fast briefing schedule: written briefs were due by 4:00 p.m. on Sunday, December 10, with oral argument set for Monday morning.

The Supreme Court's December 9 order to stop the recount had a perverse effect: it made it impossible for counties to finish their recounts by December 12, the safe harbor deadline. County officials had already questioned whether they could finish their recounts on time. Halting the recount provided a blunt answer: they simply couldn't.

The oral arguments, heard on the morning of Monday, December 11, were relatively bland and boring, at least for a case with such monumental importance regarding who would be the next president of the United States. Ted Olson, Bush's lawyer, began the argument by droning on about how the Florida Supreme Court had "changed statutory deadlines" and "changed the meaning of words such as 'shall' and 'may' into 'shall not' and 'may not.'"[8] The argument then devolved into the question of whether the Supreme Court had jurisdiction to hear the case, parsing complicated issues of constitutional adjudication.

The parties ultimately focused on two main points: First, did the Florida Supreme Court's ruling, which allowed each county to determine the "intent of the voter," violate the federal Equal Protection Clause? Differing standards for whether to count certain ballots might have the effect of treating voters unequally according to where they lived. Second, if the Florida Supreme Court's decision was wrong in some way, what was the proper remedy, given that the safe harbor deadline was the following day, December 12?

A 7–2 RULING

The Supreme Court issued its ruling on Tuesday, December 12—an extremely rushed timetable given that the oral arguments had taken place just the day before. The majority opinion, an unsigned ("per curiam") ruling, rested on the equal protection issue and the proper remedy. Although the Court did not list an author, subsequent research revealed that Justice Kennedy was primarily responsible for this per curiam opinion.[9]

The Court first stated that the Constitution does not explicitly confer the right to vote: "The individual citizen has no federal constitutional right to vote for electors for the President of the United States unless and until the state legislature chooses a statewide election as the means to implement its power to appoint members of the Electoral College."[10] But, the Court continued, once a state grants its citizens the right to vote for president, it must do so on "equal terms." The Florida Supreme Court's decision to order a statewide recount without a uniform standard for determining the intent of the voter, the Court said, violated this ideal. The varying processes and standards that election officials across the state were applying to the recount failed to ensure equal treatment between voters.

This portion of the opinion was 7–2, not simply a 5–4 ruling along ideological lines, as many people may think. In addition to the conservatives on the Court (Chief Justice Rehnquist and Justices Thomas, Scalia, O'Connor, and Kennedy), two liberal justices, Souter and Breyer, also agreed that the Florida Supreme Court's decision did not provide enough guarantees of equal protection given that counties had differing standards for discerning the intent of the voter for each ballot. Some counties might count a pregnant chad as a valid vote but other counties might reject that ballot. There was even evidence of differences between election officials in the same county. For example, Palm Beach County switched their rule during the process, first counting a ballot only if at least two corners of the chad were dislodged, but later accepting ballots with dimpled chads.[11] These differing standards, the seven justices said, violated the ideal of equality in ballot counting.

But the rest of the opinion was 5–4. The five conservative justices refused to fix the problem of having uneven standards across the state, instead simply stopping the recount. The Florida legislature, the majority found, wanted to comply with the safe harbor deadline and resolve any disputes about the state's Electoral College votes by December 12. "That date is upon us, and there is no recount procedure in place under the State Supreme Court's order that comports with minimal constitutional standards."[12] Instead of sending the case back to the Florida Supreme Court to correct the constitutional problem, the majority chose to stop the recount entirely.

This disposition is radical. Normally, when a lower court makes a mistake, the proper course is for the appeals court to instruct that court to fix the problem. Often the Supreme Court provides precise standards to use on remand. But here, the majority refused to send the case back at all. It more or less threw up its hands. Most perversely, this same majority had created the very problem that it relied upon to claim that there was no longer enough time to complete the recount by December 12. If the Court had not put the Florida Supreme Court's decision on hold on December 9, the counties likely could have finished their recounts in time. And December 12 was not even a hard deadline: the electors were not meeting until December 18 and Congress would not gather to tally Electoral College votes until January 6, 2001. The majority elevated a desire to have the election resolved by December 12 above protecting voters—with the Court's own delay the biggest reason for the state's inability to complete the count in the first place. By stopping the recount, some ballots that indicated a vote for president but which were not picked up by the machine were essentially thrown out.

There's a line in the majority's opinion that proved particularly controversial: "Our consideration is limited to the present circumstances, for the problem of equal protection in election processes generally presents many complexities."[13] Normally, Supreme Court decisions are binding precedent, setting out legal rules for all courts to use in the future. But here the Court pretty much said that *Bush v. Gore* was good for one day only. Indeed, although lower courts have used principles from the decision in subsequent election disputes, the Supreme Court itself did not cite the case in a majority opinion for over twenty years.[14] That is, unlike most other Supreme Court cases, the Court has basically ignored its ruling in *Bush v. Gore*. It's not as if the Court didn't hear any election disputes in the two decades after the case! The one-off aspect of the ruling generated immense criticism, as it suggests the Court was being lawless, simply deciding a political, not legal, dispute.

Chief Justice Rehnquist wrote a separate concurrence, joined by Justices Thomas and Scalia, to explain his view that the Florida Supreme Court had acted too much like a "legislature" in its decision, taking authority away from the state legislature to determine the manner of appointing presidential electors in violation of Article II of the U.S. Constitution. This is the same argument conservatives used in 2020 and beyond under the so-called "independent state legislature" theory, discussed later in this book, which suggests that state courts cannot invalidate state election laws.

All of the four liberals on the Court (Justices Stevens, Ginsburg, Souter, and Breyer) wrote their own dissents to highlight the incorrectness of the majority's opinion (though Justices Souter and Breyer agreed with the majority on the equal protection portion). I like Justice Stevens's dissent the most: "Although we may never know with complete certainty the identity of the winner of this year's Presidential election, the identity of the loser is perfectly clear. It is the Nation's confidence in the judge as an impartial guardian of the rule of law."[15]

The decision to halt the recount cemented Bush's certified win in Florida by 537 votes. The next night, Al Gore said that he would accept the results and not continue his challenge in Congress, promising not to take back his concession this time. "Now the U.S. Supreme Court has spoken. Let there be no doubt, while I *strongly* disagree with the Court's decision, I accept it."[16]

DID BUSH ACTUALLY WIN FLORIDA?

Five hundred thirty-seven votes out of 6 million cast is a minuscule number. A bevy of things going slightly differently could have changed the outcome. The confusingly designed butterfly ballot in Palm Beach County surely caused some people, especially older voters, to vote for Pat Buchanan when they intended to choose Al Gore, but there wasn't any legal remedy for that mistake. Improper voter purges, too, took away some people's right to vote, and those voters could have tipped the balance. We will never know who would have won Florida in 2000 if everyone who was eligible to cast a proper, easy-to-understand ballot had been able to do so.

That's not to say, however, that we can't speculate as to who should have won on the basis of all ballots cast. The Supreme Court deprived the country of this knowledge by stopping the recount, but the media was undeterred. A consortium of news organizations, including *USA Today* and the *Miami Herald*, examined over 175,000 Florida ballots that counting machines had rejected.

The outcome?

It depends.

If, as Gore had requested, the recount had included only the under-votes—those ballots the machines read as having no vote for president—then Bush still would have won by a few hundred votes. If the recount had also included all overvotes—ballots the machine rejected because they registered *two or more* votes for president, even though on examination the intent of the voter was clear to choose one person—then Gore likely would have won by a very small margin. But Gore never asked for a recount of all overvotes![17]

Thus, it's not entirely accurate to say that the Supreme Court simply decided the presidential election in favor of George W. Bush. It's likely that Bush still would have won had the recount proceeded in the way Gore wanted. There were enough problems in Florida, however, to suggest that Gore might have been the preferred candidate of most people in the state. We just can't say for sure.

Bush v. Gore has had an immense effect on the law of democracy. It goes beyond the Bush presidency or the fact that we'll never know who received the most votes for president in Florida. Justice Scalia had a snarky response to those who continued to object years later: "Get over it."[18] But we shouldn't just "get over" the case—not because of its result, but because of its pernicious effects on our elections to this day.

AN EXPLOSION OF LITIGATION

Election lawyers love *Bush v. Gore*, at least for their bottom line. After all, these days you can't run a campaign without hiring a lawyer. Planning for litigation is now a routine part of campaign strategy.

Election law wasn't really a field of study before *Bush v. Gore*. Few law schools had professors who focused on the area or courses on the topic. Even closely contested presidential races with serious questions about the result in some states—such as the allegation of improprieties in Illinois during the 1960 election between Richard Nixon and John F. Kennedy—didn't end in protracted litigation.[19] Now, thanks to the effects of *Bush v. Gore*, many law schools have someone like me whose entire scholarly agenda involves election law and voting rights.

The number of election law cases bears this out. As Professor Rick Hasen of the UCLA Law School has documented, the rate of election litigation ballooned to three times more lawsuits after *Bush v. Gore* than before that case. The year 2020 saw a record high number of election law cases with 424—which was 26 percent more filings than the 337 cases in 2016.[20] There has also been a surge in money spent on election litigation.[21] Political operatives know that a close election might come down to the specific rules in play, and they are using courts to manipulate those rules.

Bush v. Gore has certainly been good for legal business, but it's been bad for the country. You shouldn't need a law degree or be wealthy enough to hire a lawyer just to run for office. And it has contributed to the feeling that an election is never really over on Election Day.

EXTRA INNINGS

Postelection lawsuits have increased in part because of the sheer fact of close outcomes and in part because candidates are now more likely to turn to the courts. A margin of a few hundred votes out of millions cast is essentially a statistical tie. Given that it's pretty much impossible to know who *really* won these extremely close elections, Professor Mike Pitts offered, somewhat tongue-in-cheek, a better solution for a very tight race: flip a coin. He even suggested that NFL referees conduct the coin flips, as that's who our society trusts most to flip coins fairly![22]

The years 2000 and 2020 are both famous for their presidential election disputes, but virtually every election year in between also saw contests go into extra innings. Here are some of the most contentious:

In 2004, the Washington gubernatorial election came down to 129 votes out of 2.8 million ballots cast, ending with Democrat Christine Gregoire narrowly defeating Republican Dino Rossi.[23] The recount and subsequent litigation lasted until June of the following year, when Rossi finally conceded after a state trial judge ruled against him. (Gregoire, as the certified winner, was serving as governor during the litigation.) Yet the trial uncovered various problems with the state's election administration, such as individuals convicted of felonies casting ballots, even though state law had disenfranchised them. There were also issues with the ballot-counting process, such as the inclusion of provisional ballots in the count without fully checking the voters' eligibility. Any of these problems might have changed the result; the trial court highlighted the messiness of the election but concluded that there was not enough evidence to overturn the certified result in favor of Gregoire.[24]

In 2008, the election in Minnesota for a seat in the U.S. Senate came down to a margin of just a few hundred votes between Norm Coleman, the Republican incumbent, and comedian Al Franken, his Democratic challenger. The initial count showed Coleman up by 215 votes. A recount, however, gave Franken the lead by 225 votes. Subsequent judicial rulings on challenged ballots increased that lead to 312. Part of the dispute involved whether to count absentee ballots, even if the voters had not complied precisely with every rule when filling them out. For instance, if the voter signed the envelope in the wrong spot, does that ballot not count? Interestingly (or perhaps predictably), the lawyers' arguments flipped during the litigation: when Coleman was ahead, his lawyers argued for a "strict compliance" standard that would reject ballots that did not exactly follow the law, but after the recount, when Coleman was down by a few hundred votes, his lawyers argued for a "substantial compliance" rule to count more ballots. Franken's lawyers initially wanted a more lenient standard when Franken was behind, but then argued for strict compliance once he pulled ahead. The Minnesota Supreme Court ultimately decided the case in Franken's favor on June 30, 2009, more than six months after the election. Franken took his oath of office on July 7, 2009, meaning that Minnesota did not have full representation in the U.S. Senate for over six months.[25] Franken won reelection in 2014 but resigned his seat in December 2018 during the #MeToo movement after several women accused him of sexual misconduct.

The biggest dispute in 2010 involved the U.S. Senate race in Alaska. The incumbent, Republican Lisa Murkowski, lost the Republican primary in 2010 to a Tea Party candidate, Joe Miller. But refusing to go gently into that good night, Murkowski launched a write-in campaign. First, she had to register as a write-in candidate. Then she had to convince voters to write in her name—which is not easy to spell. For instance, voters might forget that it ends in an *i*, not a *y*. After Alaska election officials declared her the winner over Miller and Democrat Scott McAdams, Miller filed suit to invalidate thousands of votes because the voters had not spelled Murkowski's name correctly. The Alaska Supreme Court, however, construed state law broadly to effectuate a voter's intent, even if there were minor misspellings or abbreviations. Being a good speller is not a qualification to vote. The court ruled the ballots valid so long as election officials could discern the voters' intent. Murkowski ultimately retained the seat.[26]

The year 2012 saw renewed allegations of voter fraud, though there was no evidence to support these claims. Representative Allen West, a Tea Party favorite, peddled voter fraud speculation when he contested his loss in—where else?—Florida. The challenger, Patrick Murphy, a Democrat, was ahead by about 2,500 votes in the South Florida congressional district election. West demanded a recount and cited "nefarious actions" by Democratic officials. Court battles ensued, but two weeks later West finally conceded the race after acknowledging he didn't have enough evidence to change the outcome.[27]

The 2016 presidential election saw demands for recounts in Michigan, Pennsylvania, and Wisconsin alongside a flurry of lawsuits, most brought by the Green Party candidate, Jill Stein. Hillary Clinton's campaign also joined the effort in Wisconsin to question the vote totals, which Donald Trump won by about 22,000 votes. Trump's lawyers responded with attempts to halt the recounts. Only Wisconsin conducted a full recount, which strengthened Trump's victory in the state by 131 additional votes. In Pennsylvania, the judge denied a recount by noting that it would force the state to be late in certifying its vote totals and that "[s]uch a result would be both outrageous and completely unnecessary; as I have found, suspicion of a 'hacked' Pennsylvania election borders on the irrational."[28] Stein, undeterred, claimed that the recounts and lawsuits were intended to shine a light on the states' election machinery. But that strategy is dangerous for our democracy: losing candidates who refuse to accept election results undermine the public's perception of the winner's legitimacy.[29]

That's what happened in 2018 in Georgia's gubernatorial election. Democrat Stacey Abrams claimed that her loss to Republican Brian Kemp for the Georgia governor's office was illegitimate. There's a lot about that election that should cause concern. For one, Kemp was serving as secretary of state at the time and was therefore overseeing an election in which he was a candidate—an obvious conflict of interest. In the three months before Election Day, the state, with Kemp leading the charge, purged more than 85,000 voters from its rolls, a disproportionate number of whom were minorities. The weekend before the election, Kemp announced an "investigation" into the state Democratic Party for "cybercrime," despite having zero evidence of malfeasance, suggesting that he was using his office to peddle a political storyline in the final days of the campaign. In a close battle, Kemp won the most votes, though the recount lasted over a week. To her credit, Abrams did not file a lawsuit to contest the results but instead sued the state in an effort to change election laws based on what she said was the state's "gross mismanagement" of the election. Abrams, however, declined to recognize Kemp as the proper winner. While she stated that Kemp would be the "legal Governor of Georgia," she refused to acknowledge the election itself as legitimate. The difference matters. By failing to accept Kemp's victory as legitimate under the rules in place that year, Abrams cast a pall over the finality of the election itself. It also gave Republicans fodder for making the same kinds of claims two years later, when Donald Trump refused to admit his defeat in the 2020 presidential election.[30]

THE BIGGEST ATTACK ON OUR DEMOCRACY SINCE THE CIVIL WAR

Donald Trump and his supporters took the concept of postelection litigation to the extreme in 2020 in the most brazen attempt to undermine our
democracy in over a century.

Joe Biden decisively won the 2020 presidential election, with no
evidence that there were any problems sufficient to call the result into
question. Even so, Trump's team and other Republicans filed over seventy
lawsuits in federal and state courts to challenge various aspects of the election. Trump lost all but one of those cases. His only victory was in Pennsylvania, where a judge ruled that voters could not go back to "cure" their
ballots three days after the election if they had failed to show a proper ID.
That decision impacted very few voters and did little to touch Joe Biden's
win by over 81,000 votes in the state.[31] Suffice to say that Trump was a big
loser in the courts.[32]

Many of those lawsuits were farcical, at best. Trump lawyer Sidney
Powell promised to "release the Kraken" (referencing a famous movie
quote) to reveal numerous election irregularities, but she had no evidence whatsoever. She ulitimately pleaded guilty to criminal charges in
Georgia for interfering with the election. A lawsuit in Michigan alleged
a "wide-ranging interstate—and international—collaboration involving
multiple public and private actors" to record "thousands of illegal, ineligible, duplicate or purely fictitious ballots."[33] Lawyers brought a case in
Colorado, purportedly on behalf of 160 million registered voters, against
governors and election officials in four states as well as Facebook CEO
Mark Zuckerberg and his wife, Priscilla Chan. They sought $160 billion
in damages—which was, as the court noted, larger than the GDP of Hun-
gary.[34] Judges ultimately sanctioned these lawyers for bringing these frivolous lawsuits, but the lawyers still kept their law licenses.[35] In another
case, the state of Texas brought a suit against Pennsylvania and other
states directly to the Supreme Court, arguing that purported problems
with Pennsylvania's election administration somehow impacted Texas.
The Court swiftly rejected the case.[36] The lawyers were looking for any
avenue to contest the results, but they were also using the courts to further
their narrative of a stolen election. As one study explains, "In the courtroom, these lawsuits yielded no meaningful success for plaintiffs. In the
court of public opinion, however, they contributed to an erosion of trust
in the democratic process."[37] The spurious litigation created an outraged

atmosphere that helped to spark the Capitol riots on January 6, 2021. In the ultimate grift, Trump also used the existence of these lawsuits to raise millions of dollars, imploring his supporters to donate to the cause.[38]

Candidates and their supporters now routinely look to the courts to avenge their election losses. Donald Trump used the judiciary to peddle his Big Lie that he had actually won the election, manufacturing an election dispute even though the result wasn't close. Virtually every court rejected his claims, but the very presence of dozens of lawsuits contributed to the apparent legitimacy of his contentions, at least among his supporters. "If courts are looking at it," the argument goes, "then there must be something there." Many courts properly rejected the lawsuits on procedural grounds, such as the fact that Trump often sued the wrong officials, but that only added to the conspiratorial suspicion. Election deniers disingenuously asserted that the courts didn't actually consider Trump's arguments of election irregularities because they didn't rule on the merits.[39] Many courts did, in fact, reach the substance of the claims and found them wholly lacking. Yet as Trump demonstrated frequently, if you say something enough times, people will start to believe it. The barrage of lawsuits created the narrative that something was amiss. If the courts won't fix the problem, well, the people would have to themselves—even through violence at the nation's Capitol. In this way, the seeds planted in *Bush v. Gore* blossomed in 2020, to disastrous results for the country.

Bush v. Gore resolved a hotly disputed presidential election through peaceful means, not violence, and for that we should be grateful. As former federal judge and legal scholar Richard Posner suggested, maybe the Court had to step in to give a definitive answer so that the two sides would not take to the streets.[40] But the case also created an environment that encourages candidates to continue to fight an election loss. Now, *no one* can run for office without having a lawyer by their side, ready to fight both in the lead-up to Election Day and after voting is over. Perhaps *Bush v. Gore* was damaging in its result, at least if you were an Al Gore voter. Yet the case has had even worse consequences for our democracy: politicians know an electoral loss is never truly over if the courts are open to air one's grievances. Had the Court let the recount continue, elevating all voters' voices, then perhaps future candidates would not see the judiciary as a political tool to alter election outcomes. Maybe finishing the recount, under a fair and equal standard, would have lowered the temperature of future election disputes, leading losers to accept defeat more readily instead of continuing the fight in the courts.

The decision also continued the trend of deferring to state politicians in voting rules. Recall the Supreme Court's ultimate holding: the recount would take too long, frustrating the Florida legislature's supposed desire to finalize its Electoral College submission by a certain date. The Court elevated this unstated precept from the legislature over the rights of many voters, who were indisputably denied their right to have their votes count. The message is stark: the state legislature has greater rights than voters in our democratic system.

Essentially, the Court's approach means that state legislatures should have little oversight from the courts, regardless of whether it's before or after an election. That idea also played a large role in the Court's invalidation of a major portion of the Voting Rights Act in the famous (or perhaps infamous) *Shelby County* decision in 2013, to which we turn next.

CHAPTER 7

THROWING AWAY YOUR UMBRELLA
DURING A RAINSTORM

Shelby County v. Holder (2013)

	JUSTICE	APPOINTED BY
MAJORITY	Roberts, John G., Jr. (chief justice) *(authored majority opinion)*	Bush, George W. (R)
	Scalia, Antonin	Reagan, Ronald (R)
	Kennedy, Anthony M.	Reagan, Ronald (R)
	Thomas, Clarence *(authored concurring opinion)*	Bush, George H. W. (R)
	Alito, Samuel A., Jr.	Bush, George W. (R)
DISSENT	Ginsburg, Ruth Bader *(authored dissent)*	Clinton, Bill (D)
	Breyer, Stephen G.	Clinton, Bill (D)
	Sotomayor, Sonia	Obama, Barack (D)
	Kagan, Elena	Obama, Barack (D)

"Things have changed in the South."[1]

In 2013, according to a majority of Supreme Court justices, extreme racism in voting policies was a thing of the past. The legacy of Jim Crow was apparently eradicated.

Try telling that to the Reverend Kenneth Dukes and Bobby Pierson, two civil rights champions who support the Voting Rights Act. Every year on June 25—the anniversary of the *Shelby County v. Holder* decision, which gutted the act—Dukes and Pierson take to the steps of the Shelby County,

Alabama, courthouse to protest the ruling and the continued assault on minority voting rights. Dukes founded the local NAACP chapter after the *Shelby County* ruling to raise the voices of those in the community, noting that the ruling "affected the whole nation" and that "not everybody is bad, but there are those with bad agendas."[2] As Pierson, the first vice president of the local NAACP, put it, "If your vote didn't count so much, they wouldn't try and take it away from you."[3]

BLOODY SUNDAY

John Lewis was an American hero. On March 7, 1965, Lewis, then twenty-five years old, joined hundreds of other community members at the Edmund Pettus Bridge in Selma, Alabama, to march to the state capitol in Montgomery to call out the plight of Black people, who were systemically denied the right to vote, especially in the South. "We're marching today to dramatize to the nation and to the world that hundreds and thousands of Negro citizens of Alabama, particularly here in the Black Belt area, are denied the right to vote."[4] When Lewis and other marchers reached the Edmund Pettus Bridge, they faced Alabama state troopers in riot gear, who advanced on the protesters and beat them with their clubs. "I lost all consciousness," Lewis said later. "I saw death. I really thought I was going to die. I thought it was the last protest."[5] Television coverage of this "Bloody Sunday" event made the atrocities a nationwide story. The protesters persevered, regrouping for a second march to the bridge two days later under the leadership of Martin Luther King Jr. Facing Alabama troops blocking their way and a pending federal court order that would prohibit the march until there was federal protection, King led the marchers to the site of the violence at the bridge, asked everyone to kneel and pray, and then turned around. A week and a half later, the marchers, then numbering in the thousands, completed the fifty-four-mile journey to Montgomery under the protection of federal law enforcement. Lewis went on to serve in Congress for more than three decades, dedicating his career to the fight for civil rights—including, of course, the fundamental right to vote.

Every Supreme Court justice should visit Selma, Alabama. In the summer of 2022, my family and I made our own pilgrimage to the Edmund Pettus Bridge. It was a transformative experience. You can feel the history of the place. I spoke with people who were there in March 1965, including Sam Walker, the historian for the National Voting Rights Museum, a small building at the base of the bridge with artifacts and pictures from the marches. Walker was eleven years old at the time and recounted, with vivid detail, how he and his classmates first went to school in the morning but left to join the community to advocate for the right to vote, even though he couldn't exercise it for another seven years. As we left the museum, Walker offered a parting message, which he attributed to his friend, Pastor Thomas Threadgill: "No generation can expect to see the end of struggle. But each generation has a responsibility to advance the struggle."

John Lewis and the other marchers were advancing the struggle by protesting Jim Crow laws that kept Black people from registering to vote and casting a ballot. Literacy tests and poll taxes were pervasive during that time. Consider a few of the questions from the 1964 literacy test that some places in Louisiana gave to Black individuals:

"Draw a line around the number or letter of this sentence."

"In the space below, write the word 'noise' backwards and place
    a dot over what would be its second letter should it have
    been written forward."

"Spell backwards, forwards."[6]

The test admonishes that "one wrong answer denotes failure of the test" and that the individual has ten minutes to complete all twenty-three questions. I give the test to my law students to see if anyone can pass—they all fail (who wouldn't?). Of course, white voters never had to take this exam to register to vote.

The "Bloody Sunday" violence in Selma made national news and put pressure on President Lyndon Johnson to act. Eight days later Johnson introduced the Voting Rights Act of 1965. In his speech to a joint session of Congress, Johnson implored, "Many of the issues of civil rights are very complex and most difficult. But about this there can and should be no argument: every American citizen must have an equal right to vote." He also praised the protesters, including Lewis: "Their cause must be our cause too. Because it's not just Negroes, but really it's all of us who must overcome the crippling legacy of bigotry and injustice. And we shall overcome."[7] Several months later, President Johnson signed the Voting Rights Act into law. It's been one of the most consequential civil rights statutes in U.S. history.

AN EXTRAORDINARY REMEDY FOR AN EXTRAORDINARY PROBLEM

The Voting Rights Act sought to eradicate racial discrimination in our electoral processes at every turn. As journalist Ari Berman recounted in his seminal book, *Give Us the Ballot*, the law "suspended literacy tests across the South, authorized the U.S. attorney general to file lawsuits challenging the poll tax, replaced recalcitrant registrars with federal examiners, dispatched federal observers to monitor elections, forced states with the worst histories of voting discrimination to clear electoral change with the federal government to prevent future discrimination, and laid the foundation for generations of minority elected officials."[8]

Black voter registration soared, as did the number of Black elected officials. But along with that progress came continued attacks on minority voting rights. These attacks weren't quite as explicit as before; states weren't asking Black people to tell them the number of soap bubbles in a bar of soap to register to vote, as they had previously done. Instead, states passed "second-generation" barriers to the ballot box: strict voter ID laws, cutbacks of early-voting opportunities, purges of the voter rolls, and redistricting maps that made it harder for minority voters to elect their preferred candidates. Despite congressional action, the right to vote was still under attack.

The Voting Rights Act included a unique tool to help disenfranchised populations that reversed the normal course of litigation and stopped new oppressive laws in their tracks. Before the act, states or localities would enact a law and a plaintiff could challenge that law in court, but the government could usually implement the new rule during the pendency of the lawsuit. Litigation takes a while to make its way through its various stages. Thus, even if a plaintiff had challenged a new law, the state or locality could use it in an upcoming election, potentially harming voters. The court might eventually rule the voting practice unlawful and prohibit the government from implementing it in the next election—but there was nothing to stop the jurisdiction from passing a new restriction, perhaps tweaking the old, prohibited one slightly. A court rules a literacy test invalid? A slightly different test can take its place. Then the process starts all over again, with the jurisdiction enforcing the harmful rule while litigation plods along.

A major element of the Voting Rights Act, Section 5, sought to reverse this process via a mechanism called preclearance. Instead of waiting for litigation to conclude or forcing plaintiffs to convince a judge to issue a preliminary order that halts the law (which courts rarely do), Section 5 prevented jurisdictions with a history of voting discrimination from implementing a new voting rule unless the jurisdiction could prove that the law would not discriminate against minority voters. States and localities that had systematically violated minority voting rights had to seek preclearance from either the federal Department of Justice or a federal court composed of three judges before using a new election law. To gain preclearance, those jurisdictions had to prove that the new rule would not negatively impact the ability of minority voters to exercise their rights.

This unique system changes the ordinary course of litigation in two ways. First, the law automatically puts new election rules on hold. In other words, a state or locality can't pass a new law and begin implementing it right away. They must gain federal approval. Second, the burden of proof is shifted. Normally, a plaintiff must prove that a voting practice is unlawful. The typical presumption is that a law is valid unless the plaintiff brings sufficient evidence to challenge it. Under Section 5, however, the *jurisdiction* must prove that the law will *not* harm minority voters. Because of their history of discrimination, they essentially have to prove a negative—that the new law won't discriminate.

Because of the extraordinary nature of this remedy, Congress limited its scope to states and localities with a history of discriminatory voting practices: those that used a "test or device" for voting and registration or had turnout rates of less than 50 percent in the 1964 presidential election. This formula meant that the preclearance mechanism applied to any rules for elections in seven states and all local jurisdictions within those states (Alabama, Alaska, Georgia, Louisiana, Mississippi, South Carolina, and Virginia), as well as to the elections in certain political subdivisions in four additional states (Arizona, Hawaii, Idaho, and North Carolina). Any time one of these states or political subdivisions sought to implement a new voting rule, it first had to submit the new law to either the Department of Justice or a federal court in D.C. and demonstrate that the intent of the law was not to disadvantage minorities and that the law would not have that effect.

Congress recognized that imposing federal oversight over certain places was extreme, but so was the discrimination in these areas. To address these concerns, the preclearance requirement was originally set to expire after five years. That is, the preapproval process was initially supposed to last only until 1970, when Congress would reevaluate whether these places still needed federal oversight. In 1970 Congress extended the time period for an additional five years and then extended it again in 1975—this time until 1982. That 1975 extension also included a revision to the law that addressed discrimination against "language minority groups" and pegged the relevant data for determining which states and jurisdictions were covered to the 1972 election. This inclusion of language minorities as protected constituencies added Alaska (again), Arizona, and Texas to the list of covered states, as well as parts of California, Florida, Michigan, New York, North Carolina, and South Dakota.[9] Any new voting rule in these jurisdictions required preclearance from the DOJ or the D.C. federal court before implementation.

Even though Congress used data from 1972 to determine which jurisdictions were subject to preclearance, the coverage formula was not static. Congress included a mechanism to let jurisdictions out of Section 5 oversight if they had a clean record, with no findings of discrimination in the recent past. In addition, federal courts could put new jurisdictions under the preclearance regime if there was a judicial finding that they had engaged in intentional discrimination against minority voters. These mechanisms are known as "bail out" and "bail in." The key point is that the law was dynamic regarding which jurisdictions were required to submit voting changes for preclearance: it started with an initial list based on metrics that spoke to prior racist practices and low turnout rates but let jurisdictions out of oversight if they proved they had stopped discriminating.

This portion of the Voting Rights Act was set to expire in 1982, but that year Congress extended it for another twenty-five years, maintaining the same baseline for the coverage formula from the 1972 data. Then, in 2006, Congress extended Section 5 once again for an additional twenty-five years, with a vote of 390–33 in the House and 98–0 in the Senate.[10] Congress did not touch the coverage formula in this reauthorization, so the 1972 baseline remained in place, under the theory that covered jurisdictions still needed the deterrent effect of preclearance and that they could bail out if they had a clean record on the right to vote. Republican President George W. Bush signed the law amid much fanfare. A bipartisan supermajority had once again supported minority voting rights.

THE SUPREME COURT'S INITIAL PROTECTION OF THE VOTING RIGHTS ACT

Southern segregationists immediately challenged the Voting Rights Act of 1965 after its enactment, taking the case directly to the U.S. Supreme Court. The Court heard arguments in January 1966, lasting for seven hours over two days. The challengers, led by a delegation from South Carolina, argued that the law violated principles of state sovereignty. The federal government, they claimed, should not have the ability to encroach upon a state's right to run its elections as it wished. On March 7, 1966— exactly a year after the Bloody Sunday march in Selma, Alabama—the Court upheld the law by an 8–1 vote. Chief Justice Warren wrote for the majority, "The Voting Rights Act was designed by Congress to banish the blight of racial discrimination in voting, which has infected the electoral process in parts of our country for nearly a century."[11] The opinion also acknowledged that certain jurisdictions had continued to defy the con- stitutional command, embodied within the Fifteenth Amendment, that "the right of citizens of the United States to vote shall not be denied or abridged by the United States or by any State on account of race, color, or previous condition of servitude." The Court acknowledged that "Con- gress felt itself confronted by an insidious and pervasive evil which had been perpetuated in certain parts of our country through unremitting and ingenious defiance of the Constitution."[12] The Court elaborated further: "Congress knew that some of the [covered] States had resorted to the extraordinary stratagem of contriving new rules of various kinds for the sole purpose of perpetuating voting discrimination in the face of adverse federal court decrees. Congress had reason to suppose that these States might try similar maneuvers in the future in order to evade the remedies for voting discrimination contained in the Act itself. Under the compul- sion of these unique circumstances, Congress responded in a permissibly decisive manner."[13]

This decision wasn't the only time the Supreme Court endorsed the remedy of preclearance to cure the ills of racist voting laws. Each time

Congress updated and extended the Act—in 1970, 1975, and 1982—the Court upheld its constitutionality.[14]

Then a tiny utility district in Texas entered the fray.

SETTING THE GROUNDWORK TO OVERRULE THE ACT

The initial challenge to the 2006 reauthorization of the Voting Rights Act came from a small utility district in Austin, Texas. The Northwest Austin Municipal Utility District Number One provided city services— water, sewer, garbage removal, and the like—to about 3,500 residents on the northern edge of the city. Those residents elected the five members of the district's board. The utility district, however, didn't conduct its own voter registration, instead partnering with Travis County on election administration.

Because the utility district was in Texas, a state with a history of voting discrimination and therefore subject to preclearance, the utility district was also a covered jurisdiction that had to seek preapproval before making any changes to its voting practices. Even small things such as moving the location of a precinct required the utility district to go to the DOJ or a federal court in D.C. to preclear those changes. Its board thought it unfair that it was subject to this federal oversight, so it sued.

The district filed its lawsuit just days after Congress enacted the renewed version of the Voting Rights Act in 2006, and the primary goal was to undo the law. The utility district had powerful backers. Edward Blum, a former stockbroker and the head of a group called the Project for Fair Representation, was the main person driving the suit; Blum would later go on to initiate the *Shelby County* litigation as well. Blum has long opposed race-based decision-making and is also the individual behind the push to outlaw affirmative action in university admissions. Blum has ties to conservative funding groups, including DonorsTrust, which one media organization referred to as the "dark money ATM of the right" and which helps him employ well-regarded conservative lawyers to bring his cases.[15] A *New York Times* profile colorfully explained that "Blum has been called many things, including a courageous man of the moment willing to take on entrenched, politically correct policies, and a tool of rich conservatives trying to extinguish efforts to help historically oppressed minorities overcome the long shadow of racism."[16]

Blum's interest in the interplay of race and voting stems, at least in part, from his unsuccessful run for Congress in 1992. He lamented that his Houston-area district was drawn in an odd shape to make it easier for a minority candidate to win. He joined a lawsuit against racial gerrymandering and eventually won a ruling at the Supreme Court to strike down a map.[17] That victory emboldened him to engage in additional litigation.[18] As the *New York Times* recounted, Blum is not a lawyer but "is a one-man legal factory with a growing record of finding plaintiffs who match his causes, winning big victories and trying above all to erase racial preferences from American life."[19]

The Northwest Austin Municipal Utility District made for a good plaintiff because it had never engaged in any kind of racial discrimination in voting; it was simply a covered jurisdiction by virtue of being in Texas. The district wasn't even created until 1987, well after Congress enacted the Voting Rights Act of 1965. Moreover, back in 2004, it was required to seek preclearance when it wanted to move a polling place from a private home to a school to make voter participation easier, and it found the preclearance process for such a small change onerous and unnecessary.[20]

In *Northwest Austin Municipal Utility District No. 1 v. Holder*, the utility district, as the plaintiff, asked the Court to declare that it should no longer fall within the preclearance formula because it had no history of discrimination. In the alternative, it argued that the law itself was unconstitutional. The Court punted on the constitutional question, however, saying that the utility district could "bail out" from the Voting Rights Act's coverage formula and would no longer have to seek preapproval for its voting changes.[21]

The constitutional question should have been relatively easy—in favor of upholding the law. The Court had approved of the preclearance process in four prior cases, and in 2006 Congress held numerous hearings and gathered extensive evidence on the more latent but still present discrimination in many areas of the country. But Chief Justice Roberts, who had argued against the Voting Rights Act as a young lawyer in the Department of Justice, saw things differently, planting the seeds to overturn the act in a future case. His opinion in *Northwest Austin* said that the Court had "serious misgivings" about the act's constitutionality. He suggested that "[t]hings have changed in the South" because Black voters had made great strides in voter registration, voter turnout, and election to office. He also highlighted the "federalism concerns" when the federal government treats states differently. "The evil that Section 5 is meant to address may no longer be concentrated in the jurisdictions singled out for preclearance," he opined.[22] All of these findings would be useful when the Court would squarely face the constitutional question. The justices could simply point to the statements in *Northwest Austin* and say they were following precedent.

And that's exactly what they did.

OVERTURNING THE CROWN JEWEL OF THE CIVIL RIGHTS MOVEMENT

It didn't take long for Edward Blum, the conservative Supreme Court "matchmaker" who had initiated *Northwest Austin*, to strike again soon after the Supreme Court essentially invited another lawsuit to challenge the act.[23] Blum was searching the internet for localities that had endured recent issues with preclearance and came across Shelby County, Alabama. He cold-called the county's attorney, Frank "Butch" Ellis, to ask about challenging the act's constitutionality. After several phone conversations, Blum went down to Shelby County to meet with the county commissioners and pitch his case.[24] Ellis admitted that decades ago the county had employed literacy tests and the like, but he claimed the county should no longer be under federal supervision given its current policies. The preclearance process required the county to spend "pretty large amounts of taxpayer money that could have gone to something like schools," he said.[25] Ellis and the county commissioners agreed to have Blum file suit.

Shelby County was an ideal plaintiff because it could present the constitutionality of the Voting Rights Act squarely before the Court. The county didn't seek to bail out, as the Northwest Austin utility district had done, probably because there had been recent Voting Rights Act issues within the county, making it ineligible for bailout. For instance, in 2004, the city of Calera, within Shelby County, had redrawn its city council district lines to eliminate the only majority-Black district and unseat the city's second-ever Black city council member and then had failed to seek preclearance for the new lines (probably because it knew that it would fail). The Department of Justice ultimately rejected the new lines and required the city to hold another election, and that Black city council member regained his seat.[26] There was also a cruel irony in having a county in

Alabama, near the site of the Bloody Sunday protests that were the catalyst for the passage of the Voting Rights Act, serve as the entity to take it down.

The defendant in *Shelby County v. Holder* was once again the federal government, specifically Attorney General Eric Holder. Holder was the country's first Black attorney general, nominated by the first Black president, Barack Obama. Local civil rights activists hired an attorney, NAACP Legal Defense and Educational Fund lawyer Debo Adegbile, to defend the law (Adegbile had first seen success as a child actor on *Sesame Street* in the 1970s). He was the only Black person to argue before the Supreme Court that year.[27] The racial implications of the case could not have been clearer.

Both the federal trial court and the court of appeals rejected Shelby County's claims and upheld the law. Congress, the courts said, had amassed a huge record that justified the continuation of the preclearance regime. Everyone knew, however, that those lower court decisions were simply a prelude to the real action at the U.S. Supreme Court.

The writing was on the wall on February 27, 2013, when the Court heard oral arguments in the *Shelby County* case. Justice Antonin Scalia summed up the skeptical views of the conservatives on the Court: Congress, he said, keeps reauthorizing the act because of "a phenomenon called perpetuation of racial entitlement." Several people in the audience gasped in shock. "Even the name of it is wonderful: The Voting Rights Act. Who is going to vote against that in the future?" he pondered, distain dripping from his voice.[28] That sentiment echoed what Justice Scalia had said four years earlier in the *Northwest Austin* oral argument. He highlighted the fact that Congress had passed the reauthorization in 2006 by a 390–33 vote in the House and a unanimous vote in the Senate and then openly mused, "You know, the Israeli Supreme Court, the Sanhedrin, used to have a rule that if the death penalty was pronounced unanimously, it was invalid, because there must be something wrong there. Do you ever expect . . . do you ever seriously expect Congress to vote against a re-extension of the Voting Rights Act?"[29] Ironically, Justice Scalia himself had been confirmed to the Supreme Court by a unanimous vote.[30]

Most Court observers saw what was coming next: the Court had avoided the constitutional question four years prior in the *Northwest Austin* case, but this time it wouldn't punt again. The formula to determine which jurisdictions were required to submit to preclearance was unconstitutional. By a 5–4 vote, with Chief Justice Roberts writing for the majority, the Court had just overturned one of the most important civil rights laws in history.

True, Roberts acknowledged, the Voting Rights Act "employed extraordinary measures to address an extraordinary problem" of pervasive racial discrimination, particularly in the South. But, Roberts declared, "Things have changed in the South."[31] His source for this statement? The *Northwest Austin* case from 2009, four years prior.

The *Northwest Austin* decision was all over Roberts's majority opinion in *Shelby County*. In *Northwest Austin*, the Court had cited a "fundamental principle of equal sovereignty" to question Congress's practice of treating states differently. That principle, however, had previously applied only when Congress admitted a new state into the Union; as a 1911 case had held, Congress cannot impose harsher rules on new states.[32] The doctrine had nothing to do with Congress's enforcement of different obligations on states based on their specific history of discrimination. In fact, the Court had rejected this very same argument in *South Carolina v. Katzenbach* when it initially upheld the Voting Rights Act in 1966, ruling that "[t]he doctrine of the equality of States, invoked by South Carolina, does not bar this approach [in the act], for that doctrine applies only to the terms upon which States are admitted to the Union, and not to the remedies for local evils which have subsequently appeared."[33] Chief Justice Roberts never even cited or quoted this passage in his *Shelby County* decision, instead briefly acknowledging the case but then saying simply that, as indicated in *Northwest Austin* (which he had also written), "The fundamental principle of equal sovereignty remains highly pertinent in assessing subsequent disparate treatment of States."[34] That conclusory statement fails to grapple with the prior case law, which had already answered the question in the opposite way. Was that portion of the 1966 case now silently overruled?

It's not uncommon for Congress to allocate different benefits or burdens on states, such as funding for specific projects, according to those states' unique circumstances. Roberts ignored that reality to invent a new "equal sovereignty" principle, suggesting that—at least for attempts to improve minority voting rights—Congress cannot single out certain states for greater oversight even if those states have a history of discrimination.[35]

Then came the crux of the decision: racial discrimination in voting apparently isn't that bad anymore. "Things have changed dramatically" in the fifty years since the Court had upheld the Voting Rights Act in 1966.[36]

Voter registration and turnout among white and Black people in the covered jurisdictions are roughly the same. Direct poll taxes or literacy tests are outlawed. Black individuals have been elected to office at higher levels than in the past. Of course, the elephant in the room was the 2008 election and 2012 reelection of the nation's first Black president, Barack Obama. Roberts didn't say this explicitly, but it underlay his opinion: If we can elect a Black president, then aren't we now in a postracial society?

The biggest problem, according to Roberts, was that Congress had not updated the coverage formula or eased the preclearance requirement of Section 5, even though the nation had made great strides in minority voting opportunities. Relying again on the 2009 *Northwest Austin* case, the Court said that the "current burdens" that Section 5 imposes "must be justified by current needs, and any disparate geographic coverage must be sufficiently related to the problem that it targets."[37] Using old data on racial discrimination from the early 1970s, when reauthorizing the act in 2006, was unconstitutional.

But Roberts failed to credit two key points. First, the coverage formula is dynamic, in that jurisdictions could "bail out" if they showed they had not discriminated recently, while a court could "bail in" a jurisdiction if it engaged in intentional discrimination. Second, many of these places were still adopting rules that harmed racial minorities. They were just doing so in less direct and more subtle ways.

Roberts was not convinced. "[H]istory did not end in 1965," he wrote. Voter discrimination today is not "pervasive," "flagrant," "widespread," or "rampant," as it was in 1965 when Congress first enacted the law. Congress had to justify treating states differently based on "current conditions." That was one of the lessons of *Northwest Austin*, Roberts said, but Congress had failed to update the law in the four years since that decision. It turns out that the *Northwest Austin* case, in laying the foundation for *Shelby County*, wasn't narrow after all. Roberts could feign being narrow and minimalist in *Northwest Austin*, all the while knowing that the effect of the decision would be monumental. Of course, given the increasing polarization in Congress, Roberts also knew that Congress was highly unlikely to pass a new coverage formula. Section 5 of the Voting Rights Act was functionally dead.

Once again, underlying the entire ruling is deference to states to run their elections as they wish. Roberts lamented the big brother mentality of the federal government overseeing state election rules: under the Voting Rights Act, some "[s]tates must beseech the Federal Government for permission to implement laws that they would otherwise have the right to enact and execute on their own."[38] We should trust states not to discriminate, Roberts seemed to be saying. They know best how to run their elections. The federal government shouldn't oversee state voting rules, even if there was a history of voter suppression in certain places. After all, states are no longer blatantly turning away Black people from the ballot box, so racial discrimination is a thing of the past. Right?

SECOND-GENERATION BARRIERS

Justice Ruth Bader Ginsburg announced her dissent, on behalf of herself and three other justices (Breyer, Sotomayor, and Kagan), orally from the bench to an open Court—a rare practice that signals a justice's extreme displeasure with the majority's decision. Wearing her famed white jabot over a black robe, her voice sounding calm in restrained anger, she invoked the words of Martin Luther King Jr. to explain why the Court's approach was wrong: "The great men who led the march from Selma to Montgomery, and their call for the passage of the Voting Rights Act, foresaw progress even in Alabama. 'The arc of the moral universe is long,' [King] said, 'but it bends toward justice'—if there is a steadfast commitment to see the task through to completion. That commitment has been disserved by today's decision."[39]

Justice Ginsburg pulled no punches in her fiery thirty-seven-page written dissent. The Court's majority was wrong on the law, wrong on the facts, and on the wrong side of history.

The right to vote was a key promise of the end of the Civil War. The Fifteenth Amendment, ratified as part of Reconstruction in 1870, says that no state may deny the right to vote on the basis of race. Yet more than a hundred years after the ratification of that amendment, minority voters still suffer immense discrimination. As Justice Ginsburg recounted, "Early attempts to cope with this vile infection resembled battling the Hydra. Whenever one form of voting discrimination was identified and prohibited, others sprang up in its place."[40] That's why the preclearance idea was so ingenious: it stopped voting discrimination before it started. Although the Voting Rights Act helped to improve things, "Congress determined, based on a voluminous record, that the scourge of discrimination was not yet extirpated."[41]

True, the act was a resounding success. Minority turnout and representation in Congress, state legislatures, and even local offices soared after jurisdictions could no longer blatantly discriminate against minority voters. But, as Justice Ginsburg explained, that fact does not mean that there is no longer discrimination. Instead of overt means to harm minorities, recalcitrant politicians have resorted to "second generation" barriers to equal participation and representation. These second-generation barriers include racial gerrymandering, where politicians draw the lines to minimize the number of districts where a majority of the voters identify as racial minorities. They include at-large election systems, where everyone votes for all seats on a city council, such that a white majority can control every seat. Strict voter ID laws disproportionately impact minorities, given the disparities in who has compliant IDs. The elimination of early voting days, such as on Sundays, when many Black churches employ "Souls to the Polls" initiatives, targets key voting opportunities. None of these measures are as explicit as poll taxes or literacy tests, but they are just as pernicious. As a congressional committee wrote when endorsing the reauthorization of the Voting Rights Act in 2006, "Discrimination today is more subtle than the visible methods used in 1965. However, the effect and results are the same, namely a diminishing of the minority community's ability to fully participate in the electoral process and to elect their preferred candidates."[42] The preclearance requirement served as an important deterrent to these limits on voting opportunities.

The majority's opinion in *Shelby County* unduly ties Congress's hands to protect the right to vote. Yet the Fifteenth Amendment—as well as other constitutional amendments about the right to vote—expressly authorizes Congress to enact "appropriate legislation" to enforce the commands of the amendment. Justice Ginsburg criticized the Court for aggrandizing its own role while at the same time undermining Congress's authority in this area. If Congress has a rational reason for enacting a law to root out racial discrimination in voting, Justice Ginsburg explained, then the Court has no basis to overturn Congress's judgment. At least, that's what the Court's prior cases had said. *Shelby County* turned all of that on its head. Instead of trusting politicians in states with a history of discrimination, the Court should have deferred to Congress's extensive findings on the continued need for federal oversight.

Those congressional findings were specific and thorough. Justice Ginsburg recounted, in page after page and in meticulous detail, numerous proposed changes to election rules that the preclearance procedure had prevented from going into effect. As one commentator noted, Congress relied on a "15,000 page record produced after 21 congressional hearings [that] included testimony from dozens of witnesses and numerous reports evaluating conditions for minority political participation both in covered jurisdictions and nationwide."[43] It was not as if Congress acted imprudently and without evidence. Moreover, Shelby County itself, as well as Alabama as a whole, had engaged in discriminatory practices in the recent past. If any state still needed preclearance, it was Alabama, the site of the Bloody Sunday march that led to the initial passage of the Voting Rights Act. "Hubris is a fit word for today's demolition of the VRA," Ginsburg lamented.

Removing preclearance would lead to backsliding in minority voting opportunities. The act was working to improve minority voting rights. It made no sense to eliminate those protections now, as discrimination was still ongoing, even if it was more subtle than before. Justice Ginsburg explained the majority's backward-thinking approach in one of the most famous lines she ever wrote: "Throwing out preclearance when it has worked and is continuing to work to stop discriminatory changes is like throwing away your umbrella in a rainstorm because you are not getting wet."[44]

IMMEDIATE EFFECTS OF THE DECISION

Within minutes of the Court's *Shelby County* ruling, some politicians announced plans to impose strict new voting rules immediately.

In 2011, Texas governor Rick Perry signed a law to impose a strict photo ID requirement for voting, limiting the kinds of IDs that were permissible to show at the polls. For instance, as recounted earlier in the chapter on photo ID laws, student IDs from state universities in Texas didn't count—although gun licenses did. In August 2012, a federal court found that the law would make it harder for Black and Latino voters to cast a ballot because they are less likely to have compliant IDs. The court denied preclearance under Section 5, meaning that the law could not go into effect.[45] The court highlighted one study suggesting that the law might reduce turnout by around 10 percent. Some experts estimated that over 600,000 registered voters did not have a qualifying ID.[46] The court therefore refused to allow Texas to implement the law.

A few hours after the Supreme Court handed down its *Shelby County* decision on June 25, 2013, however, Governor Perry announced that the state would immediately enforce the new strict photo ID law given that it was suddenly free of Section 5's strictures.[47] Without the preclearance regime, Texas was no longer subject to a requirement to prove that the law would not harm minority voters before implementation—and it was eager to impose the law right away. The state also announced that it would put into force new redistricting maps, even though a federal court had previously denied preclearance for them because of their discriminatory nature.[48] Lengthy litigation ensued, and courts eventually invalidated the voter ID law and aspects of the redistricting maps, but not before several election cycles had passed.[49] (Texas then tweaked its ID law and drew new maps, leading to further litigation.) Thus, because of *Shelby County*, Texas was able to use election rules that courts eventually found to be unlawful.

The story was the same in North Carolina. There, the state's legislative leaders first proposed a mild photo ID bill in early 2013. Because certain counties in North Carolina were subject to preclearance, the state would have had to demonstrate that the law would not discriminate against minority voters before using it in upcoming elections. That's probably why they initially kept their proposal narrow. The day after *Shelby County*, however, Republican leaders announced they would go much further, planning an "omnibus" election bill that would curtail voter registration, cut back on early-voting opportunities, and impose a strict voter ID requirement. Under preclearance, the state would have been prohibited from immediately implementing the law. But freed from federal oversight, the Republican leaders in the state decided to go as far as they could.[50]

Once again, after lengthy litigation, a federal court eventually struck down the North Carolina law, saying that it targeted minority voters "with almost surgical precision."[51] The court wrote, "[I]n what comes as close to a smoking gun as we are likely to see in modern times, the State's very justification for a challenged statute hinges explicitly on race—specifically its concern that African Americans, who had overwhelmingly voted for

Democrats, had too much access to the franchise."[52] That decision, however, came down over three years after *Shelby County*. A federal court had put parts of the law on hold for the 2014 midterms, but not all of it, meaning that North Carolina voters were stuck with a restrictive, illegal voting regime for that election. Requiring preclearance would have prevented the politicians from manipulating the voting rules in this way.

The biggest effect of *Shelby County* and the loss of preclearance is probably at the local level, where jurisdictions can now enact voting rules and redistricting plans without having to show that the new rules will not harm minority voters. There are scores of examples. Augusta-Richmond County, Georgia sought to shift its local elections from November to July—which likely would have depressed turnout among minorities, given historical voting patterns. The Department of Justice denied preclearance, citing evidence that changing the date of Election Day would disproportionately affect Black voters.[53] Just four days after the Supreme Court issued its opinion in *Shelby County*, however, the county revived its efforts to move Election Day, passing the new rule in early 2014. A federal court eventually rejected a challenge to this change, meaning that the county could move Election Day to July.[54] The legal standard was now different, making it easier for the locality to justify its new rule.

Shelby County has significantly hindered equality in our voting processes. At bottom, the decision says that we should just trust elected officials to do the right thing. They don't need oversight from the federal courts or the Department of Justice, even if they have a history of discriminatory practices. It's simply another way to defer to lawmakers on the very rules that keep them in office.

At every turn, and despite a bevy of evidence, the Supreme Court has said that we should have faith in state legislators not to craft voting rules that will harm certain constituencies. State legislators, however, are political actors. For most of them, the number one concern is to win reelection and stay in power. If that means discriminating against racial minorities, whether due to lingering racism or simply because minorities tend to vote for the other party, then so be it. *Shelby County* is just another mechanism to take courts out of the voting rights business by making it harder for advocates to challenge unfair rules.

The Supreme Court has been clear: we can't rely on it to ensure a fair democracy. After decades of oppression, racial minorities continue to fight for equal representation. The Court seems oblivious to the fact that we are still in the rainstorm of oppressive voting laws that harm minorities.

But the damage didn't end there. *Shelby County* gutted Section 5 of the Voting Rights Act. Would Section 2—the other major portion of the crown jewel of the civil rights movement—be next on the chopping block?

CHAPTER 8

AN ACTIVIST COURT

Brnovich v. Democratic National Committee (2021)

	JUSTICE	APPOINTED BY
MAJORITY	Alito, Samuel A., Jr. *(authored majority opinion)*	Bush, George W. (R)
	Roberts, John G., Jr. (chief justice)	Bush, George W. (R)
	Thomas, Clarence *(joined Gorsuch's concurrence)*	Bush, George H. W. (R)
	Gorsuch, Neil M. *(authored concurring opinion)*	Trump, Donald (R)
	Kavanaugh, Brett M.	Trump, Donald (R)
	Barrett, Amy Coney	Trump, Donald (R)
DISSENT	Kagan, Elena *(authored dissent)*	Obama, Barack (D)
	Breyer, Stephen G.	Clinton, Bill (D)
	Sotomayor, Sonia	Obama, Barack (D)

A rizona's presidential primary in 2016 was a disaster. On March 22, many voters left work to go to the polls only to find astonishingly long lines. Some voters, especially in areas with a high population of minority individuals, waited for more than five hours and didn't cast their ballots until after midnight.[1] The problems occurred mostly in Maricopa County, the state's largest county and home to Phoenix. The main culprit was the county's decision to cut the number of polling places from more than 400 in the 2008 primary to fewer than 60 in 2016.[2] The stated goal was to reduce costs, but voters suffered the consequences. Many voters made it to the front of the line only to find out they were mistakenly registered as independents, meaning they couldn't vote in the Republican or Democratic presidential primaries. One voter recounted that their five-hour wait to vote was "made even more unpleasant and upsetting because the one bathroom at the voter center was overwhelmed and leaked raw sewage onto the sidewalk and the adjacent grass."[3] As an Arizona newspaper put it on the day after the election, "Maricopa County voters woke up with an election hangover Wednesday morning, and it wasn't pretty."[4] Phoenix mayor Greg Stanton called it a "fiasco" and asked the Department of Justice to investigate. Arizona governor Doug Ducey, a Republican, said it was "unacceptable."[5] The Arizona debacle made national news, offering a clear example of how cuts to voting opportunities can have tangible effects, especially on minority communities.[6]

Prior to 2013, Maricopa County would not have been allowed to reduce the number of polling sites from 400 to 60 without first proving the change would not harm minority voters. That's because Arizona, with a long history of voter suppression, was a "covered jurisdiction" under Section 5 of the Voting Rights Act. Recall that under Section 5, jurisdictions with a record of discrimination had to seek preclearance for any voting changes by demonstrating that the new election rule would not make minority voters worse off. With the Supreme Court's decision in *Shelby County* in 2013, however, Arizona was freed of this preclearance requirement. The state and its subdivisions could make any changes they wanted to the voting process without first seeking federal approval.

Maricopa County therefore did not need to seek preclearance before it reduced the number of polling places for the 2016 primary. After the disaster, the head of Maricopa County's elections, Helen Purcell, promised more polling sites for subsequent elections, but voters denied her another term in November 2016, terminating her twenty-eight years in the office.[7]

THE CHALLENGE TO ARIZONA'S VOTING POLICIES

Just a few weeks after the March 2016 primary, Democrats and voting rights advocates filed a lawsuit to challenge various aspects of Arizona's election regime. The case became known as *Brnovich v. Democratic National Committee* ("Brnovich" is pronounced "Burn-o-vitch," which is the last name of Arizona's attorney general at the time, Mark Brnovich). The

March 2016 primary had exposed numerous deficiencies in election administration that plaintiffs wanted the courts to fix before the November presidential election that year.

In addition to seeking court supervision of Maricopa County's plan for November 2016, the voting rights advocates challenged two specific aspects of Arizona's voting procedures. First, with respect to mailed ballots, Arizona changed its law in 2016 to prohibit a person from delivering someone else's completed ballot to the ballot box, with several exceptions. Specifically, it is a felony for anyone besides a caregiver, family member, household member, mail carrier, or elections official to collect and deliver another person's ballot. About 80 percent of the state's voters cast their ballots using vote-by-mail, so this rule affected a lot of people who relied on others to drop off their completed ballots for them. Political parties and voting rights organizations have sophisticated operations to collect and deliver ballots. The plaintiffs in this case were concerned in particular about Native American voters, who do not have very good access to the postal service and rely heavily on ballot collectors. The ban on ballot collection could make it a lot harder for many of these voters to return their ballots, thereby hindering their ability to exercise their right to vote.

Second, the plaintiffs challenged a longstanding Arizona law that required officials not to count a ballot if the voter cast it in the wrong precinct. Imagine that your county requires you to vote at a specific precinct if you want to vote in person on Election Day instead of voting by mail. You show up to what you think is your correct precinct, only to find your name not on the voter roll. Instead of turning you away, federal law requires poll workers to offer you a provisional ballot. Then, after voting is over, election officials determine whether the voter roll was wrong and if your ballot should actually count. Since 1970, Arizona law has specified that the ballot will not count if the voter was at the wrong precinct. The voter should have gone to the correct place.

Figuring out where to vote is sometimes easier said than done. Voters obviously think they are in the right location, and some voters might have shown up to the wrong place just before the polls closed, with no time to go elsewhere. Counties exacerbated the problem by changing or consolidating polling locations on a regular basis. Arizona, in fact, was the worst state in throwing out provisional ballots, tossing around 40,000 total votes in all elections between 2008 and 2016.[8] In 2012, one in three discarded ballots nationwide was from Arizona.[9] These tossed ballots included votes for both statewide and local offices. Of course, all Arizonans are eligible to vote in statewide races regardless of where in the state they live or cast their ballot. But the state still threw out the entire ballot, including the votes in the statewide races. The plaintiffs challenged this rule as unconstitutional and invalid under the Voting Rights Act.

The *Brnovich* case was, in many ways, a logical follow-up to *Shelby County*, which we covered in the previous chapter. After *Shelby County*, Arizona no longer had to seek preapproval for its new voting laws and could implement its new election rules immediately. The plaintiffs therefore needed another approach. They invoked Section 2 of the Voting Rights Act.

Section 2 applies to all jurisdictions nationwide. It says that the government may not impose a voting rule if the law "results" in the denial or abridgement of the right to vote because of someone's race or color. The text of the law is a little technical. To prove a violation of Section 2, a plaintiff must show that, "based on the totality of circumstances," the election processes "are not equally open to participation" by minority voters because these voters "have less opportunity than other members of the electorate to participate in the political process and to elect representatives of their choice."[10] Essentially, a plaintiff must prove that a voting rule has the effect of making it harder for minorities to vote and that based on the "totality of circumstances"—meaning, anything relevant to the question—minority voters can't participate in the election in the same way as other voters.

Here, the plaintiffs argued that the two Arizona laws at issue—about ballot collection and provisional ballots cast in the wrong precinct—denied the right to vote to some people on a discriminatory basis. This is a claim for "vote denial." A state might pass a law that sounds neutral—closing polling places to save money, for example—but the effects of the law fall disproportionately on minority voters given socioeconomic factors and geographic living patterns. Section 2 was intended to outlaw those kinds of rules.

SETTING THE STAGE

The plaintiffs had a good case that these two Arizona voting rules hurt some voters, especially minority individuals. On the first rule, many voters who relied on ballot collectors, whether they were from a political party or a voting rights organization, would have to find another way to send in their ballots. On the second rule, regarding votes cast at the incorrect location, voters who sought to vote in person on Election Day might find their ballot thrown out if they were at the wrong precinct. Voting is already complicated enough; these rules made it even harder for many individuals to cast a ballot that would count.

One of the plaintiffs' main lawyers was Bruce Spiva, who has fought for voting rights for decades. Spiva and I chatted over Zoom a couple of weeks after he lost the 2022 Democratic primary for D.C. attorney general; he had been retrieving campaign yard signs from his neighbors just before our talk. He explained to me how the facts in the case were particularly compelling, especially given the testimony from actual voters on the difficulties they faced because of these laws. Spiva recalled, with a wry smile, one of the witnesses in the case, a die-hard Trump supporter who became part of the litigation because election officials had thrown out her vote in the Republican primary after she had mistakenly gone to the wrong precinct to vote. Spiva and the woman met for breakfast at Starbucks to prepare for her testimony, but she steered the conversation mostly to social issues, such as how she disliked the politics of Starbucks and its owner (they soon left and went elsewhere) and her criticism of athletes who kneel during the national anthem. Spiva recalled that he and the woman disagreed on virtually everything, except for this: everyone's vote should count.[11]

But in other respects the plaintiffs' case was weak. Arizona offered multiple paths to the ballot, so a voter who encountered hurdles with one method could always try another. A voter who previously relied on ballot collectors, for example, could ask a family member, household member, or caregiver to deliver their ballot for them. Or they could simply drop it in the mail. Or they could go to one of the in-person voting sites during the twenty-seven days of early voting or on Election Day itself. A voter concerned about showing up to the wrong precinct could request a mailed ballot, fill it out at home, and then deliver it to a vote center. Although the two challenged rules made participation harder for some voters, these individuals had other mechanisms available to cast a valid vote.

The case went before District Judge Douglas L. Rayes, an Obama appointee whom Arizona Republican senator John McCain also supported for the bench. Judge Rayes held a ten-day trial in which he heard from 51 witnesses and considered over 230 evidentiary exhibits. He then wrote an 83-page opinion to uphold the state's rules. He began by noting that the right to vote is not absolute, citing the *Anderson* and *Burdick* cases (discussed in chapters 1 and 2) for the idea that states have significant leeway to regulate their elections as they see fit. Judge Rayes also cited *Crawford*, the voter ID case discussed in chapter 3, to highlight how the state can place burdens on the right to vote. Thus, the court's starting place was deference toward Arizona's rules, citing *Burdick* for the proposition that "[c]ommon sense, as well as constitutional law, compels the conclusion that government must play an active role in structuring elections."[12] That is, Judge Rayes read Supreme Court precedent to require narrow protection for the right to vote.

The court then faulted the plaintiffs for failing to offer clear evidence of voters who suffered disenfranchisement because of these Arizona laws. Regarding the limits on ballot collection, the court said, "The socioeconomic circumstances cited by Plaintiffs might explain why this process is more difficult for some voters than others, but those circumstances are not themselves the burden imposed by the challenged law."[13] The court highlighted the various paths for casting a ballot, such as the twenty-seven days of no-excuse early voting.

Yet the court also recognized that the state did not present any evidence to support its desire to ban ballot collection. "[T]here has never been a case of voter fraud associated with ballot collection charged in Arizona," Judge Rayes acknowledged.[14] There was also no indication that Arizona voters believed that banning ballot collection was necessary to secure the state's elections. But, the court said, given that the burden on voters was not too onerous, the state need not offer a precise rationale for its rules.

Regarding Section 2 of the Voting Rights Act, the court employed a two-part test and rejected the plaintiffs' claim. This two-part test— which asks (1) whether a law disproportionately harms minorities and (2) whether the "totality of the circumstances" suggests there is discrimination—is important because it comes directly from the text of the Voting Rights Act itself. First, Judge Rayes determined that the two laws did not create a disparate impact on minority voters. The plaintiffs had not provided enough evidence that the law harmed minority voters more than non-minorities; it also "does not impose burdens beyond those traditionally associated with voting."[15] The court further noted that the overall number of rejected provisional ballots was small, even if minority voters were slightly more likely to have their ballots thrown out. Second, the court looked at the totality of the circumstances, which essentially asks whether social or historical conditions of discrimination within the state contributed to the discriminatory result. Here, the court went through various factors to find that, although Arizona voters had suffered from discrimination, the plaintiffs had not made their case—demonstrating that litigants must have real evidence of discrimination to bring a viable claim. "Plaintiffs' causation theory is too tenuous to support their [Voting Rights Act] claim because, taken to its logical conclusion, virtually any aspect of a state's election regime would be suspect as nearly all costs of voting fall heavier on socioeconomically disadvantaged voters."[16]

Ultimately, the court strongly rejected the plaintiffs' claims and upheld Arizona's laws in a clear, detailed, and thoughtful opinion. The two Arizona laws may have been unfair and may have harmed some minority voters, but the court was unconvinced given the lack of evidence that the law actually created discriminatory results in the ability to participate in Arizona elections.

Because they lost, the next step for the plaintiffs was to appeal to a higher court. Some scholars have questioned the strategy to appeal this case, especially given the strength and thoroughness of Judge Rayes's opinion. Nonetheless, the next stop was the Ninth Circuit Court of Appeals, which the plaintiffs thought might be more amenable to voting rights claims because of that court's more progressive makeup. But everyone knew that if Arizona lost at the appeals court, the state's leaders would take the case all the way to the Supreme Court, which had been quite hostile to voting rights claims. Noted election law scholar Rick Hasen said that he considered the Arizona case to be "extremely weak" in light of the lack of evidence.[17] After the drubbing at the district court, perhaps the idea to go to higher courts was imprudent at the time; in retrospect it seemed disastrous. Advocates know that the Supreme Court is not friendly to claims by voters. Perhaps those who seek to protect voting rights for all shouldn't give the Court the opportunity to further gut pro-voter statutes.

Bruce Spiva, the plaintiffs' lawyer, strongly disagreed with this assessment. He thought he had an extremely compelling factual record that showed real disenfranchisement. Walking away would have meant abandoning those 40,000 voters whose ballots the state had thrown out.

Failing to use the Voting Rights Act for its intended purpose would be a self-inflicted wound on the voting rights community.

The plaintiffs appealed, at first suffering another loss. The Ninth Circuit Court of Appeals initially agreed with the district judge, on a 2–1 vote, to uphold the laws.[18] That court focused even more on Arizona's justification of preserving the integrity of the election process—despite no real evidence of fraud—to support the state's election rules. The opinion showed how plaintiffs have a higher evidentiary burden than states do: the court chided the plaintiffs for not presenting evidence of racial disparities in ballot collection but found no problem with the state's lack of evidence of fraud that the law sought to prevent.

The Democrats who initially brought the lawsuit then asked a larger panel of the Ninth Circuit Court of Appeals to reconsider the case in what is known as an "en banc" hearing, where all or most of the appeals judges on that court review a judicial decision.[19] The larger appeals court agreed to rehear the case and issued a 7–4 ruling in favor of the plaintiffs, noting, "For over a century, Arizona has repeatedly targeted its American Indian, Hispanic, and African American citizens, limiting or eliminating their ability to vote and to participate in the political process."[20]

They won!

But not really. The court's decision just set the stage for the Supreme Court to mess things up even further.

THE SUPREME COURT MAKES UP THE LAW

The oral argument in *Brnovich* was unique for several reasons. For one, the justices heard from the lawyers via telephone, instead of in the courtroom, because of the Covid-19 pandemic. Instead of a normal colloquy where the justices frequently interrupt the lawyers—and each other—to probe their contentions, the arguments proceeded in a more orderly style, where each of the lawyers made a short presentation followed by questions from the justices in order of seniority. Many arguments go for about an hour, but this one lasted almost two.

Jessie Amunson, who argued the case on behalf of Arizona's secretary of state, Katie Hobbs (who became the governor of Arizona in 2023), told me that the oral argument logistics were strange because of the telephonic hearing. She conducted the argument from her basement after having a landline installed. She put a sign on the front door of her house telling people not to ring the doorbell; she even checked with her neighbors to make sure they didn't have any yard work scheduled. She implored her kids to be quiet the entire time. In an amusing twist, the audio they were listening to upstairs was slightly delayed, so when Amunson came up from the basement, her kids were still tuning in—and were shocked to see their mom already done.[21]

Even over the telephone, astute listeners could hear the disdain for the Democratic plaintiffs' arguments in the justices' comments. Amunson explained that the proper test for Section 2 of the Voting Rights Act—which exists to protect minority voters in all aspects of the voting process—should "take a functional view of the political process and look to a holistic view of—of how it is actually affecting the voter on the ground."[22] Justice Alito derisively retorted, "Well, those are a lot of words. I really don't understand what they mean."[23]

Most people predicted that the voting rights plaintiffs would lose this case. They would probably lose big. Even Amunson acknowledged that, although she obviously wanted to win the case, she at least sought to minimize the damage if a loss was truly inevitable. But I'm not sure people were ready for just how bad the opinion would end up. The *New York Times* called it "among the most consequential in decades on voting rights."[24] The League of Women Voters decried the opinion as "a significant blow to the freedom to vote."[25] "The Supreme Court Has Neutered the Voting Rights Act," read a headline in *The Atlantic*.[26] Professor Guy-Uriel Charles of Harvard Law School, the author of that column, lamented, "The Voting Rights Act regime as we knew it is gone, and it's not coming back." Charles continued: "Crucially, America's racially stratified society did not happen by chance; it is the product of a long history of intentional discrimination, including voting discrimination. This history of discrimination and the reality of current discrimination should mean that the scales must tip in favor of voters of color and voting equality."[27] But the scales had now tipped in the complete opposite direction.

What was so bad about the Court's 6–3 decision to uphold Arizona's laws and reject the plaintiffs' contention that they violated Section 2 of the Voting Rights Act—the very provision that prohibits discriminatory voting policies?

Justice Samuel Alito made up the law.

I don't make that statement lightly. The word "activist" to describe a judge is thrown around a lot. It often simply signals that the person disagrees with a judicial decision. Attacking the judge as "activist" is an easy trope. But here, I think we can agree on a more precise definition of an activist judge as one who, in their written opinion, adds language to a statute. That's where Justice Alito's activism took off. Recall that the lower courts all used a two-part test to analyze Section 2 of the Voting Rights Act: (1) Did the plaintiffs prove that the voting law in question creates a disparate impact on minority individuals? And (2) under the totality of the circumstances, did historical or societal factors cause or contribute to that disparity? This test comes directly from the language of Section 2. To analyze the totality of the circumstances, lower courts for years had focused on specific measures, detailed within a Senate report that accompanied the Voting Rights Act, which spoke to the kind and level of discrimination in the jurisdiction. But Justice Alito ignored that formulation, saying it applied only to redistricting cases (where did he come up with that?) and instead created his own framework that he apparently made up out of whole cloth. He essentially rewrote the text of the Voting Rights Act and devised a new standard that makes it virtually impossible for voting rights plaintiffs to bring successful claims against discriminatory voting laws.

Justice Alito claimed that he was not creating a new test. Yet he spent several pages outlining five "guideposts" that plaintiffs must now satisfy to win a suit for vote denial under Section 2 of the Voting Rights Act. These guideposts, he posited, were simply part of the inquiry into the totality of the circumstances. He disregarded the factors from the Senate report, which many courts had relied upon over the years, and substituted his own views on what measures were most important. There were few citations to legal authorities in these paragraphs. He literally made them up. Every measure he chose tilts the scales significantly in favor of the state.

Let's consider each of Alito's five so-called guideposts in turn (I will explain what they mean in more detail below):

- "First, the size of the burden imposed by a challenged voting rule is highly relevant."
- Second, "the degree to which a voting rule departs from what was standard practice when Section 2 was amended in 1982 is a relevant consideration."

- Third, "the size of any disparities in a rule's impact on members of different racial or ethnic groups is also an important factor to consider. Small disparities are less likely than large ones to indicate that a system is not equally open."
- Fourth, "courts must consider the opportunities provided by a State's entire system of voting when assessing the burden imposed by a challenged provision."
- Fifth, "the strength of the state interests served by a challenged voting rule is also an important factor that must be taken into account."[28]

Why are these "guideposts" so dangerous? Because they suggest we should simply trust states not to discriminate, basically removing federal judicial oversight. They make it virtually impossible for voting rights plaintiffs to win their cases. And they keep in place election rules that result in discrimination.

Take the first consideration, the extent of the burden on voters. Although any election rule might cause some burden—voters might have to travel to visit their precinct or deliver their ballot—this factor suggests that it's fine to have a rule that discriminates against racial minorities so long as the hurdles are not too hard for people to overcome. It's apparently OK to make voting a little bit difficult. The Court cited *Crawford*, the voter ID case, to accept the "usual burdens of voting" as normal and routine. Notice how all of these cases reinforce each other? The justices used their approval of voter ID laws to justify other burdens on the fundamental constitutional right to vote.

The second guidepost—whether a voting rule was routine in 1982 when Congress amended the Voting Rights Act—is even more problematic. This standard essentially locks into place a voting rule if it has been around for a long time. It's seemingly irrelevant if present conditions cause the voting law to produce current disparities. The overall voting processes in many states are immeasurably different today than they were over forty years ago, but the Court insulated a rule that's been around for a while even if modern day realities make it harder for minority individuals to participate in our democracy. Once again, the mantra here seems to be to "trust the states"—or more accurately, trust the entrenched state politicians who have every incentive to maintain unfair voting laws that help them stay in power.

The third factor, the size of the impact on minority voters as compared to non-minorities, also should be irrelevant. A law that harms only a handful of minorities is still discriminatory. Is Justice Alito saying that it's OK to disenfranchise some voters so long as there aren't too many affected? This guidepost essentially approves election laws that suppress the vote only a little bit. But any discrimination that affects the fundamental right to vote is abhorrent to the ideal of equality within a democracy.

The fourth and fifth factors then double down on the idea that we should simply trust state politicians not to discriminate against voters. The fourth guidepost directs courts to consider a state's overall election system; the fifth says we must accept the state's justification for its challenged voting rule. Neither of these factors tells us whether the law creates a discriminatory impact on minority voters. It shouldn't matter if the state makes it relatively easy to vote in one manner if most minorities already vote in another way. Curtailing the method of voting that most minority voters use harms their ability to exercise the franchise. And the state's rationale for its law is even further afield. This point should be obvious: a state should not be able to give a good enough reason to discriminate.

The result of these five guideposts is that it will be virtually impossible for voting rights plaintiffs to bring successful claims of vote denial. We are no longer in a period of explicit voter restrictions through literacy tests or poll taxes, so it's unlikely a state would pass a law that overtly discriminates. Voter suppression is (usually) more subtle. Many laws still discriminate, just in less obvious ways. That doesn't make those laws any less concerning. Older laws might now have discriminatory effects if people change how they interact with the voting system. Or maybe the rules discriminated all along. Yet the first three guideposts cut off a plaintiff's case unless the burdens of a new law are abundantly clear and impossible to deny. The last two guideposts elevate the state's interests to a superpower that can insulate it from virtually all attack. Almost any election rule, after all, helps to make election administration easier and fraud less likely. At least, that's what the state can always claim to make the plaintiff's case disappear.

Let me reiterate: Justice Alito cited no legal sources—no statutes, case law, legislative history, nor even scholarly articles—to support the creation of his five "guideposts." He just made them up. As Justice Elena Kagan put it in her fiery dissent, "The majority fears that the statute Congress wrote is too 'radical'—that it will invalidate too many state voting laws. So the majority writes its own set of rules, limiting Section 2 from multiple directions."[29] As the journalist Ian Millhiser wrote in *Vox*, "The Supreme Court isn't even pretending that it's bound by legal texts in its voting rights cases."[30]

Judicial activism, indeed.

THE AFTERMATH

Perhaps the Supreme Court's opinion in this case wasn't as bad as some had feared. Justice Alito expressly disclaimed that he was creating a new test for Section 2 of the Voting Rights Act, instead saying he was merely offering "guideposts." As a result, some lower court judges have refused to follow the guideposts explicitly. However, that reprieve is likely to be short-lived. Other lower courts have already invoked them to reject challenges to voting laws.

We've seen this story before. The Court issues a ruling that it claims to be narrow and reasonable, but in a subsequent decision, it elevates the restrictive rule to a controlling constitutional principle. The justices then say they are merely following precedent. That's what happened in *Shelby County* on Section 5 of the Voting Rights Act, as the previous chapter recounted: the Court pretended it was simply adhering to the prior *Northwest Austin* case, failing to acknowledge that *Northwest Austin* shifted the law. That's probably what will happen here too. When the other shoe drops on Section 2—perhaps invalidating the law entirely or otherwise gutting it further—the Court will cite *Brnovich* and claim that it is only following precedent.

In 2023, the Court issued a surprise 5–4 ruling in another Section 2 case, with Chief Justice Roberts and Justice Kavanaugh joining three liberals to uphold the act for now when applied to redistricting maps that harmed Black voters.[31] But the four-justice dissent for the other conservative justices vigorously opposed the ruling. Justice Kavanaugh, in his concurring opinion, also gave states a blueprint for a future challenge to this section of the act.[32] Thus, even though Section 2 of the Voting Rights Act enjoyed a reprieve in the redistricting context for now, it's not hard to imagine a future ruling when it does not fare as well. Either way, the Court is unlikely to admit that *Brnovich* was essentially made-up law.

That's not judging. It's politics wrapped up in law as a disguise.

Some of the Democratic lawyers aren't as nervous. As they noted, the *Northwest Austin* case expressed "concerns" about the constitutionality of Section 5, which the Court then pointed to in *Shelby County*. By contrast, the Court said nothing about Section 2's constitutionality in *Brnovich*, instead focusing on the meaning of the statute. Moreover, lower courts were already considering many of the so-called "guideposts" from Justice Alito's opinion, just not as explicitly. Even Mark Brnovich himself, the Arizona attorney general who argued to defend the state's law and whose name is on the case, said he thought Justice Alito was simply trying to provide bright line rules for an ambiguous statute and that people who don't like it can just ask Congress to change the law.[33] That's technically true, though he failed to acknowledge that effecting congressional change is difficult and that voters will be harmed in the process. That said, even failed lawsuits can spark social change. The Democratic lawyers noted that several Arizona counties switched to a Vote Center model—where there are no assigned precincts and voters can deliver their ballots to any Vote Center in the county—to avoid the out-of-precinct problem in the wake of this case. There was also a movement for a ballot initiative to expand voting access, which would include legalizing ballot collection.[34]

But I'm still worried. The Court overreached in deciding the Arizona case. It could have written a careful opinion affirming the district court's decision to uphold the laws without creating new standards to narrow the protection of Section 2. It could still transform those "guideposts" into firmer rules that severely limit the Voting Rights Act even further. This is not a narrow, incremental ruling from a careful Court. It's another bold opinion aiming to reshape our democracy by trusting those already in power instead of scrutinizing the voting rules they enact.

Moreover, *Brnovich* continues the trend of removing judicial protection for voting rights. As Rick Hasen, an election law scholar, wrote soon after the Court announced its decision:

When you couple this opinion with the 2008 ruling in the *Crawford* case, upholding Indiana's voter ID law against a Fourteenth Amendment equal protection challenge, the 2013 ruling in *Shelby County* killing off the preclearance provision of the Voting Rights Act for states with a history of discrimination, and today's reading of Section 2, the conservative Supreme Court has taken away all the major available tools for going after voting restrictions.[35]

Perhaps there is one saving grace: although the *Brnovich* case harmed voting rights protection, Section 2 is still technically alive, even if much weaker than before. Its very presence leaves the door open to lawsuits, which are expensive for governments to defend against. The Supreme Court has severely narrowed the protection of the Voting Rights Act, but the law still might deter some bad actors from passing rules that harm minority voters.

That's more than we can say about claims of partisan gerrymandering under the U.S. Constitution. As we will see in the next chapter, those cases are now completely dead.

CHAPTER 9

POLITICIANS GONE WILD

Rucho v. Common Cause (2019)

	JUSTICE	APPOINTED BY
MAJORITY	Roberts, John G., Jr. (chief justice) *(authored majority opinion)*	Bush, George W. (R)
	Thomas, Clarence	Bush, George H. W. (R)
	Alito, Samuel A., Jr.	Bush, George W. (R)
	Gorsuch, Neil M.	Trump, Donald (R)
	Kavanaugh, Brett M.	Trump, Donald (R)
DISSENT	Kagan, Elena *(authored dissent)*	Obama, Barack (D)
	Ginsburg, Ruth Bader	Clinton, Bill (D)
	Breyer, Stephen G.	Clinton, Bill (D)
	Sotomayor, Sonia	Obama, Barack (D)

What's the most eccentric wedding cake you have ever seen? Odds are, it probably isn't as unique (in the most loving way) as the cake for the wedding of two voting rights champions, Nick Stephanopoulos and Ruth Greenwood, who have been in the trenches to fight partisan gerrymandering. Their courtship started with redistricting: they met at a conference about how to draw district lines. Their wedding cake depicted a strangely shaped and apparently gerrymandered district in Illinois, where they lived, which connected two different communities of Latino voters through a small strip of land. The caption on the cake said, "Nick and Ruth: combining communities of interest." The comedian John Oliver even showed their cake on his show.[1]

Both Stephanopoulos and Greenwood are now at Harvard Law School, focusing on voting rights. They are a tag-team couple that fights gerrymandering, which is the practice of drawing district lines in ways that ensure a particular outcome. Greenwood directs the school's Election Law Clinic; Stephanopoulos teaches Election Law and his scholarship helps to provide legal theories to fight for equal representation. They have partnered (along with other organizations and groups) to take gerrymandering cases all the way to the Supreme Court. Their dinner conversations must be wild!

They are passionate about this work because of how skewed our democracy has become. States must redraw their legislative lines every ten years in a process known as redistricting, and in most places, self-interested politicians choose their voters, not the other way around. Not long ago, a majority of Supreme Court justices thought the Court should stop egregious partisan gerrymandering, which occurs when politicians draw unfair and often convoluted maps to boost their chances of remaining in power. But they needed a legal theory to employ. Stephanopoulos and Greenwood, together with other voting rights champions such as Anita Earls (who is now a justice on the North Carolina Supreme Court), have worked tirelessly to offer a viable theory and persuade the justices to stop partisan gerrymandering.

EVEN KIDS UNDERSTAND THE PROBLEM

In 2018, three teenage siblings from Austin, Texas, created a board game they called Mapmaker. They used a Kickstarter campaign to fund the project, which gained national attention after Arnold Schwarzenegger tweeted about it. The trio—two in college and one in high school—had grown up playing board games in a gerrymandered district that sprawled from Austin to Houston, and they sought to educate people about gerrymandering in a fun, engaging way. Mapmaker: The Gerrymandering Game was born.[2]

I've played the game numerous times; my preteen daughter especially likes it. In a four-person game, each player represents the Red Elephants, Blue Donkeys, Yellow Porcupines, or Green Leaves. Voters for your "party" are then spread randomly across the board. The goal is to place wooden borders around the board to create districts that your party controls with the most voters. The incentive is to draw districts that are oddly shaped or that sprawl across the board to pick off voters from different areas so that you can control the most districts.

The game shows just how intuitive (and downright easy) it is to draw unfair maps if you want—and how wrong it is if we seek a fair democracy. Kids understand this point inherently: if you start a game with the rules stacked in favor of one side, then that side is bound to win more often, cutting against an innate sense of playground fairness.

Of course, democracy is not a game. It's the way we govern ourselves so the majority's votes can prevail.

Our legislatures are composed of lawmakers who represent us, and so we split voters into districts to elect them to the legislature. (There are other models to elect representatives, including parliamentary systems with proportional representation, but this is the system we have.) The starting place is to draw those lines, which must be recalibrated every ten years after the new census data reveals population changes in each state. "One person, one vote" means that each district must be roughly equal in population so that each lawmaker will represent about the same number of people. Ever since our founding, politicians have tried to manipulate the maps to help themselves and their own political parties. In fact, the very term "gerrymander" comes from a mash-up between the name of Massachusetts governor (and eventual vice president) Elbridge Gerry and "salamander," stemming from a political cartoon that likened the maps Gerry supported to the shape of the amphibian. (See next page for cartoon.)

What's different now is the sheer sophistication and preciseness of today's gerrymanders. Computer technology, along with the increased polarization of our society, has made it extremely easy to predict how people will vote. Map drawers can use algorithms to discern the political makeup of a neighborhood, down to the block. They use that data to engage in what is known as packing and cracking. With packing, the goal is to smoosh as many of your opponent's voters as possible into one or two districts, so that they won't be in the neighboring districts that you control. For example, District 1 might be 90 percent Democratic and 10 percent Republican, while all of the surrounding districts might be 49 to 51 percent in favor of Republicans. Republicans, who will likely win each of the close districts with just barely a majority, can control the most seats. With cracking, on the other hand, the mapmakers draw lines through a cohesive neighborhood to split it into multiple districts. In this way, an

THE GERRY-MANDER.

Political cartoon from an 1812 Boston Gazette
showing a salamander-shaped voting district.

area that has a cluster of one kind of voter cannot come together to elect a representative because the map breaks them up.

Both sides are at fault for engaging in these practices, though Republicans have been worse offenders recently given that they have controlled more state legislatures, which draw both congressional and state legislative lines in most states. For the 2010 elections, Republicans engaged in a massive project known as REDMAP, or the Redistricting Majority Project, to focus on state legislative races. The goal was to win key districts and thereby give Republicans control of state houses just as the 2010 round of redistricting began. It worked. Republicans won a majority in about two-thirds of state legislative chambers, and they used their newfound authority to draw district maps to entrench themselves in power. It's how, to use just one example, Barack Obama won Pennsylvania's Electoral College votes in 2012 with 51 percent of the vote but Democrats won only 28 percent of the state legislative seats.[3]

How does one draw maps in this way? The simplified diagram below shows how to create voting districts to achieve a particular outcome.

It's hard to stop these practices at the ballot box. The familiar refrain of "vote the bums out" doesn't work when the system is set up to keep the bums in. State legislators draw maps that they know will help to elect them again even if they fall out of favor with the majority of voters. Unless we take power away from legislators to draw the lines—something that a handful of states have done with independent redistricting commissions—politicians are going to act politically, crafting maps that are favorable to

How to Gerrymander Voting Districts

40% GRAY **60% WHITE**	
0 GRAY DISTRICTS **5 WHITE DISTRICTS** **WHITE WINS**	
2 GRAY DISTRICTS **3 WHITE DISTRICTS** **WHITE WINS**	
3 GRAY DISTRICTS **2 WHITE DISTRICTS** **GRAY WINS**	

themselves and their political parties. That skewed representation affects every aspect of our society. As Allison Riggs, who argued the *Rucho* case at the Supreme Court and who is now a state supreme court justice in North Carolina, noted, "If we don't protect the right to vote, our ability to help shape every other policy in this country is undermined."[4]

Courts, therefore, are vital in analyzing maps to ensure they don't abridge the right to vote and create an unfair democracy. The right to vote is a constitutional precept; equality in elections is the backbone of democratic representation. If the courts won't police gerrymandering, then no one will.

So, what did the Supreme Court do on this issue?

You guessed it.

THE COURT GIVETH . . .

Lawyers who practice before the Supreme Court have a mantra on how to win a case: "Count to five." Five justices out of nine constitute a majority for a ruling. Unfortunately, those who seek a remedy for egregious partisan gerrymandering still haven't been able to count to five.

The Supreme Court had heard several cases about partisan gerrymandering in the decades before 2019's *Rucho v. Common Cause*. In 1986, in *Davis v. Bandemer*, six justices agreed that the Court could hear claims of partisan gerrymandering and that judges could (and should) determine when unfair maps violated the Constitution. After all, as the Court put it, "unconstitutional discrimination occurs . . . when the electoral system is arranged in a manner that will consistently degrade a voter's or a group of voters' influence on the political process as a whole."[5] The Court noted that the relevant question is "whether a particular group has been unconstitutionally denied its chance to effectively influence the political process."[6] The Court found, however, that the plaintiffs in *Davis v. Bandemer* had not presented sufficient evidence to render the Indiana map in question unconstitutional. Moreover, there were not five votes for a single standard for courts to apply, as the justices split on the proper approach to take, with four using one test and two proposing another.

Voting rights activists tried again in 2004, challenging a Pennsylvania map for being unfair. As the Court explained, "[T]he Republican party controlled a majority of both state Houses and held the Governor's office.

Prominent national figures in the Republican Party pressured the General Assembly to adopt a partisan redistricting plan as a punitive measure against Democrats for having enacted pro-Democrat redistricting plans elsewhere."[7] The map had irregularly shaped districts and ignored local government boundary lines, all in an effort to help Republicans win more seats.

Once again, the plaintiffs who brought the case couldn't count to five. Four conservative justices, led by Justice Scalia, said that federal courts are powerless to do anything about partisan gerrymandering, declaring the problem "nonjusticiable." That's a fancy word for saying that the issue isn't one for judges to decide—that the concept isn't judicially manageable because there are no clear tests to apply. After all, according to Justice Scalia, any kind of line drawing requires political choices, which legislators, not judges, should make. Legislators are accountable to the people through elections, while federal judges are appointed for life. If you don't like the way the lines are drawn, then vote out the people who drew them! Of course, that simplistic idea ignores the fact that politicians draw the lines in ways that make it much harder to vote them out. It also runs directly contrary to *Davis v. Bandemer* from 1986, which said that courts *could* hear these cases, not to mention several earlier cases in which the Court did enter the "political thicket."[8] Nevertheless, four justices proclaimed that courts should not enter the "political thicket" of partisan gerrymandering and should instead leave the problem for others to tackle. Congress, for instance, could theoretically place limits on how to draw new maps, but federal courts should not.

Four justices—the traditional liberals—vehemently disagreed, using *Davis v. Bandemer* as well as other redistricting precedents to explain how and why courts should declare an egregious map unlawful. Each justice offered their own clear rule for judges to apply to root out the worst partisan gerrymanders. Justice Stevens, for example, suggested that the Court look to its precedents on racial gerrymandering, which prevent mapmakers from unfairly considering race too much, to inform an approach to partisan gerrymandering. Racial gerrymandering cases, after all, are well settled. Moreover, the very fact that these dissenters offered legal tests—rules that judges use all the time to decide cases—disproved the Scalia faction's argument that there were no judicially manageable standards for this area of law.

Justice Anthony Kennedy didn't join either side. He disagreed with the four conservatives that the Court should never entertain partisan gerrymandering claims and thought courts could rule a particularly egregious gerrymander unlawful. As he noted, "If a State passed an enactment that declared 'All future apportionment shall be drawn so as most to burden Party X's rights to fair and effective representation, though still in accord with one-person, one-vote principles,' we would surely conclude the Constitution had been violated. If that is so, we should admit the possibility remains that a legislature might attempt to reach the same result without that express directive."[9] Yet he also disagreed with the four liberals on the various tests they proposed. He didn't think any of them were sufficient for courts to adopt without the risk of making the judiciary look too partisan. Staying in the middle, he said that perhaps a suitable standard would emerge in the future, leaving the door open for that possibility. Justice Kennedy's position—not fully with the conservatives and not fully with the liberals—deprived both sides of a five-vote majority.

Political scientists and legal scholars attempted to heed Justice Kennedy's call. They set out to discern a precise standard to identify maps that were outliers and only explainable by pure partisan motivation. They came up with lofty-sounding measures like the "partisan symmetry test" and the "mean-median difference," all with an eye toward convincing Justice Kennedy to provide a fifth vote for finally declaring the worst partisan gerrymanders unconstitutional. They failed again in 2006 in a case called *League of United Latin American Citizens v. Perry*, though several justices (including Kennedy) expressed interest in some kind of "partisan symmetry" standard, or a measure that would look at whether a map treated both major political parties fairly.[10] Law professor Nick Stephanopoulos (of wedding cake fame) and political scientist Eric McGhee wrote an article on a new metric they created called the "efficiency gap," which they hoped would persuade Justice Kennedy.[11]

They came close—or so they thought. In 2018, the Court considered *Gill v. Whitford*, a case involving partisan gerrymandering in Wisconsin, where Republicans had crafted a map that ensured they could control the state legislature even if they did not win a majority of votes statewide. In 2012, Republican candidates received 48.6 percent of the two-party statewide vote but won sixty of the ninety-nine seats in the state Assembly. Republicans increased their majority in 2014 to sixty-three of the ninety-nine seats with just 52 percent of the statewide vote. Using mathematical formulas such as the efficiency gap, the plaintiffs showed that the map was severely skewed to favor Republicans. They won a favorable ruling at the lower court to strike down the map.[12]

But after the state appealed, the Supreme Court punted on the issue, dismissing the plaintiffs' case for a procedural reason. In an opinion by Chief Justice Roberts—notorious for his supposedly "narrower" decisions that are used later to make bolder pronouncements—the Court ruled unanimously that the plaintiffs' in that case did not have standing, which is the legal right to bring a case, because they had not suffered a personal injury. The problem, according to the Court, was that the main Democratic plaintiff lived in a strong Democratic district, so the Wisconsin map didn't harm him. A Democrat would still represent him in the legislature. He had no basis, according to the Court, to complain about districts in other parts of the state.[13] He wasn't allowed to assert a statewide injury based on the overall effects of the map. Of course, state legislatures pass laws collectively, so the overall statewide skew is exactly what causes the unfair representation. Changing the lines for one district necessarily alters the lines in other districts. But that didn't seem to matter much to the Court, which held steadfastly to the idea that only plaintiffs who directly suffered a harm within their own district had the right to sue.

Justice Elena Kagan wrote a separate opinion in which she detailed how a future plaintiff could win a case, focusing on the arguments and evidence they might present. It was basically a road map for the next lawsuit. As she acknowledged, "[W]hen legislators can entrench themselves in office despite the people's will, the foundation of effective democratic governance dissolves."[14] The Court needed to provide a remedy for this constitutional harm, especially because self-interested legislators would continue to pass egregious maps to help keep themselves in power. Only the other liberals (Justices Ginsburg, Breyer, and Sotomayor) joined Kagan's separate opinion. Justice Kennedy did not; if he had, there would have been five votes for Kagan's approach.

Was Kennedy not convinced by any of the legal theories Kagan espoused? We'll never know.[15] The Court issued its decision in this Wisconsin case on June 18, 2018, and only nine days later, on June 27, Kennedy announced that he would retire from the Court, handing Donald Trump another vacancy to fill. With Kennedy retiring—Brett Kavanaugh would take his place—counting to five for a constitutional ruling against partisan gerrymandering became that much harder.

...AND THE COURT TAKETH AWAY

The Supreme Court opened the door to claims of partisan gerrymandering in 1986 in the *Davis v. Bandemer* case, though the justices never coalesced around a single test to root out the worst abuses. The Court slammed the door shut in 2019 in the *Rucho* case by a 5–4 vote. The biggest reason? The Court's composition had changed. Justice Kennedy had indicated he was open to invalidating a map—or at least the worst districts within a map—when evidence of partisan shenanigans was abundant. But he was no longer on the Court. In his place, Justice Kavanaugh joined the other conservative justices in outright refusing to hear these claims.

The *Rucho* case actually involved two lawsuits, one stemming from extreme Republican gerrymandering in North Carolina and the other involving blatant Democratic gerrymandering in Maryland.

In North Carolina, Republicans won nine of the thirteen congressional seats in 2012, even though their congressional candidates received only 49 percent of the vote statewide. In 2014, they won 55 percent of the statewide vote, which translated to controlling ten of the thirteen seats, all because of partisan gerrymandering. They weren't shy about their goals. One of the principal map drawers, Republican state representative David Lewis, admitted, "I think electing Republicans is better than electing Democrats. So I drew this map to help foster what I think is better for the country."[16] He also explained that he drew a ten–three map because he couldn't find a way "to draw a map with eleven Republicans and two Democrats."[17] Lewis served in the state legislature for seventeen years, eventually resigning in disgrace in 2020 after pleading guilty to two federal charges of campaign finance violations. He apparently set up a scheme to funnel $50,000 from his campaign account to another account he created for his own personal use.[18]

The trial in *Rucho* occurred in Greensboro, North Carolina, which itself was symbolic as the site of iconic protests during the civil rights era. It was also perhaps the most gerrymandered corner of the state, splitting the predominantly Democratic and Black city right down the middle. Anita Earls, a civil rights champion who founded the Southern Coalition for

Social Justice to fight for racial equality (and who later became a justice on the North Carolina Supreme Court), helped to litigate the dispute. Earls went to Charlotte after law school to take on voting rights cases, telling me how she had seen firsthand the power of the right to vote as "foundational and fundamental to all of the other issues people care about."[19] She worked in communities and witnessed tangible changes when people began to enjoy representation in a way they never had before. Earls was masterful in her opening and closing arguments in this case, demonstrating her fervent belief in equality and justice. The lawyers meticulously walked through statistical analyses and evidence of partisan skew. Ruth Greenwood and Nick Stephanopoulos, the anti-gerrymandering couple, were also part of the team, with Stephanopoulos focused on drafting the written briefs and Greenwood handling the witnesses. (As Stephanopoulos put it, boasting about his wife, Greenwood "annihilated" the state's expert witness during cross-examination.)[20] Greenwood recalled fondly what happened when she was prepping one of the voters she represented for a deposition. A standard question that lawyers ask their witnesses ahead of time is whether the person has ever been arrested, as the opposing lawyer is sure to bring it up. The voter seemed embarrassed when she responded, "Yes." "What for?" Greenwood inquired gently. "Protesting the gerrymander," was the response. "I've never been so excited for a defense counsel to try to beat up on my plaintiffs as criminals!" Greenwood exclaimed.[21]

The lengthy lower court opinion in North Carolina struck down the state's map, explaining in great detail just how unfair the map was to the state's Democratic voters. A court in Maryland used similar reasoning to invalidate that state's gerrymander. The Maryland case involved a district that a Republican had won for two decades. The 2010 census results required the district to shrink by about 10,000 individuals to achieve the legal requirement of equal population among all districts in a state. Maryland Democrats decided to fix the population disparity in a way that would simultaneously flip the district to Democratic control: they drew lines that relocated about 360,000 voters to surrounding districts and moved 350,000 other individuals into the district. A solid red district became blue overnight.

The lower courts in both North Carolina and Maryland each coalesced around a legal standard that could root out the worst partisan gerrymanders. All told, fifteen federal judges across five states appointed by both Democratic and Republican judges had ruled against partisan gerrymandering by the time the Supreme Court took up the issue.[22]

THE COURT DECLARES: GERRYMANDERING IS CONSTITUTIONAL

The cases from North Carolina and Maryland, which reached the Supreme Court at the same time, offered the justices every permutation they would need to tackle the problem of gerrymandering. There was both a Republican and a Democratic gerrymander, so the Court wouldn't look political by ruling them both unlawful. There was a map that was skewed statewide (North Carolina's) and a map that focused its attention on a specific district (Maryland's), offering the Court different legal theories under both the Fourteenth Amendment and the First Amendment to the U.S. Constitution. (In fact, the lawyers for the various groups squabbled over which was the best theory to advance.) Both maps were egregiously unfair, and everyone knew that state lawmakers were simply trying to draw maps favorable to their side. It was undeniable—they even admitted it openly.

As Justice Kagan explained in her dissent:

> The partisan gerrymanders in these cases deprived citizens of the most fundamental of their constitutional rights: the rights to participate equally in the political process, to join with others to advance political beliefs, and to choose their political representatives. In so doing, the partisan gerrymanders here debased and dishonored our democracy, turning upside-down the core American idea that all governmental power derives from the people. These gerrymanders enabled politicians to entrench themselves in office as against voters' preferences. They promoted partisanship above respect for the popular will. They encouraged a politics of polarization and dysfunction. If left unchecked, gerrymanders like the ones here may irreparably damage our system of government.[23]

But Chief Justice Roberts and the other conservative justices weren't convinced. Roberts, writing for the majority, claimed that federal courts are not the proper venues for complaints about partisan gerrymandering. The Framers, he posited, never would have fathomed the courts taking on a role in what he deemed to be a political dispute; instead, they would have left the problem to Congress to solve. Of course, the Framers never could have imagined the preciseness of today's gerrymanders, either. Leaving the issue to Congress presents the same problem as letting state legislators draw the maps: lawmakers are too self-interested and therefore have little incentive to limit the practice.

It's not as though the Court has washed its hands clean of all redistricting litigation. The familiar one person, one vote cases require districts to have roughly equal populations. That was never a constitutional requirement until the Court imposed the one person, one vote rule in the 1960s. Its decisions upended redistricting practices in virtually every state. There is also a large body of case law involving racial gerrymandering to ensure appropriate minority representation—though Republicans have also used the doctrine to attack maps that consider race *too much*. Either way, the Court is well versed in redistricting cases. To say that the Framers left the problem of partisan gerrymandering to the elected branches is essentially to ignore all history after the founding era.

That history includes decades of case law in which the Court required fair maps. Reflecting that history, a lawyer for Common Cause, a pro-democracy group that brought the North Carolina case (alongside other organizations such as the League of Women Voters), was eighty-two-year-old Emmet Bondurant, who was involved in one of those earlier disputes. Bondurant is a civil rights champion who had argued before the Supreme Court in 1963, at the age of twenty-six, in *Wesberry v. Sanders*. That case was one of the precedents that established the one person, one vote principle. Bondurant returned to the Court fifty-five years later to argue *Rucho*, underscoring the fact that the Court had previously stopped unfair redistricting practices and could do so again.[24] He told me, in his southern drawl and gentlemanly manner, that proving partisan intent in this case "would be like shooting a bird on the ground."[25] A graph the plaintiffs presented to the court to visualize the partisan effect of the North Carolina congressional map showed how the version the legislature adopted was quite literally off the chart.[26] The case was that easy, at least if the Court were willing to say that a legislature cannot ignore all concepts of fairness in drawing a new map.

But Chief Justice Roberts, for the majority, refused to recognize the inherent constitutional requirement of a fair democracy. Even though the

Constitution forbids states from drawing districts with unequal populations or engaging in racial discrimination, he wrote that "a jurisdiction
may engage in constitutional political gerrymandering."[27] Read that sentence again. The Supreme Court of the United States announced that
political gerrymandering is *perfectly constitutional*. The Court gave a green
light to legislators to draw maps to help themselves stay in office. Politicians are political actors, the argument goes, so they will always act politically. And given that the Constitution says that state legislators determine
the "time, place, and manner" of running elections, it should come as no
surprise that their decisions are political. The majority here posited, "The
central problem is not determining whether a jurisdiction has engaged in
partisan gerrymandering. It is determining when political gerrymandering has gone too far."[28] That inquiry, the Court held, is one the judiciary
isn't equipped to make, as any ruling would require judges to wade too
much into politics. It's the overwrought concern of the Court entering the
political thicket all over again.

A DISINGENUOUS SUPREME COURT OPINION

Just because state legislators or Congress have the first cut at election
laws doesn't mean that courts must stay out of the business entirely. Politicians enact all sorts of laws that courts strike down for violating the
Constitution. The whole point of judicial review is for judges—who aren't
supposed to be political actors—to check politicians and ensure that laws
do not violate the protections within the Constitution. "Constitutional
partisan gerrymandering" should be an oxymoron.

This judicial abdication is the fundamental flaw of the Court's opinion
in *Rucho*, where it simply refused to intervene to stop egregious partisan gerrymandering: the majority claimed that because elected legislators
typically draw the lines, then that process is inherently (and appropriately)
political. If it's political, then it's not suited for judicial oversight. The
courts must stay out of it.

The Court was unnecessarily concerned that a ruling against these
maps would let judges impose their own political theory on our entire
democracy without constraint. Despite various careful tests that the plaintiffs and Justice Kagan's dissent offered, the majority convinced itself that
there was no "limited and precise standard that is judicially discernible

and manageable."[29] That finding ignored the reality that lower courts were already employing easy-to-administer tests to determine whether a map was a true outlier, using simulations and formulas to see if political opportunism was really the only explanation for how the lines were drawn. One expert in the North Carolina case simulated three thousand maps and found that, even when controlling for the state's geography and demographics, the one the legislature adopted was at the far extreme of partisan advantage. As Justice Kagan pointed out in her dissent, the map was an outlier compared "to the other maps the State could have produced given its unique political geography and its chosen districting criteria."[30] In allowing that one egregious map to remain in force, the justices failed to acknowledge that by refusing to rule against blatant partisan gerrymandering, they were effectively imposing a political theory of their own: those in power can use every resource imaginable to rig the system and remain in power.

Roberts also engaged in some sleight of hand in his opinion. He claimed that the dissent "essentially embraces the argument that the Court unanimously rejected in *Gill*," the partisan gerrymandering case out of Wisconsin from the prior year, that "this Court *can* address the problem of partisan gerrymandering because it *must*."[31] But *Gill* said no such thing. Roberts left out key language. The full sentence in *Gill* says, "At argument on appeal in this case, counsel for the plaintiffs argued that this Court *can* address the problem of partisan gerrymandering because it *must*."[32] The Court didn't reject the idea in *Gill*; it didn't address it, instead holding that the plaintiffs did not have the legal right to bring suit. To say that the Court rejected the contention—unanimously, no less—is quite disingenuous. Roberts literally quoted only the second half of a sentence to try to make the dissenters look bad. Most rookie lawyers wouldn't (or at least shouldn't!) make that kind of mistake. This error exemplifies the majority's slipshod approach to the entire case. As Emmet Bondurant, the octogenarian lawyer who argued the case for Common Cause, wrote, "*Rucho v. Common Cause* is intellectually dishonest and fundamentally incorrect in at least thirteen distinct ways."[33] The legal scholars Guy-Uriel Charles and Luis Fuentes-Rohwer remarked that the opinion is "an amalgam of misdirections, distortions and less-than-pellucid thinking."[34]

"Our conclusion does not condone excessive partisan gerrymandering," Roberts claimed.[35] Don't be fooled. That's exactly what it does by letting politicians manipulate maps without any federal judicial oversight. Roberts then offered two so-called solutions to the problem: state courts can strike down bad maps under state constitutions, and voters can enact ballot initiatives to require independent redistricting commissions. The problem with the state courts solution is the looming "independent state legislature" idea (discussed in the next chapter) that would give the U.S. Supreme Court the final say once again, as well as certain state courts that simply follow the U.S. Supreme Court's lead even when analyzing their differently-worded state constitution. The problem with the independent redistricting commission idea is that many states, including North Carolina and Maryland, don't let their voters pass an initiative to create a commission without first securing legislative approval. There's literally no way to go around the legislature in these places. Yes, independent redistricting commissions are a good idea where they are possible, but that's no solution for places that would require politicians to give up their power to draw their own districts. The Democratic-controlled House has twice passed bills recently to mandate independent redistricting commissions for drawing congressional lines, but the proposals died in the Senate; after all, many members of Congress are self-interested, too.[36]

There should be no such thing as constitutional partisan gerrymandering. The courts are the only actor in our democracy that has the proper incentives and power to stop it. The plaintiffs were not asking judges to be "omnipresent players in the political process," as Justice Kagan explained. They just sought a ruling that would stop the "worst-of-the-worst cases of democratic subversion, causing blatant constitutional harms."[37] Justice Kennedy had opined, back in that 2004 case from Pennsylvania, that the Court would surely find a constitutional violation if a legislature explicitly said it was trying to harm the other party's right to fair and effective representation.[38] That's exactly what happened in both North Carolina and Maryland. But instead of upholding the Constitution and promoting a fair democracy, Roberts deferred to state politicians once again.

Reflecting back on the case she helped to litigate, Anita Earls, from her new perch as a justice on the North Carolina Supreme Court—where she ruled against the state's maps under the state constitution—was still frustrated with the Court's opinion. The evidence of unfairness was just so overwhelming. "If all nine members of the Supreme Court had been in the courtroom during the week of the trial," she said, "maybe they wouldn't have reversed" the lower court's ruling that invalidated the map. But she also said that there's nothing she would have changed about how she presented the case: "There are cases I've lost that I could tell you what I would have done differently. This is one where I can't think of anything I would have done differently to win. We did our clients proud in presenting the best possible case."[39] The evidence was overwhelming that North Carolina's gerrymander harmed equal representation and the people's right to vote and govern themselves. The maps were extreme outliers under any possible measure of fairness. Five justices on the Supreme Court simply wouldn't listen.

THE 2020 REDISTRICTING CYCLE

Freed of any and all constraints from the Supreme Court, politicians did exactly what one would expect after the 2020 census in the first redistricting cycle after *Rucho* came down: they gerrymandered the heck out of their maps. Nationwide, Republicans did not gain as many seats through gerrymandering as pundits initially expected, but that's only because Democrats drew strong maps for themselves in places like Illinois and New York. State courts also stopped some of the worst gerrymanders, including in North Carolina, putting into place a fairer court-drawn congressional map instead. (We will discuss that North Carolina Republican-skewed map in a different—but related—context in the next chapter.) Perhaps most tellingly, the number of swing districts—those that have roughly the same number of Democrats and Republicans such that either candidate had a chance of winning—declined for the 2022 election, which reduced electoral competition. In addition, experts predicted that the maps would sustain the dire underrepresentation of racial minorities in Congress throughout the next decade.[40]

Numerous measures—the kinds of tests the Court should have adopted—prove that gerrymandering continues to run amok. Various voting rights experts such as Nick Stephanopoulos and Ruth Greenwood, along with Eric McGhee and Michal Migurski, created PlanScore, a website that allows policymakers and the public to rate various maps to determine the level of partisan gerrymandering. Anyone can upload a proposed map to evaluate its fairness. PlanScore considers mathematical formulas such as the efficiency gap, partisan bias, the mean-median difference, and the declination metric (definitions for all of these measures are available on the PlanScore website). The data is illuminating. Based on partisan bias, the Texas congressional map for 2022 would have allowed Republicans to win 10.6 percent extra seats in a hypothetical, perfectly tied election. The Ohio congressional map—which the state supreme court determined was unlawful under the state constitution but a federal court ordered to be put in place for 2022 because the election was imminent—would have given Republicans 19.7 percent extra seats in a hypothetical, perfectly tied election. The Maryland congressional map gave Democrats a 10 percent advantage.[41] The story is much the same for the state legislative maps. Most favor Republicans, although Democrats aggrandized their power in the states they controlled. The upshot: the redder places will become even redder and the bluer places will become even bluer because of the way the politicians drew the maps.

Yet the Supreme Court's response was, essentially, "Not our problem."

That sentiment exemplifies the Court's overall approach to the right to vote. Violations of the core principle that the *people* should govern go unaddressed. The conservative justices seem to think that elections can fix the problems—just vote the bums out!—without acknowledging that the "bums" are creating the rules that make it so much harder to oust them from office. Sure, a motivated electorate can unseat an incumbent politician, but a skewed map makes the task so much harder. Deference to state legislators—because they are more responsive to the people—might sound good as a democratic theory, but it doesn't work in practice, especially for the very rules of the game that help to keep them in office. The powerful can become even more powerful.

And as for the rest of us? We are left figuring out how to save our democracy without a Supreme Court we can trust.

CHAPTER 10

THE NEXT LOOMING CASE

" **T** his is ridiculous." The message on the cardboard sign said it all.
Jennifer Taff, a Wisconsin voter, had requested an absentee ballot
in April 2020 just as the Covid-19 pandemic began to disrupt everyone's
lives, but it never arrived. Her father was fighting lung cancer, so she was
particularly concerned about exposing herself—and then him—to the vi-
rus. Nevertheless, she greatly valued her right to vote, so she bundled
up to withstand the cold Milwaukee weather, donned a mask, and wrote
"This Is Ridiculous" in blue marker on a large piece of cardboard to hold
up as she waited in line to vote.

Patricia McKnight, a college senior and an intern at the *Milwaukee
Journal Sentinel*, saw Taff holding the sign as McKnight approached the
polling place on her way to vote. She pulled out her iPhone and snapped
a picture. She sent it in to her editors and then waited over an hour and
a half to cast her own ballot in the election for state supreme court justice and other races at the beginning of the pandemic. The newspaper
published the photo online and it immediately went viral. As McKnight
recounted, the photo resonated with people because of its simple yet
forceful message: "It was completely ridiculous to have hundreds [and]
hundreds of people in a mile-long line wrapping around a couple blocks
to go vote. It *is* ridiculous."[1]

The day before, the Wisconsin Supreme Court had reversed an order
from Governor Tony Evers to delay the election until June because of the
pandemic.[2] Taff, McKnight, and thousands of other Wisconsin voters were
therefore waiting in a long line to vote. To make matters worse, the U.S.

Supreme Court issued a ruling on that same Monday to reverse a lower federal court decision that had extended the absentee ballot deadline. Because of the newly emerging pandemic, thousands of Wisconsin voters had requested absentee ballots but had never received them. A federal judge had required the state to accept late ballots because of the unprecedented nature of the pandemic, but the Supreme Court majority said that doing so would "fundamentally alter the nature of the election."[3] Voters like Taff, who never received their absentee ballot, had to choose between sacrificing their fundamental right to vote and risking their health by voting in person during the early stages of the Covid-19 pandemic, when almost everything else had shut down. Ridiculous, indeed.

Thus began a series of cases in 2020 about running elections during a pandemic. Predictably, the Supreme Court consistently ruled against voters. In these cases, several justices also revived a little-known, rarely used, and legally dubious idea called the "independent state legislature" theory. The ramifications for the sanctity of the right to vote are massive.

THE U.S. CONSTITUTION VERSUS STATE CONSTITUTIONS

As we've seen previously, the U.S. Constitution does not explicitly confer the right to vote. The Supreme Court has used that lack of an express textual right to give states great leeway to regulate their voting processes as they see fit. The Court has deferred to state legislatures and failed to uphold a voter's interest in easy access to the ballot.

Pursuant to the Court's approach in cases like *Anderson*, *Burdick*, and *Crawford* (covered in chapters 1–3), the Court has too narrowly construed the Constitution's protection for the right to vote. The Court has generally said that election rules must treat voters equally, yet jurisprudence under this equality principle has allowed states to enact a whole suite of voter restrictions.

State constitutions, by contrast, are not as limited. Every state has its own constitution that provides various rights to people living in those states. Forty-nine of the fifty state constitutions, in fact, affirmatively grant the right to vote. The constitutions use language saying that every citizen "shall be entitled to vote at all elections" or "shall be an elector." (Only Arizona's constitution does not include this explicit language, but its state courts have interpreted its constitution as conferring voting rights as well.)[4] Furthermore, about half of state constitutions include language saying that elections must be "free," "free and equal," or "free and open." Thus, textually, state constitutions go beyond the U.S. Constitution in granting the right to vote and protecting voters.[5]

In the wake of the U.S. Supreme Court's narrow voting rights jurisprudence, advocates began looking toward state constitutions, arguing for state courts to protect the fundamental right more robustly under their express provisions. There was some success on this front! Several state courts invoked their state constitutions to strike down voter ID laws, partisan gerrymanders, and other voter restrictions.[6]

Conservative activists then came up with another bright idea: maybe state courts shouldn't be allowed to use their state constitutions at all, at least when it comes to voting in federal elections. Here is where the legal arguments become bolder—and weirder. The contention is that a state supreme court—supposedly the highest authority in interpreting state law—actually has no authority to rule a state voting law unconstitutional when that voting rule is used in federal elections. State election laws, the argument goes, are immune from attack and can even outright violate the state constitution.

How could this be? The hypertextualist argument revolves around the word "legislature" in the U.S. Constitution. Article I, Section 4, also known as the Elections Clause, says, "The Times, Places and Manner of holding Elections for Senators and Representatives, shall be prescribed in each State by the Legislature thereof."[7] That is, *state legislatures* have the authority to regulate federal elections. The Constitution goes on to say that Congress can "make or alter" election regulations, but states have the first crack at it. Similarly, when it comes to electing the president, Article II says that "Each State shall appoint, in such Manner as the Legislature thereof may direct," the presidential electors for their state.[8] The *state legislature* directs how to determine the state's presidential electors, meaning that, paradoxically, the state supreme court does not have authority over the state legislature in this context. Every state allows their voters to cast ballots for presidential candidates, but technically they are voting for presidential electors pledged to those candidates. At the founding, many state legislatures simply declared who would receive the state's presidential electors. The Constitution would even allow state legislatures to take that power back if they wanted instead of allowing the voters to choose the electors.

We therefore have a state-focused structure for election administration. And if you take the Constitution's text ultra-literally, the authority to regulate voting and elections flows to the state legislatures. It says "legislature," after all. This reading underpins the independent state legislature theory.

Does that mean a state legislature can do whatever it wants, without limit, when crafting rules for federal elections?

EARLY—AND CONSISTENT—REJECTION OF THE INDEPENDENT STATE LEGISLATURE THEORY

Some conservative litigants have tried to argue that legislature means legislature, and only legislature, such that no other state authority can limit what the legislature does. Normally, a state supreme court can invalidate a state law by declaring it violative of the protections found within the state constitution. The bold argument here is that for rules about federal elections, state legislatures are essentially free agents because the U.S. Constitution says that only the legislature of a state can dictate those rules, meaning that state courts have no power over the legislature. This concept is known as the independent state legislature theory of election law.

The U.S. Supreme Court has rejected this idea several times. In 1932, in *Smiley v. Holm*, the Court considered whether a congressional redistricting plan passed by the Minnesota legislature but not approved by the governor was still valid. The legislature, after all, had enacted the map, so under this textualist reading of the U.S. Constitution it should be immaterial that the governor had refused to accept it. The Supreme Court held, however, that the state constitution required the governor to sign any laws (and allowed the legislature to override a gubernatorial veto) as part of the state's general lawmaking function. The legislature had not enacted the new map according to the state constitution's rules. That is, the Court unanimously rejected the idea that the state legislature could pass a voting rule for federal elections by itself, separate from the governor's approval or legislative override of the governor's veto. The state constitution required the typical legislative process, and the U.S. Constitution did not replace that basic understanding of the state legislature's function.[9] Note that the Court in *Smiley* was considered pretty conservative—four of the justices from the unanimous ruling were nicknamed the Four Horsemen of the Apocalypse for opposing FDR's New Deal legislation—and it still rejected this ultra-textual interpretation of the state legislature's role in crafting election rules.[10]

The modern era of the independent state legislature theory of election law began with three justices who floated it in *Bush v. Gore*. Recall (see chapter 6) that the U.S. Supreme Court was reviewing the Florida Supreme Court's decision regarding the recount process for the 2000 presidential election. The majority declared that the Florida Supreme Court's ruling to continue the recount statewide violated the federal Equal Protection Clause because different canvassing boards across the state were creating their own standards as to whether to count a ballot as a valid vote (a hanging chad, a pregnant chad, and so on). Chief Justice Rehnquist wrote a separate opinion, joined by Justices Thomas and Scalia. In that *Bush v. Gore* concurrence, Rehnquist raised another problem he saw with the Florida Supreme Court's decision: it took away authority from the state legislature by "significantly depart[ing] from the legislative scheme for appointing Presidential electors."[11] Article II of the U.S. Constitution lets the "legislature" direct the appointment of presidential electors, and Rehnquist thought that the Florida Supreme Court's opinion to continue the recount would "frustrate" the state legislature's desire to finalize the vote totals by the date Congress had set (the so-called "safe harbor" deadline). He also believed the Florida Supreme Court's interpretation of Florida statutes was incorrect. In essence, Rehnquist was saying that the Florida Supreme Court was acting like a legislature and imposing its own views, contrary to the actual legislature's commands.

This is a strange interpretation. The Florida Supreme Court, as the highest court in the state, should have the ultimate authority to interpret Florida laws. It's odd for a justice on the U.S. Supreme Court to tell the Florida Supreme Court that it's wrong about Florida law. But that is basically what Rehnquist said. The Florida Supreme Court, he posited, shouldn't be allowed to interpret the Florida election laws contrary to how the state legislature would want, because the U.S. Constitution gives sole authority to the "legislature" to determine the rules for appointing presidential electors.

If you found the previous two paragraphs confusing, you're not alone. It's a confusing doctrine that flips the law on its head. Here's one way to think about it: normally, the state supreme court has the last word on state law. It is "supreme," after all. But here, Rehnquist was saying that the state supreme court was not allowed to rule against the legislature because the U.S. Constitution says the legislature—and by implication no one else— can determine the rules for federal elections. In this one area of law, the state legislature is higher than the state supreme court.

Only three justices latched on to this idea in *Bush v. Gore*. Four agreed with it in 2015 in a case called *Arizona State Legislature v. Arizona Independent Redistricting Commission*, but that was still one justice shy of a majority. Back in 2000, Arizona voters approved a ballot proposition to create the Arizona Independent Redistricting Commission. The goal was to "end . . . the practice of gerrymandering and improv[e] voter and candidate participation in elections."[12] The initiative took power away from the legislature to draw district lines, instead placing it within a newly formed five-member commission. The majority and minority leaders of each house of the state legislature have a nominee, and those four people select a fifth person to be the chairperson, who must not be registered with either political party. Thus, the commission has two Democrats, two Republicans, and a chair from neither party. The commission drew Arizona's maps after the 2000 census and again after the 2010 census. The Republican-controlled legislature, however, was not pleased with the congressional map for 2012, fearing that it unduly favored Democrats, so it sued. Its argument was that the commission itself was invalid because it unconstitutionally took away power from the legislature to draw the map.[13]

Once again, this argument might seem simple if one looks at the text of the Constitution and nothing else: the Elections Clause says that the "legislature" can dictate the "times, places, and manner" of running congressional elections, and the Arizona Independent Redistricting Commission was not the "legislature." A majority of the Court, however, rejected that argument in an opinion written by Justice Ruth Bader Ginsburg. She noted that the state constitution explicitly gives the people of Arizona lawmaking power through a ballot initiative. The people had engaged in "direct" lawmaking when it created the commission and therefore were acting as a "legislature" by invoking these powers via the ballot. The Arizona Constitution even says, "Any law which may be enacted by the Legislature under this Constitution may be enacted by the people under the Initiative."[14] The Court pointed out, "Nothing in that Clause instructs, nor has this Court ever held, that a state legislature may prescribe regulations on the time, place, and manner of holding federal elections in defiance of provisions of the State's constitution."[15]

Chief Justice Roberts disagreed in a fiery dissent, joined by Justices Scalia, Thomas, and Alito. He claimed that the majority was "gerryman-der[ing] the Constitution" by "interpret[ing] the constitutional term 'the Legislature' to mean 'the people.'"[16] The people had taken authority to draw maps away from the state legislature through a ballot initiative, mean-ing the "legislature" was no longer in charge, contrary to the U.S. Consti-tution's commands. It was a "magic trick" of constitutional interpretation.[17]

There are many problems with Roberts's view, especially given the history of the Constitution's Elections Clause, but here is a practical one: Roberts was in the minority. A majority of the Court strongly rejected his interpretation, instead ruling that "legislature" in the Constitution means the state legislature, *as created and constrained by the state constitution.* Thus, the precedent was clear: the U.S. Constitution gives authority to state legislatures to regulate federal elections, but those legislatures must act within the bounds of their state constitutions.

Roberts himself even alluded to this concept in 2019's *Rucho v. Com-mon Cause* (discussed in chapter 9), the North Carolina case about partisan gerrymandering in which the Court closed the federal courthouse doors to these claims. He said that although the federal courts could not (or at least would not) invoke the U.S. Constitution to stop partisan gerryman-dering, "provisions in state statutes and state constitutions can provide standards and guidance for state courts to apply."[18] That statement would make no sense if state constitutions could *not* bind state legislatures in how they draw district lines.

VOTING DURING A PANDEMIC

The idea that state legislatures are essentially free agents kept reappearing among a subset of justices and litigants. The Covid-19 pandemic, break-ing out during a presidential election year, brought the concept to the forefront.

Covid-19 disrupted much of everyday life. The pandemic quickly changed the voting process in so many ways, from delaying primaries in some states to altering the methods of voting. The demand for mail-in balloting soared while states scrambled to find enough poll workers to staff polling locations. Mail slowdowns and threatened cuts to the postal service budget made voters nervous about whether their ballots would arrive on time. Simply put, the election infrastructure was not initially equipped to handle a record number of voters casting a ballot during a pandemic, especially with an influx of mailed votes.

Voting rights advocates sued in numerous states that were unresponsive to the need for voters to have a safe and reliable method of voting. The 2020 election set a record for litigation in this field of law, and Wisconsin was one of the key battlegrounds. In light of concerns about Covid-19 and postal slowdowns, in late September 2020 a federal district judge ordered Wisconsin to count all ballots that were postmarked by Election Day, so long as they arrived within six days after Election Day. An appeals court put that order on hold in a split ruling. The dissenting judge noted that without the extension of the date when ballots could arrive, "It is a virtual certainty that current conditions will result in many voters, possibly tens of thousands, being disenfranchised absent changes to an election code designed for in-person voting on election day. We cannot turn a blind eye to the present circumstances and treat this as an ordinary election. Nor can we blindly defer to a state legislature that sits on its hands while a pandemic rages."[19] She ended her opinion, "Good luck and G-d bless, Wisconsin. You are going to need it."[20] The plaintiffs sought review at the Supreme Court, which agreed with the appeals court to deny the ballot receipt extension by a 5–3 vote (Justice Ginsburg had recently passed away, which is why only eight justices ruled on the matter).

The Court's ruling meant that some Wisconsin voters would not have their votes counted despite placing their ballots in the mail by Election Day. But some of the justices went even further in this case, signaling that they were open to an interpretation of the Constitution that gives unfettered discretion to state legislatures to run elections however they want. Justice Gorsuch, joined by Justice Kavanaugh, cited the Elections Clause and said, "The Constitution provides that state legislatures—not federal judges, not state judges, not state governors, not other state officials—bear primary responsibility for setting election rules."[21] Justice Gorsuch reiterated this view in a case from North Carolina a few days later, this time joined by Justice Alito.[22] And in the week before the election, in a case from Pennsylvania also involving the absentee ballot deadline, Justice Alito, joined by Justices Thomas and Gorsuch, again said that state courts cannot invoke state constitutions to alter the rules as set out by state legislatures: "The provisions of the Federal Constitution conferring on state legislatures, not state courts, the authority to make rules governing federal elections would be meaningless if a state court could override the rules adopted by the legislature simply by claiming that a state constitutional provision gave the courts the authority to make whatever rules it thought appropriate for the conduct of a fair election."[23]

Counting noses from the 2020 litigation, then, we see at least four justices—Thomas, Alito, Gorsuch, and Kavanaugh—who embraced the idea that state legislatures essentially have superpowers when regulating federal elections. Under this view, state courts cannot impose different election rules, even to effectuate the right to vote under the state constitution, because doing so would take away the power given to the "legislature" within the Elections Clause of the U.S. Constitution. State election boards or chief election officials also may be hamstrung while administering elections if only the "legislature" can determine election rules.

Notably, Chief Justice Roberts—who embraced an aspect of the independent state legislature concept in his dissent in the 2015 Arizona redistricting case—didn't join these other opinions in the 2020 pandemic disputes. Justice Amy Coney Barrett, confirmed soon before the 2020 election, didn't participate in these cases. The question remained: Was there a fifth vote for this "independent state legislature" idea?

BACK TO THE TAR HEEL STATE

I could teach an entire seminar solely based on North Carolina's gerrymandering battles and I still wouldn't have enough time to cover the myriad lawsuits from the past few decades. There were cases in both federal and state courts after the 1980, 1990, 2000, 2010, and 2020 rounds of redistricting. The litigation sometimes took the entire decade to resolve, only to have the redistricting process start up once again after the next census, when states must redraw their maps. That's what happened in the 2010s. After lengthy litigation spanning many years, the Supreme Court refused to invalidate the state's map in the *Rucho* case in June 2019, yet the state supreme court struck the map down using the state constitution later that year. The court ordered a new map for 2020, and then the process started all over again with the new census data.

In 2021, North Carolina's Republican-controlled legislature once again drew a congressional map that, by all measures, was an extreme gerrymander. The map essentially ensured that ten Republicans and four Democrats would win congressional seats even if the state voted about fifty-fifty between the Republican and Democratic candidates. Plaintiffs sued under the state constitution, contending that the map was unfair and violated several provisions of the North Carolina Constitution. They argued that a map that so severely skews representation violates the constitutional command that a government derives its power from popular sovereignty and must treat everyone equally.

The North Carolina Supreme Court, which elects its justices in partisan races, struck down the map in February 2022 on a 4–3 party-line vote, with all Democrats in the majority (including new Justice Anita Earls, who had litigated the *Rucho* gerrymandering case in the previous decade) and all Republicans in dissent. The majority opened its thorough 143-page opinion with a stark reminder that the case was really about democracy itself:

> Today, we answer this question: does our state constitution recognize that the people of this state have the power to choose those who govern us, by giving each of us an equally powerful voice through our vote? Or does our constitution give to members of the General Assembly, as they argue here, unlimited power to draw electoral maps that keep themselves and our members of Congress in office as long as they want, regardless of the will of the people, by making some votes more powerful than others?[24]

The Court answered that question emphatically on the side of the people: "We hold that our constitution's Declaration of Rights guarantees the equal power of each person's voice in our government through voting in elections that matter."[25]

The majority then engaged in a thorough discussion of the applicable state constitutional protections and the ways in which a skewed map violates the constitutional commands that "[a]ll elections shall be free," that the people have the right to freedom of speech and assembly, and that "[n]o person shall be denied the equal protection of the laws."[26] The language "[a]ll elections shall be free" is particularly important, for there is no analogous clause in the federal constitution. It shows that the North Carolina constitution offers stronger protection for voters than does the U.S. Constitution. A map that essentially dictates the results ahead of time because of how the legislators drew the lines violates these state constitutional commands.

One of the state's arguments to uphold the map invoked the independent state legislature theory to say that the North Carolina Supreme Court did not have the authority to render this decision. The court wholeheartedly rejected the contention: it "is inconsistent with nearly a century of precedent of the Supreme Court of the United States affirmed as recently as 2015. It is also repugnant to the sovereignty of states, the authority of state constitutions, and the independence of state courts, and would produce absurd and dangerous consequences."[27]

The North Carolina Republicans appealed the North Carolina Supreme Court's ruling to the U.S. Supreme Court. Normally, the Supreme Court would not review a decision that involves purely state issues, as the state's highest court is the final arbiter of state law. But the justices found a federal hook to hear the case in the independent state legislature idea. Never mind that the concept is contrary to all reasonable interpretations of separation of powers and state sovereignty. As two law professors put it, the idea is a "seemingly plausible but ultimately preposterous constitutional theory."[28]

The Court heard oral argument in December 2022. The lawyers on both sides advocated passionately for how they thought the Court should rule. The justices asked probing questions on the implications of the concept. The voting rights community waited with bated breath in early 2023 to find out if the justices would add another barrier to voting rights protection, this time cutting off challenges in state courts.

POLITICIANS IN ROBES

As we discussed previously, the North Carolina Supreme Court had struck down the severely gerrymandered map in February 2022 under the state constitution, and the U.S. Supreme Court had agreed to review that decision. But in November 2022, North Carolina held an election for two of the seats on the state supreme court, and two Republicans won.[29] Overnight the court went from a 4–3 Democratic majority to a 5–2 Republican tilt. Almost immediately, the Republican majority announced that it was going to rehear the prior gerrymandering decision.[30]

This move was unprecedented. In the previous thirty years, the North Carolina Supreme Court had agreed to rehear only two cases out of the 214 requests it had received. Both of those cases involved routine matters, not fundamental disagreements with the outcome of a highly charged political case. The only change in this instance had been the court's composition. Justice Anita Earls, dissenting from the rehearing order, lamented that "it took this Court just one month to send a smoke signal to the public that our decisions are fleeting, and our precedent is only as enduring as the terms of the justices who sit on the bench."[31]

The North Carolina Supreme Court heard oral argument on the rehearing in March 2023, but the outcome was preordained: by a 5–2 party-line vote, the court reversed itself, upheld the gerrymandered map, and curtailed the force of the state constitution to protect voters, all in the name of giving more power to state legislators.[32] The court, mimicking the U.S. Supreme Court's decision in *Rucho*, disclaimed any ability for the courts to rein in partisan gerrymandering.

The cruel irony is that there are no longer any judicial checks on partisan maps in North Carolina: the U.S. Supreme Court said that federal courts can't rule against these maps under the U.S. Constitution, and now the state supreme court, after a change in composition, reversed itself and said that state courts were also closed, even when the plaintiffs invoked the fuller protection of the state constitution. So much for adhering to precedent.

Justice Earls once again issued a powerful dissent:

> I dissent from this Court's majority opinion and its shameful manipulation of fundamental principles of our democracy and the rule of law. I look forward to the day when commitment to the constitutional principles of free elections and equal protection of the laws are upheld and the abuses committed by the majority are recognized for what they are, permanently relegating them to the annals of this Court's darkest moments. I have no doubt that day will come.[33]

The North Carolina Supreme Court's decision to reverse itself raised another thorny question: What would happen to the case pending before the U.S. Supreme Court on the independent state legislature idea? Previously, the North Carolina Supreme Court had used the state constitution to strike down the map, and the Republican-controlled legislature had appealed, saying that the state courts were powerless under the U.S. Constitution to render election decisions that limited state laws as applied to federal elections. Now the North Carolina Supreme Court had reversed itself, meaning that the state constitution did not restrict the legislature at all when drawing congressional lines. What would the U.S. Supreme Court do?

A WIN THAT'S NOT REALLY A WIN

Many legal observers (myself included) expected the U.S. Supreme Court to dismiss *Moore v. Harper* after the North Carolina Supreme Court reversed itself because the case was now moot: there was no longer a state-level ruling that rejected the map under the state constitution. In June 2023, however, the Court surprised most people by ruling on the matter—and rejecting the North Carolina Republicans' arguments to fully limit the state supreme court's power. By a 7–2 vote (with Justices Thomas and Alito in dissent), the Court held, "The Elections Clause does not insulate state legislatures from the ordinary exercise of state judicial review."[34] That statement seemed like a big victory. Progressive advocates breathed a sigh of relief, as the Court had ostensibly rejected the independent state legislature theory. The Court looked at precedent and historical practice "to confirm that state legislatures remain bound by state constitutional restraints when exercising authority under the Elections Clause."[35] That is, the stronger protection for voters within state constitutions would still bind state lawmakers when they craft rules for federal elections. State courts could strike down gerrymandered maps under state constitutions.

But Chief Justice Roberts, writing the majority opinion, offered an important and nefarious caveat. He said that "state courts may not transgress the ordinary bounds of judicial review such that they arrogate to themselves the power vested in state legislatures to regulate federal elections."[36] Roberts did not say what he meant by the "ordinary bounds of judicial review." He did not specify when state courts might "arrogate to themselves the power vested in state legislatures." The standard is extremely murky. At some point, it appears, the U.S. Supreme Court can step in to reverse a state court ruling on election law, but we don't know where that point is. The Court therefore did not fully reject the independent state legislature theory. It instead adopted a "weaker" form of the idea, placing power in itself to discern, in future cases, when state courts have gone too far in invalidating a state law under the state constitution. Justice Kavanaugh doubled down on this idea in his concurrence, explaining that "a state court's interpretation of state law in a case implicating the Elections Clause is subject to federal court review."[37]

The implications of this power grab by the Supreme Court justices are immense. The Court gave to itself the authority to determine when a state court has gone too far in ruling on a state law under the state constitution. The Court offered no guidance to state judges on what are the "ordinary bounds of judicial review." It even refused to decide whether the North Carolina Supreme Court had somehow exceeded its authority in this case, saying that the North Carolina Republicans had not sufficiently presented the argument.

By noting that state courts might issue rulings that "transgress the ordinary bounds of judicial review," the Court opened the door to the next battleground for the 2024 election and beyond. As Professor Rick Pildes noted in the *New York Times*, "No great feat of lawyering will be required to transform disputes in federal elections about the actions of state election officials or state courts into federal constitutional claims that assert those state actors have 'gone too far' in their interpretation of state constitutions or state statutes."[38] Will every state judge now be looking over their shoulder, worrying that the U.S. Supreme Court will declare that their decision was not "judicial" in nature? Will the Supreme Court justices overrule state court decisions under state constitutions? No one knows. The broadest form of the independent state legislature idea—the concept that state courts had no power to rule under state constitutions—was bad enough. The vague form of the theory the Court embraced adds the promise of future litigation to the mix, which could even happen during a heated presidential election dispute.

Imagine this scenario: A presidential candidate contests the close election results in a particular state, perhaps basing the challenge on the operation of a state law. Maybe a state court has extended the absentee balloting deadline or struck down a voter ID law under the state constitution to protect the right to vote. Will the U.S. Supreme Court reverse the state court if the justices do not like the state court's outcome? All they would need to cite is the sentence in *Moore v. Harper* that the state court had "transgress[ed] the ordinary bounds of judicial review." The justices have declared themselves to be the final arbiter of the fairness of American democracy. Perhaps that prospect would be less concerning if the Court had consistently demonstrated a commitment to all voters. But, as we have seen, current jurisprudence favors those already in charge.

Ultimately, voters have fewer places to turn to vindicate their rights. The Court had already narrowed the protection for the right to vote under the U.S. Constitution. The justices then said that state supreme courts might go too far in interpreting their state constitutions, but the U.S. Supreme Court has, at least for now, refused to say where the line is between a permissible interpretation of a state constitution and an invalid one. Any curtailment of the authority of a state supreme court to use its state constitution closes off an important avenue of rights protection. Both textually and historically, state constitutions are stronger than the U.S. Constitution in the safeguards they offer to voters. Stripping state supreme courts of their authority to uphold these rights will only hurt voters and help politicians. It will mean that state legislators have little oversight in the election rules they can pass. They will have every self-interested incentive to enact rules to help keep themselves in office. Power has devolved away from voters and into the hands of state legislators. Those legislators—many of whom won their seats thanks to extreme gerrymandering—will inevitably pass rules that make it harder to vote them out.

State legislatures can pass unfair maps, strict voter ID rules, limits to early voting, or other restrictive election measures without meaningful judicial oversight. Both federal courts and state courts present uphill battles for the protection of the fundamental right to vote. Plaintiffs can't turn to federal courts and invoke the U.S. Constitution or the federal Voting Rights Act because the Supreme Court's rulings, which offer extreme deference to state legislatures, have made it so much harder for voters to win these cases. State courts might be a viable avenue for voters to vindicate their rights—until the U.S. Supreme Court steps in to push back against a state court's interpretation of its own state constitution. Whichever way voters turn, the Supreme Court has used fancy-sounding legal theories to make it harder for voters to win. As a result, democracy loses.

The advocacy for the independent state legislature theory, even in the weaker form that the Court embraced, is the culmination of a several-decades push to take the courts out of the election business altogether. That approach might make sense under an extreme federalist theory of government that suggests power should flow to state legislators, as those elected officials are closest to the people. The problem is that in election law, the interests of politicians and the interests of voters often clash. State legislators want to stay in power, and achieving that goal might mean suppressing the vote of those who will oppose them. The Court used to recognize that, in the unique realm of election law, legislators need more scrutiny, not less. But the era when we could count on the Supreme Court to vindicate our rights is over. Because of the Court's rulings, our governmental structure is much less focused on "We the People."

"We the Politicians" is, unfortunately, more accurate.

CONCLUSION

I t was the perfect storm. First, conservative Justice Antonin Scalia passed away in February 2016, a presidential election year, creating a key vacancy on the Supreme Court. Instead of holding the necessary hearings for Merrick Garland, President Barack Obama's eminently qualified nominee, Senate Majority Leader Mitch McConnell stonewalled, saying that the "American people should have a voice" in who will appoint the next justice.[1] Against all odds, Donald Trump won the presidency and immediately selected conservative Neil Gorsuch for the spot. Step one of the plan to transform the Court was complete.

Next, the then-current swing justice, Anthony Kennedy, resigned from his seat in 2018, and President Trump appointed Kennedy's former law clerk and protégé, Brett Kavanaugh, as his replacement. Step two, done.

Finally, Justice Ruth Bader Ginsburg—the "notorious RBG," as her fans called her—passed away in September 2020, less than two months before the next presidential election. But instead of giving the American people "a voice" by letting the winner of the 2020 election choose her successor, McConnell pushed through Trump appointee Amy Coney Barrett a mere week before Election Day and after millions of Americans had already cast their ballots through early voting. That gave the Supreme Court—which had more or less been a 5–4 Court with the centrist Justice Anthony Kennedy in the middle—a solid 6–3 conservative majority. Think of it this way: if the Senate had confirmed the moderate Merrick Garland, and had Ruth Bader Ginsburg lived just a few months longer— allowing new president Joe Biden to fill her seat—then the Court today would have a 5–4 liberal or moderate tilt.

Instead, the Court is much more conservative than it has been in decades. That reality has stark consequences for our democracy. The cases profiled in this book—and others that rest upon them—have skewed our democracy toward the wealthy and entrenched. Politicians will continue to use the Court to craft strict rules that help to keep themselves in power. Everyday voters—and the overall structure of American democracy—remain the victims.

Although the Supreme Court has narrowed the protection for the right to vote under the U.S. Constitution, state constitutions can still safeguard democracy, even with the potential of the Court invoking the supposedly milder form of the independent state legislature theory to cabin their reach. All fifty state constitutions demand fair elections and offer more robust protection for voters than what's found in the U.S. Constitution, as limited by the U.S. Supreme Court. Calling upon state constitutions is therefore still a viable legal path to uphold the fundamental right to vote, at least for state and local elections. Lawyers should double down on state constitutional litigation and activists should continue to push for broader voting rights enhancements within state constitutions.

Even with state constitutions as a bulwark, however, it's difficult to envision a fair democracy—where voters reign supreme—with a Court that is anti-democracy. We could, of course, throw up our hands about the current state of the law and lament the democracy that was. We could retreat into our everyday lives, figuring that we can't change the system. That's the easy path. But that's not my style. Instead, we must find tangible solutions to create a democratic structure that is truly reflective of the will of the people. We can stop asking "What might have been?" and instead ask "What might be possible?"

I see three paths, which we should pursue simultaneously: (1) the voting rights community should seek compromise in voting legislation and avoid the Supreme Court altogether, if possible; (2) we must have a serious conversation about meaningful—and reasonable—Court reform; and (3) we should further mobilize the electorate, using these anti-democracy cases as the linchpin for a new movement.

The Supreme Court has harmed American democracy, but there's still a path to fix it. A better election system is within reach.

THERE'S SOMETHING IN THE WATER (OR BOURBON) IN KENTUCKY

In 2021, Kentucky—a reliably red state—made national news for bucking the trend: it expanded the right to vote. The state enacted a bipartisan bill to both improve access to the ballot and tackle election security. Among other reforms, the state adopted three days of early voting—up from zero—while also mandating paper ballots, which are more secure. Passing the law took a conscious effort to seek common ground, reach across the aisle, ask for input from election experts, and make reasonable compromises. I would have liked seven days of early voting, for example, but three is certainly better than none. The result was a bill that both sides could support. Everyone had a stake in making it better. The law was not challenged in court, as hardly anyone felt aggrieved by the final product. Even if someone had sued, the courts probably would have upheld the law given how reasonable it is.

Republican Secretary of State Michael Adams, a pro-democracy conservative who led the effort, focused on reforms that would improve election administration. I had the good fortune of informally advising him on Kentucky election law, and what I noticed from those conversations was a real desire to serve the voters and the election system as a whole—while convincing lawmakers, especially of his own party, that the voting changes were good policy and also made political sense.

While election rules are undoubtedly polarized, there are seeds in this Kentucky story of what I call a Grand Election Compromise. This framework could help us craft better election rules while also avoiding the Supreme Court altogether. If there is true compromise, with both sides achieving some of what they want, then it's less likely that someone would sue to strike down a law. Yes, this approach requires a recommitment to democratic ideals from both sides. Perhaps there is a silent virtue to the Court's too-narrow jurisprudence on voting rights: it forces us to double down on bipartisanship and compromise so that we can keep these issues away from the Court.

The Grand Election Compromise entails four ideals that Democrats, Republicans, and everyone else should acknowledge and accept as a foundational starting point for our conversations:

1. Every eligible citizen should be allowed to vote with minimal burden.

2. The system should acknowledge concerns about the potential for fraud and set up ways to deter it.
3. Voters should be as educated as possible.
4. Elections should be won by ideas, not by the rules of the game or the partisanship of election officials. This also means that losers should readily accept their defeat.

These propositions are not controversial—or at least, they shouldn't be! They all derive from an understanding that democracy requires the consent of the governed, which is a fundamental principle enshrined in our Declaration of Independence. They were at the heart of the compromise deal in Kentucky, and they can provide a baseline for future discussions. We can use that compromise as a seed for further conversations on the harder questions: abolishing the Electoral College, fixing Senate (mis)representation, and the like. We can tackle the most difficult issues only if we relearn how to talk to each other first. American democracy requires two viable political parties who are both committed to the ideal that the voters decide who is in power. Finding compromise in election rules, that both sides will see as legitimate, is a virtue—and can sustain our democracy. We should rightly brand anyone who opposes them as anti-democracy.

Who could reasonably object to the idea that election rules should satisfy the dual goals of making it easier to vote for those who are eligible and creating a system that deters fraud? Who could oppose a rule that promotes voter education or that focuses our elections on the voters instead of the politicians? Shouldn't the losers always graciously admit their defeat, fighting their battles in the next election by convincing voters of their cause? These ideals are somewhat vague, but they provide a framework for evaluating a proposed election rule. If a new law does not promote these goals—and if it goes directly contrary to any of them—then it should be rejected as anti-democracy.

A majority of justices on the Supreme Court have proved time and time again that they will issue rulings that help politicians and harm voters. So, let's just avoid the Court altogether. Let's join conservatives and liberals through the Grand Election Compromise. Let's allow the four ideals of the Grand Election Compromise to guide future policymaking. Sure, we should sue if legislatures enact laws that harm voters, ideally in state courts using state constitutions, but maybe we can follow Kentucky as a template to find compromise that makes litigation not as necessary.

JUSTICES SHOULD NOT SERVE FOR DECADES

I'm not so naïve to believe that the Court will never issue additional, harmful election law rulings. There will, of course, be litigation as states continue to pass restrictive voting rules. Not everyone will embrace the Grand Election Compromise. We need a solution that focuses directly on the anti-democracy forces that control the Court.

In the wake of Senator McConnell's refusal to let the Senate consider Judge Merrick Garland, President Obama's nominee to the Court, followed by President Donald Trump's successful nominations of three conservative jurists, many on the left called for Court packing, or the addition of more justices to the Court. At least one (and maybe more) of the justices received their spots in illegitimate ways, the argument goes, so it makes sense to counter them with additional justices. Plus, the threat of Court packing worked in the 1930s to stop the Court from dismantling many of FDR's New Deal initiatives. The Constitution does not set the number of justices; Congress, in fact, has changed the size of the Court several times in the past, though the tradition of nine justices has continued since 1869. Congress could change it again.

I'm not convinced, however, that Court packing makes sense in this political climate. The Court could certainly use more justices. There are twelve regional circuit courts of appeals and a thirteenth subject-specific appellate court, so maybe twelve or thirteen justices makes sense. My main concern is that this move would be a pure power grab. In response, once conservatives control Congress and the presidency, they would add seats to counter the new liberal justices. Would Democrats then have to add more members to counter those new "Republican" seats? It's a tit-for-tat with seemingly no end point. Already, after what McConnell did to stymie the Garland nomination, it's reasonable to ask whether a future president could ever fill a vacancy if the opposing party controls the Senate. We might have vacancies last for years. We need to find a way to reduce the salience of these fights.

There are stronger reforms that strike more at the heart of the Court's anti-democracy forces and will help the Court function better in the long term, without risking an escalating arms race over the number of justices.

First, Supreme Court justices should be subject to term limits of eighteen years.[2] Most political scientists agree that term limits make no sense for elected officials, as they lead to weaker legislatures, increased polarization, and lower quality democratic representation.[3] But judges don't represent people in the same way. Several states have a mandatory retirement age for their state supreme court justices and the process works well.[4] In the same vein, U.S. Supreme Court justices shouldn't serve for life. The long tenure makes them too insulated from the real world. The happenstance of a justice's death or retirement shouldn't create such a monumental change in the law.

Eighteen-year term limits make sense because they would provide a natural rotation where every president will have two appointees per four-year term. Evening out Supreme Court appointments could lower the temperature of the nomination battles. Several Democratic members of Congress have introduced a bill to enact this reform, though some opponents question whether it would be constitutional.[5] There's at least a good argument that there are no constitutional hurdles so long as an outgoing justice still retains their status as a senior justice, meaning they could hear cases on the lower federal courts and keep their salary. In any event, term limits are a viable solution to make Supreme Court battles less consequential, which would hopefully reduce the incentive to nominate justices who are ideologues. And even if the Court were still populated with extreme partisans, at least they wouldn't serve for as long. True, as some scholars note, eighteen-year term limits could increase polarization by making every election a referendum on the Court—though in some ways that is already occurring.[6] Regardless, at least the rotation of justices would be a lot more regular, which scholars suggest could reduce the time when the Court suffers from extreme ideological imbalances.[7]

Second, an even better idea would be to mimic the practice of the courts of appeals by increasing the number of justices on the Court and then having them sit in smaller panels. Most federal appeals courts have between eleven and seventeen total judges (though the First Circuit has six and the Ninth Circuit has twenty-nine), who hear cases in three-judge panels that are randomly selected. The full court can sit en banc, or with all the judges on that court, to rehear a case (except for the Ninth Circuit, which holds its en banc sessions with a subset of the twenty-nine). Each court also has senior judges, who are essentially semiretired but who can hear cases in these three-judge panels as well.

The practice of sitting in three-judge panels means that one panel must pay attention to the other panels and try to conform their decisions accordingly. A panel can't go completely rogue, as the full court might decide to review that panel's decision, although the courts hold only a few of these all-judge en banc sittings each year. Each individual nomination to the appeals courts is important, but perhaps the stakes are lowered because each judge won't hear every case that comes before the court.

Congress could adopt a similar process for the Supreme Court. There could be fifteen justices who sit in panels of nine (or five or three) based on a random draw. Any panel could not overrule a prior Supreme Court decision. All fifteen justices sitting together en banc would have to consider that kind of ruling. To be sure, the most controversial cases would still likely go before the full fifteen-member Court, so combining this reform with reasonable term limits would reduce the likelihood of entrenched ideology reinfecting the Court. As two law professors who proposed a similar idea put it, a slightly larger Court that sits in panels might hear more cases each year, which "would enable the Court to provide a check against the other branches and lower courts, generate a more understandable and accurate body of law, and ensure greater consistency in the laws that govern citizens across the country."[8] On cases involving democracy itself, the random draw would lessen the likelihood of ideology driving the decisions—though there is the risk that the full en banc Court would just take all of these controversial cases, minimizing the effectiveness of this reform.

Third, again borrowing from the practice of the federal appeals courts, the Supreme Court could have a rotating cast of appellate and district court judges sit "by designation" on the Supreme Court. Currently, district court judges often sit on three-judge panels of the courts of appeals. Appellate judges also visit other courts of appeals in different parts of the country and hear cases there. This practice gives the judges valuable experience and places the focus of each decision on the law and precedent, not on the particular judges themselves. Why not let these judges visit the Supreme Court as well? There's nothing magical about the work of the Supreme Court. Its docket is almost entirely a review of federal trial and intermediate court decisions, as well as appeals from state supreme courts when there are federal constitutional issues involved. Any federal judge could do this work on occasion, which will also likely improve their decision-making processes when they return to their own courts. And, once again, a rotation of "justices" to hear cases at their final stage might reduce the extent to which ideology infects the decisions, especially if Supreme Court panels are chosen randomly from all appeals and district court judges.[9] Scholars have also proposed the requirement of a "balanced bench," with a Court composed of five Democratic-appointed justices, five Republican-appointed justices, and five additional members from the courts of appeals whom those ten select unanimously.[10]

There is a strong argument that the Supreme Court needs serious reform. None of the ideas here—term limits, a larger Court that sits in panels, and a rotation among lower-court judges—has an obvious partisan valence, though no reform will eliminate ideology entirely. It's impossible to predict how these changes would impact the Court's decisions—which is exactly the point. The current Court is out of step with American democracy. Ratcheting up the partisanship of the Court by adding additional Democratic-appointed justices is not a viable long-term answer. We should instead focus on reforms that can gain bipartisan support because they will improve the operation of the Court for all.

"END CITIZENS UNITED"

None of the ideas for Court reform will happen overnight. Although not as radical as Court packing, they still take strong political will to implement. The American polity must recognize the danger of the Court's current jurisprudence and demand real solutions. That requires a political movement. We should use the anti-democracy cases to mobilize the electorate to press for real reform.

Chapter 5 mentioned the group End Citizens United, which focuses on the problem of money in politics. This organization offers a great example of how to use a harmful Supreme Court case to focus the public's attention on a judicial decision that damages democracy. The group has made real headway.

Some of my political science friends helped me run a survey in summer 2022 to ask a representative sample of Americans about their views on important election law cases. We gave half of the respondents a list of cases from the past fifty years and asked which one has "been the most harmful to American democracy and our elections. Even if you think multiple cases have been harmful, please choose the one that you think has been most harmful to American democracy and our elections."

Twenty-seven percent of the respondents chose *Citizens United*. *Bush v. Gore* came in second, with 26 percent. Over 11 percent of the respondents clicked "other" and most wrote that they didn't know, though a handful listed something related to abortion, which was not surprising given that our survey went out just as the Court was overturning *Roe v. Wade* in the summer of 2022.

Results of Author's Survey on Most Harmful Cases to American Democracy

CASE	PERCENT
Citizens United v. Federal Election Commission (2010)	27.36
Bush v. Gore (2000)	26.43
Brnovich v. Democratic National Committee (2021)	11.29
Crawford v. Marion County Election Board (2008)	9.16
Rucho v. Common Cause (2019)	7.70
Shelby County, Ala. v. Holder (2013)	6.64
Other (please list)	11.42

We asked the other half of respondents, who had not seen the list of cases from the previous inquiry, an open-ended question: "What U.S. Supreme Court case from the past 50 years do you think has been the most harmful to American democracy and our elections?" This question helped us gauge whether there were cases that had entered the public consciousness so much that everyday Americans could name them, even without giving the respondents any case names. Not surprisingly, 57 percent of our survey takers did not identify a case, most saying they didn't know. Of those who listed a case or issue, about a third said "abortion," which again is unsurprising given the national debate on abortion rights at that time. The next listed case was *Citizens United* or a mention of campaign finance, identified by just under 14 percent of those who offered a response to this question. No other case came close in the frequency of responses.

This data suggests that *Citizens United*, or at least the issue of money in politics, remains a salient flash point for a good number of Americans. Advocates for a stronger democracy should use this information to engage in further mobilization efforts. After all, the main antidote to anti-democracy forces is to improve voter turnout by a massive amount. Americans still believe in democracy. We don't always vote, and even when we do, we often don't put democracy issues at the forefront. That needs to change.

Those who seek meaningful reform should use the anti-democracy tendencies of the Supreme Court to foster a movement in favor of pro-democracy candidates, of whatever political party. A fidelity to democratic principles should be a litmus test for any future justices. Moreover, soundly rejecting anti-democracy candidates at the ballot will demonstrate Americans' faith in democracy.

None of this is easy. The whole point of many of these judicial decisions is to enshrine rules that make it more likely for incumbents to win. Deference to state politicians on election policies produces incentives for extreme gerrymandering, restrictive voting rules, and a derogation of the laws that protect marginalized communities. It would take a true political wave to overcome these structural hurdles. But that's what is needed to defeat the anti-democracy mentality that pervades many aspects of our government.

In short, we need to vote the bums out. We need to create a political culture in which democracy issues are at the forefront. We need to strive for massive turnout. Currently, turnout in presidential elections is below 70 percent and turnout in midterms hovers around 50 percent—and those numbers are already historically high as compared to just a few years ago. Why not 90 percent turnout or higher? There are significant hurdles to the ballot box for certain constituencies. We need to find ways to help these individuals overcome those barriers. A massive political movement is a necessary response to these challenges.

———

In his famous essay in the Federalist Papers, known as Federalist #78, Alexander Hamilton wrote that the judiciary "will always be the least dangerous to the political rights of the Constitution; because it will be least in a capacity to annoy or injure them." The executive branch—the presidency—has the power of the sword; Congress has the power of the purse; but the judiciary has "merely judgment."[11]

As we have seen, however, over the five decades since the early 1970s, the Supreme Court has taken on an outsized role in curtailing political rights. It's become perhaps the *most* dangerous branch because of its effect on the makeup of the other two branches, thanks to its restrictive voting rights decisions.

But in a democracy, the people reign supreme. Although the Court has made our jobs much harder, we can still out-organize, out-mobilize, and out-vote those who espouse anti-democracy views. This is not a short-term fix. We must double down on our commitment to create an inclusive democracy, where the voters—not the Supreme Court, entrenched politicians, or restrictive voting rules—determine the outcome.

As Benjamin Franklin left the Constitutional Convention in 1787, a woman asked him whether the delegates had created a republic or a monarchy. Franklin's famous response: "A republic, if you can keep it."[12]

It's up to all of us to keep it.

ACKNOWLEDGMENTS

Writing a book is an audacious thing to do. It takes blind faith, a lot of luck, and tons of time in front of a computer screen. Thankfully, I have been fortunate to have family, friends, colleagues, and students who have all supported this endeavor. It's not hyperbole to say that this book would not be a reality without their love, guidance, and support.

First, I thank the J. David Rosenberg College of Law at the University of Kentucky for its assistance, both moral and financial. Several colleagues read draft chapters, listened to my ruminations, and offered wisdom. The university provided summer research funds to support this project. I am grateful.

I had an unrivaled team of law student research assistants who made every word, page, chapter, figure, and end note better. All of the good stuff in this book is thanks to them and all of the mistakes are my own. Faith Evans, Macin Graber, Emily Shepard, Michaela Taylor, and Whit Wiman: Thank you for all of your help! You are going to have long and storied careers and I can't wait to watch you thrive. Thanks also to the students who enrolled in my Election Law course and who endured hearing about the progress of this book as I was researching and writing.

Many people read all or part of this book and offered valuable feedback. I am particularly indebted to Bill Fortune and Tony Gaughan for reading the entire manuscript as I was writing and providing helpful suggestions. Thanks also to Jessie Amunson, Adam Bozzi, Chris Bradley, Susan Dellarosa, Allan Douglas (hi Dad!), Ben Douglas, Caitlyn Douglas, Anita Earls, Adam Eichen, Art Eisenberg, Irma Fallon (hi Mom!), George Frampton, Ruth Greenwood, Roz Heise, Kristen Janicki, Alan Kluegel, Ian MacDougall, Jim Mason, Mary Marchetto, Jenny Mitchell (and the

Washington and Lee Law Library), Laurie Nichols, Trevor Potter, Jonathan Shaub, Nick Stephanopoulos, Mark SooHoo, Franita Tolson, Roger Wallace (my sixth-grade teacher!), and Richard Winger for reading draft chapters, pointing me toward sources, talking through the issues, and offering other assistance. Thanks also to Justin Wedeking and Mike Zilis for help on the survey discussed in the Conclusion. I'm amazed at how many people from different parts of my life believed in this book and offered their time, encouragement, and assistance. I also thank the numerous people I interviewed whose stories helped the chapters come alive. I learned so much from all of you.

There's no book without a great team behind the scenes. My agent, Lucy Cleland at Calligraph, believed in this project—and in me—from the beginning. Lucy, I am fortunate to have you by my side. Joanna Green at Beacon Press embraced this project from the start and offered immensely valuable editing expertise. Susan Lumenello and Katherine Scott parsed each word to make the writing stronger.

To the loves of my life—my reason for existence: Bari, my love, I am nothing without you. What started as a late-night conversation in a college dorm room in August 1999 has blossomed into the incredible life we have created. Thank you for always supporting (almost!) every crazy idea I've ever had. When I said I planned to write a second book, you didn't bat an eye. You have been my rock forever and I'm so proud that our love story continues.

Caitlyn and Harrison: my greatest joy in life is to be your dad. I am so proud of both of you for who you are: kind, sweet, generous, fun-loving, goofy(!), incredible kids. You amaze me every day—from success in Speech Team or on the stage to solid base hits on the baseball field to simply hearing your giggles as you play with each other outside. Thanks for enduring the times when I was on my computer instead of playing with you to write this book. Let's go out for ice cream sundaes to celebrate when this book is published!

Finally, to you, the reader: thank you for reading! As a law professor of voting rights, I firmly believe that one of my jobs is to explain these vital concepts to voters, who are the lifeblood of our democracy. I hope this book provided you with the knowledge you need to keep fighting for the democracy that we all hold so dear.

NOTES

INTRODUCTION

1. "Speech by Franklin D. Roosevelt, New York (Transcript)," Dec. 8, 1941, Library of Congress, https://www.loc.gov/resource/afc1986022.afc1986022_ms2201/?st=text.

2. Karen Yourish, Larry Buchanan, and Denise Lu, "The 147 Republicans Who Voted to Overturn Election Results," *New York Times*, Jan. 7, 2021, https://www.nytimes.com/interactive/2021/01/07/us/elections/electoral-college-biden-objectors.html.

3. "ABC News/Ipsos Poll," Ipsos, Jan. 8–9, 2021, https://www.ipsos.com/sites/default/files/ct/news/documents/2021-01/topline_abc_ipsos_poll_january_10_2021_final.pdf.

4. "ABC News/Ipsos Poll."

5. "Cross-Tabs for October 2022 Times/Siena Poll of Registered Voters," *New York Times*, Oct. 18, 2022, https://www.nytimes.com/interactive/2022/10/18/upshot/times-siena-poll-registered-voters-crosstabs.html.

6. *Positive Views of Supreme Court Decline Sharply Following Abortion Ruling*, Pew Research Center, Sept. 1, 2022, https://www.pewresearch.org/politics/2022/09/01/positive-views-of-supreme-court-decline-sharply-following-abortion-ruling.

7. Alexander Keyssar, *The Right to Vote: The Contested History of Democracy in the United States* (New York: Basic Books, 2000), 24.

8. Reynolds v. Sims, 377 U.S. 533 (1964); Harper v. Virginia State Bd. of Elections, 383 U.S. 663 (1966); Kramer v. Union Free Sch. Dist. No. 15, 395 U.S. 621 (1969).

9. On the scholarly front, my approach in this book—to look at election law cases that have harmed democracy—essentially is an argument for an anti-canon of election law. On anti-canons of constitutional law, see Richard Primus, "Canon, Anti-Canon, and Judicial Dissent," 48 *Duke Law Journal* 243 (1998); Jamal Greene, "The Anticanon," 125 *Harvard Law Review* 379 (2011).

10. Stephen Fowler, "A New Georgia Voting Law Reduced Ballot Drop Box Access in Places That Used Them Most," NPR, July 27, 2022, https://www.npr.org/2022/07/27/1112487312/georgia-voting-law-ballot-drop-box-access.

11. Erik J. Engstrom and Jason M. Roberts, "A Federal Court Struck Down Much of North Carolina's Voter ID Law—But What's Left Could Still Shrink the Black Vote," *Washington Post*, Oct. 5, 2016, https://www.washingtonpost.com /news/monkey-cage/wp/2016/10/05/a-federal-court-struck-down-much-of-the -voter-id-law-in-north-carolina-but-a-remaining-provision-could-affect-the-black -vote.

12. Rebecca Leber, "In Texas, You Can Vote with a Concealed Handgun License—But Not a Student ID," *New Republic*, Oct. 20, 2014, https://newrepublic .com/article/119900/texas-voter-id-allows-handgun-licenses-not-student-ids.

CHAPTER 1: THE 1980 ELECTION AND THE BEGINNING OF THE END

1. "1980 Presidential Election," 270 to Win (website), https://www.270towin .com/1980_Election.

2. "1980 Presidential Election."

3. "1980 Presidential Election."

4. "Anderson, John Bayard," *Biographical Directory of the United States Congress*, https://bioguide.congress.gov/search/bio/a000195; Adam Clymer, "John Anderson, Who Ran Against Reagan and Carter in 1980, Is Dead at 95," *New York Times*, Dec. 4, 2017, https://www.nytimes.com/2017/12/04/us/politics/john-anderson-who-ran -against-reagan-and-carter-in-1980-is-dead-at-95.html.

5. "Statement from the Family of John B. Anderson," *FairVote*, Dec. 4, 2017, https://www.fairvote.org/statement_from_the_family_of_john_b_anderson.

6. Margot Hornblower, "Anderson: Steady and Self-Confident," *Washington Post*, Oct. 23, 1980, https://www.washingtonpost.com/archive/politics/1980/10/23 /anderson-steady-and-self-confident/6401908d-fc90-4eaa-8243-a0cec5b3989e.

7. Sara Burnett, "John Anderson, 1922–2017," Associated Press, Dec. 4, 2017, https://www.legacy.com/news/celebrity-deaths/john-anderson-1922-2017-former -longtime-illinois-congressman/.

8. Scott Simon, "Remembering John Anderson," NPR, Dec. 9, 2017, https:// www.npr.org/2017/12/09/569601024/remembering-john-b-anderson.

9. Rob Richie, "Remembering John Bayard Anderson, 1922–2017," *FairVote*, Dec. 4, 2017, https://www.fairvote.org/remembering_john_bayard_anderson_1922 _2017.

10. Hornblower, "Anderson"; Clymer, "John Anderson."

11. Jim Mason, email to author, June 8, 2022.

12. Anderson v. Celebrezze, 499 F. Supp. 121, 141 (S.D. Ohio 1980) (Appendix); Hornblower, "Anderson"; Jim Mason, *No Holding Back: The 1980 John B. Anderson Presidential Campaign* (Lanham, MD: Rowman & Littlefield, 2011), 505.

13. Clymer, "John Anderson."

14. Mason, *No Holding Back*, 12.

15. Bill Peterson, "John Anderson's 'Unlikely' Campaign an Air of Unreality at the End," *Washington Post*, Nov. 3, 1980, https://www.washingtonpost.com/archive /politics/1980/11/03/john-andersons-unlikely-campaign-an-air-of-unreality-at-the -end/d749a4b8-7e1b-454d-aede-ee9bdcc4befa; Mason, *No Holding Back*.

16. *Anderson*, 499 F. Supp. at 123.

17. Id. at 141.

18. Id. at 123.

19. David M. Ifshin and Roger E. Warin, "Litigating the 1980 Presidential Election," 31 *American University Law Review* 485, 485 (1982).

20. *Anderson*, 499 F. Supp. at 123.

21. Id. at 127.

22. George Frampton (cofounder and board chair, Partnership for Responsible Growth), author interview, Aug. 12, 2021. All interviews were conducted via Zoom unless otherwise noted.

23. See Maurice N. Nessen, "Book Review: *Stonewall: The Real Story of the Watergate Prosecution*, by Richard Ben-Veniste and George Frampton," 77 *Columbia Law Review* 963 (1977), https://www.jstor.org/stable/1121984; see also Richard Ben-Veniste and George Frampton, *Stonewall: The Legal Case Against the Watergate Conspirators* (New York: Touchstone, 1978).

24. Frampton interview.

25. *Anderson*, 499 F. Supp. at 125 (citations and quotation marks omitted).

26. Baker v. Carr, 369 U.S. 186, 208 (1962).

27. Id. at 242 (Douglas, J., concurring).

28. Reynolds v. Sims, 377 U.S. 533, 555 (1964).

29. Harper v. Virginia State Bd. of Elections, 383 U.S. 663, 667 (1966).

30. Wesberry v. Sanders, 376 U.S. 1, 17 (1964).

31. Yick Wo v. Hopkins, 118 U.S. 356, 370 (1886).

32. Kramer v. Union Free Sch. Dist. No. 15, 395 U.S. 621, 628 (1969).

33. *Anderson*, 499 F. Supp. at 125.

34. Id. at 124.

35. Id. at 127.

36. Celebrezze v. Anderson, 448 U.S. 918 (1980).

37. Memorandum from Lewis F. Powell Jr., J., U.S., to Conference of Supreme Court Justices, on 80–182 *Celebrezze*, (Sept. 12, 1980) (on file with the Washington and Lee University Library).

38. Clymer, "John Anderson."

39. Peterson, "John Anderson's 'Unlikely' Campaign."

40. Clymer, "John Anderson."

41. Peterson, "John Anderson's 'Unlikely' Campaign."

42. Peterson, "John Anderson's 'Unlikely' Campaign."

43. Frampton interview.

44. Anderson v. Celebrezze, 664 F.2d 554 (6th Cir. 1981).

45. Id. at 564.

46. Frampton interview.

47. "Anderson v. Celebrezze, Oral Argument—December 6, 1982," Anderson v. Celebrezze, 460 U.S. 780 (1983) (No. 81-1635), Oyez, https://www.oyez.org/cases/1982/81-1635, at 5:44.

48. Id. at 26:02.

49. Frampton interview.

50. Frampton interview.

51. Anderson v. Celebrezze, 460 U.S. 780, 786 (1983).

52. Id. at 786–87.

53. Id. at 792.

54. Id. at 788.

55. Id. at 789.

56. On the impact of independent candidates, see Paul R. Abramson, John H. Aldrich, Philip Paolino, and David W. Rohde, "Challenges to the American Two-Party System: Evidence from the 1968, 1980, 1992, and 1996 Presidential Elections," 53 *Political Research Quarterly* 495, 513 (2000).

57. Cody S. Barnett and Joshua A. Douglas, "A Voice in the Wilderness: John Paul Stevens, Election Law, and a Theory of Impartial Governance," 60 *William & Mary Law Review* 335, 366 (2018).

58. *Anderson*, 460 U.S. at 808 (Rehnquist, J., dissenting).

59. Id. at 818.

60. Id. at 817.

61. Papers of Justice Harry Blackmun (1982), Box 377, 81–1635, "Anderson v. Celebrezze" folder, Manuscripts Division, Library of Congress.

62. Clymer, "John Anderson."

CHAPTER 2: A VOTE FOR DONALD DUCK

1. Alan Burdick (vice president, Americans for Democratic Action Hawaii), author interview, Sept. 19, 2021; Robert Reinhold, "Hawaii Lawsuit May Test Limits of Write-In Votes," *New York Times*, Aug. 29, 1991, https://www.nytimes.com/1991 /08/29/us/hawaii-lawsuit-may-test-limits-of-write-in-votes.html.

2. Burdick interview.

3. Canaan v. Abdelnour, 710 P.2d 268 (Cal. 1985), overruled by Edelstein v. City & Cty. of San Francisco, 56 P.3d 1029 (Cal. 2002).

4. Alan Burdick, attorney, letter to Gerard Jervis, director of research for the Office of the Lieutenant Governor, State of Hawaii, June 6, 1986.

5. Charleen M. Aina, deputy attorney general, State of Hawaii, letter to Gerard Jervis, director of research for the Office of the Lieutenant Governor, State of Hawaii, July 11, 1986.

6. Burdick interview.

7. Anthony J. Gaughan, "Voting in Colonial and Revolutionary America," *Oxford Handbook of American Election Law* (forthcoming, 2024), manuscript in author's collection.

8. Burson v. Freeman, 504 U.S. 191, 200 (1992).

9. Id. at 201, n6, quoting James Lindsay Gordon, *The Protection of Suffrage* (Charlottesville, VA: Chronicle and Brand, 1891), 13, quoted in E. Evans, *A History of the Australian Ballot System in the United States* (Chicago: University of Chicago Press, 1917), 11.

10. Id. at 202 (internal quotation marks and citations omitted).

11. Information from this paragraph and the ones that precede it are derived mostly from *Burson*.

12. Cole v. Tucker, 41 N.E. 681 (Mass. 1895).

13. Oughton v. Black, 61 A. 346, 348 (Pa. 1905).

14. Debbi Wilgoren, "Murkowski Appears to Make History in Alaska," *Washington Post*, Nov. 3, 2010, https://www.washingtonpost.com/wp-dyn/content/article /2010/11/03/AR2010110302555.html.

15. In 1946, William Knowland was the first person to win an election to the U.S. Senate as a write-in candidate. California governor Earl Warren appointed

Knowland to the U.S. Senate in 1945 to fill a vacancy caused by the death of Senator Hiram W. Johnson. Knowland then won two elections on the same day in November 1946, one of them as a write-in candidate. The first election was to fill the rest of Johnson's term from November until January 1947; no candidates appeared on that part of the ballot, so Knowland won with write-in votes. He also won the regular election on the same day to a full six-year term. See "Knowland, William Fife, 1908–1974," *Biographical Directory of the United States Congress*, https://bioguide.congress.gov/search/bio/K000292; "Election History for the State of California, November 5, 1946," Join California, http://www.joincalifornia.com/election/1946-11-05.

16. "Senator Elected on a Write-in Ballot," U.S. Senate, https://www.senate.gov/artandhistory/history/minute/Senator_Elected_on_Write_in_Ballot.htm.

17. Sue Anne Pressley, "In Tennessee, a Lawmaker Dies and His Rival Vanishes," *Washington Post*, Oct. 23, 1998, https://www.washingtonpost.com/archive/politics/1998/10/23/in-tennessee-a-lawmaker-dies-and-his-rival-vanishes/bba7c955-3694-4451-8b5c-3c0c564322da; Amy Argetsinger, "Who Are You Writing In? The Overwhelming Allure of Voting for Someone Who Won't Win," *Washington Post*, Nov. 3, 2016, https://www.washingtonpost.com/lifestyle/style/who-are-you-writing-in-the-overwhelming-allure-of-voting-for-someone-who-wont-win/2016/11/03/472da8ec-9f14-11e6-a44d-cc2898cfab06_story.html; Associated Press, "Widow of Tennessee Senator Defeats Rival Accused in Slaying," *Los Angeles Times*, Nov. 4, 1998, https://web.archive.org/web/20160306193000/http://articles.latimes.com/1998/nov/04/news/mn-39309; Associated Press, "Candidate's Widow Wins in Tennessee," *New York Times*, Nov. 5, 1998, https://www.nytimes.com/1998/11/05/us/the-1998-elections-the-states-candidate-s-widow-wins-in-tennessee.html.

18. "Charlotte Burks," *Ballotpedia*, https://ballotpedia.org/Charlotte_Burks.

19. Reinhold, "Hawaii Lawsuit."

20. Reinhold, "Hawaii Lawsuit."

21. Wolfgang Saxon, "Harold Fong, 56, Judge in Center of Dispute on Write-In Ballots," *New York Times*, Apr. 22, 1995, https://www.nytimes.com/1995/04/22/obituaries/harold-fong-56-judge-in-center-of-dispute-on-write-in-ballots.html.

22. Burdick v. Takushi, No. 86-0582 (D. Haw. Sept. 29, 1986), at 5.

23. Id.

24. Burdick v. Takushi, 846 F.2d 587, 588 (9th Cir. 1988).

25. Burdick v. Takushi, 776 P.2d 824, 825 (Haw. 1989).

26. Burdick v. Takushi, 737 F. Supp. 582 (D. Haw. 1990).

27. Id. at 586–87.

28. Id. at 582.

29. Id. at 591.

30. Burdick v. Takushi, 937 F.2d 415, 419 (9th Cir. 1991).

31. Id. at 421.

32. Id. at 420.

33. Reinhold, "Hawaii Lawsuit."

34. Burdick interview.

35. Alan Burdick (vice president, Americans for Democratic Action Hawaii), email to Whittington Wiman (research assistant, University of Kentucky J. David Rosenberg College of Law), Aug. 12, 2021.

36. "Obituary of Mary C. Burdick," M. John Scanlan Funeral Home, https://scanlanfuneralhome.com/tribute/details/8667/Mary-Burdick/obituary.html.

37. Burdick interview.

38. "Gutierrez v. Ada, Oral Argument—December 06, 1999," Gutierrez v. Ada, 528 U.S. 250 (2000) (No. 99-51), Oyez, https://www.oyez.org/cases/1999/99-51, at 6:39.

39. "Burdick v. Takushi, Oral Argument—March 24, 1992," Burdick v. Takushi 504 U.S. 428 (1992) (No. 91-535), Oyez, https://www.oyez.org/cases/1991/91-535, audio recording, at 2:57.

40. Burdick v. Takushi, 504 U.S. 428, 438 (1992).

41. Arthur Eisenberg (executive counsel, New York Civil Liberties Union), author interview, Sept. 9, 2021.

42. "Burdick v. Takushi, Oral Argument—March 24, 1992," at 19:14.

43. Burdick, 504 U.S. at 432.

44. Id. at 433.

45. "Hawaii Unopposed Candidate Primary Elections, Amendment 3 (1988)," Ballotpedia, https://ballotpedia.org/Hawaii_Unopposed_Candidate_Primary_Elections,_Amendment_3_(1988); Hawaii Constitution, Article III, section 4; Burdick interview.

46. Burdick, 504 U.S. at 440 n.10.

47. Id. at 448 (Kennedy, J., dissenting).

48. Eisenberg interview.

49. Anderson v. Celebrezze, 460 U.S. 780, 789 (1983).

50. Burdick, 504 U.S. at 434.

51. Burdick interview.

52. Morris Takushi, former director of Hawaii elections, State of Hawaii, email to author, Sept. 23, 2021.

CHAPTER 3: THE FIGHT OVER VOTER ID

1. Ari Berman, "Rigged: How Voter Suppression Threw Wisconsin to Trump," Mother Jones, Nov. 2017, https://www.motherjones.com/politics/2017/10/voter-suppression-wisconsin-election-2016.

2. Berman, "Rigged."

3. Berman, "Rigged."

4. Pat Schneider, "UW Prof Points to Voter ID Law, Candidate Absence as Reasons for Drop in Student Turnout," Cap Times, Sept. 26, 2017, https://madison.com/ct/news/local/education/university/uw-prof-points-to-voter-id-law-candidate-absence-as-reasons-for-drop-in-student/article_c140d94f-22fc-5c8f-80ed-dabf7e6a050d.html.

5. Chelsea Schneider, "Longtime Indiana Lawmaker Bill Crawford Remembered as a 'Giant Among Men,'" Indianapolis Star, Sept. 25, 2015, https://www.indystar.com/story/news/politics/2015/09/25/bill-crawford-long-time-indiana-lawmaker-dies/72806814.

6. "Longtime State Rep. Bill Crawford Dies," Statehouse File, Sept. 25, 2015, https://www.thestatehousefile.com/politics/longtime-state-rep-bill-crawford-dies/article_4dd5f7dc-5b67-5970-8d1b-311828efe100.html.

7. Bill Crawford (representative, Indiana House of Representatives), author interview (telephone), May 19, 2015.

8. Joshua A. Douglas, "The History of Voter ID Laws and the Story of *Crawford v. Marion County Election Board*," in *Election Law Stories*, ed. Joshua A. Douglas and Eugene D. Mazo (St. Paul, MN: Foundation Press, 2016), 468.

9. Matt A. Barreto, Stephen Nuño, Gabriel R. Sanchez, and Hannah L. Walker, "The Racial Implications of Voter Identification Laws in America," 47 *American Politics Research* 238 (2019).

10. Crawford v. Marion Cty. Election Bd., 472 F.3d 949, 954 (7th Cir. 2007) (Evans, J., dissenting).

11. Crawford interview.

12. Joe Simpson (former treasurer, Greater Indianapolis Branch NAACP), author interview (telephone), May 19, 2015.

13. Richard A. Posner, *Reflections on Judging* (Cambridge, MA: Harvard University Press, 2013), 84–85.

14. Crawford v. Marion Cty. Election Bd., 553 U.S. 181, 191 (2008).

15. Id. at 193.

16. Id. at 195.

17. Justin Levitt, "A Comprehensive Investigation of Voter Impersonation Finds 31 Credible Incidents out of One Billion Ballots Cast," *Washington Post*, Aug. 6, 2014, https://www.washingtonpost.com/news/wonk/wp/2014/08/06/a -comprehensive-investigation-of-voter-impersonation-finds-31-credible-incidents -out-of-one-billion-ballots-cast.

18. *Crawford*, 553 U.S. at 195 n.11.

19. Id. at 197.

20. Atiba R. Ellis, "The Meme of Voter Fraud," 63 *Catholic University Law Review* 879 (2014).

21. See, for instance, "Voter Identification," MIT Election Data and Science Lab, last updated June 10, 2021, https://electionlab.mit.edu/research/voter -identification; "The Impact of Voter Suppression on Communities of Color," fact sheet, Brennan Center for Justice, Jan. 10, 2022, https://www.brennancenter.org /our-work/research-reports/impact-voter-suppression-communities-color.

22. Chris Coyles (@CoylesPolitics), "Infuriating. That law prevented my grand-mother from voting in an election that year," Twitter, Oct. 14, 2021, 2:40 p.m., https://twitter.com/CoylesPolitics/status/1448720476801470464?s=20.

23. Anderson v. Celebrezze, 460 U.S. 780, 789 (1983).

24. Burdick v. Takushi, 504 U.S. 428, 433 (1992).

25. Crawford, 553 U.S. at 209 (Scalia, J., concurring in the judgment) (internal quotation marks omitted).

26. Id. at 208.

27. Id. at 209.

28. Id. (Souter, J., dissenting).

29. Center for Democracy and Election Management, American University, *Building Confidence in U.S. Elections: Report of the Commission on Federal Election Reform*, section 2.5, Sept. 2005, https://web.archive.org/web/20070620141435/http:// www.american.edu/ia/cfer/report/report.html#sect2.

30. Spencer Overton, "Dissenting Statement," Carter Baker Dissent (website), https://web.archive.org/web/20051123074755/http://www.carterbakerdissent .com/dissent.php.

31. W. Gardner Selby, "PolitiFact: Take Gun License, but Not Student ID, to Texas Polls," *Austin American-Statesman*, Sept. 23, 2016, https://www.statesman .com/news/20160923/politifact-take-gun-license-but-not-student-id-to-texas -polls.

32. Russell Berman, "The Obvious Voting-Rights Solution That No Democrat Will Propose," *Atlantic*, Aug. 30, 2021, https://www.theatlantic.com/politics/archive /2021/08/voting-rights-national-id-card/619772.

33. Zoltan Hajnal, Nazita Lajevardi, and Lindsay Nielson, "Voter Identification Laws and the Suppression of Minority Votes," 79 *Journal of Politics* 363, 366 (2017).

34. Transportation Security Administration, "Identification," https://www.tsa .gov/travel/security-screening/identification, last visited Oct. 29, 2021; Food and Drug Administration, "Legal Requirements for the Sale and Purchase of Drug Products Containing Pseudoephedrine, Ephedrine, and Phenylpropanolamine," https://www.fda.gov/drugs/information-drug-class/legal-requirements-sale-and -purchase-drug-products-containing-pseudoephedrine-ephedrine-and, last updated Nov. 24, 2017.

35. Alan Blinder, "Election Fraud in North Carolina Leads to New Charges for Republican Operative," *New York Times*, July 30, 2019, https://www.nytimes.com /2019/07/30/us/mccrae-dowless-indictment.html.

36. Charles Stewart III, Stephen Ansolabehere, and Nathaniel Persily, "Revisiting Public Opinion on Voter Identification and Voter Fraud in an Era of Increasing Partisan Polarization," 68 *Stanford Law Review* 1455, 1479 (2016).

37. Monmouth University Polling Institute, "Public Supports Both Early Voting and Requiring Photo ID to Vote," June 21, 2021, https://www.monmouth.edu /polling-institute/reports/monmouthpoll_us_062121.

38. Monmouth University Polling Institute, "Public Supports Both Early Voting and Requiring Photo ID to Vote."

39. National Conference of State Legislatures, "Voter Identification Requirements: Voter ID Laws," Oct. 7, 2021, https://www.ncsl.org/research/elections -and-campaigns/voter-id.aspx.

40. Michael J. Pitts and Matthew D. Neumann, "Documenting Disenfranchisement: Voter Identification During Indiana's 2008 General Election," 25 *Journal of Law and Politics*, 329, 330 (2009).

41. Ethan Magoc, "Flurry of Photo ID Laws Tied to Conservative ALEC Group," *MinnPost*, Aug. 20, 2012, https://www.minnpost.com/politics-policy/2012 /08/flurry-photo-id-laws-tied-conservative-alec-group.

42. Magoc, "Flurry of Photo ID Laws Tied to Conservative ALEC Group."

43. American Legislative Exchange Council, "ALEC Voter ID Model Legislation," https://images2.americanprogress.org/campus/web/ALEC_voter_ID_model _legislation.pdf (last visited Oct. 29, 2021); Magoc, "Flurry of Photo ID Laws Tied to Conservative ALEC Group."

44. Magoc, "Flurry of Photo ID Laws Tied to Conservative ALEC Group."

45. National Conference of State Legislatures, "Voter Identification Requirements: Voter ID Laws."

46. National Conference of State Legislatures, *Voter ID Laws*, report, updated Mar. 9, 2023, https://www.ncsl.org/research/elections-and-campaigns/voter-id.aspx.

47. Will Doran, "Voter ID Is Blocked for Now in NC. Your Guide to All the Court Fights and What's Next," *News & Observer*, Sept. 19, 2021, https://www.newsobserver.com/news/politics-government/article254326153.html.

48. Brennan Center for Justice, "Texas NAACP v. Steen (Consolidated with Veasey v. Abbott)," Sept. 21, 2018, https://www.brennancenter.org/our-work/court-cases/texas-naacp-v-steen-consolidated-veasey-v-abbott.

49. VoteTexas.gov, "Identification Requirements for Voting," https://www.votetexas.gov/mobile/id-faqs.htm, accessed Feb. 22, 2023.

50. Alex Presha, "Black Woman in Rural Texas Unable to Vote, Advocates Say System Is Unfair," ABC News, Oct. 5, 2021, https://abc7ny.com/black-woman-in-rural-texas-unable-to-vote-advocates-say-system-is-/11082256/.

51. N. Carolina State Conf. of NAACP v. McCrory, 831 F.3d 204, 214 (4th Cir. 2016).

52. Applewhite v. Com., No. 330 M.D. 2012, 2014 WL 184988, at *1 (Pa. Commw. Ct. Jan. 17, 2014).

CHAPTER 4: THE STIGMA OF FELON DISENFRANCHISEMENT

1. Ramirez v. Brown, 507 P.2d 1345, 1346 (Cal. 1973).

2. Ramirez's personal information: found through Lexis public record search (death certificate); *Ramirez*, 507 P.2d at 1346; "Ex-Convicts Get Coast Vote Right," *New York Times*, Mar. 31, 1973, https://www.nytimes.com/1973/03/31/archives/exconvicts-get-coast-vote-right-california-high-court-voids-state.html.

3. *Ramirez*, 507 P.2d at 1346.

4. Death certificate found through Lexis public record search.

5. Brief for Respondent at 5, Richardson v. Ramirez, 418 U.S. 24 (1974).

6. Id.; *Ramirez*, 507 P.2d at 1346.

7. Brief for Respondent at 5; *Ramirez*, 507 P.2d at 1346.

8. Skaggs Faucette LLP, "Welcome to Skaggs Faucette LLP," https://www.skaggsfaucette.com, accessed Jan. 17, 2022.

9. Marty Glick and Maurice Jourdane, *The Soledad Children: The Fight to End Discriminatory IQ Tests* (Houston: Arte Publico Press, 2019).

10. Marty Glick (attorney, Skaggs Faucette LLP), author interview, Nov. 5, 2021.

11. *California Rural Legal Assistance*, https://crla.org/about-crla, last visited Jan. 17, 2022.

12. Skaggs Faucette LLP, "Welcome to Skaggs Faucette LLP."

13. Glick interview. The case is styled *Richardson v. Ramirez*. Ramirez is Abran Ramirez. Richardson, the named defendant, was Viola ("Vi") Richardson, who was the county clerk of Mendocino County at the time and ultimately served in that role for twenty years. She petitioned the court to intervene in the case, fearing that the other county clerks would not adequately defend California's law. She was also involved in a separate case filed by a different person with a felony conviction—strangely enough, also named Richardson—so she was interested in the resolution of the issue. Clerk Richardson ultimately became the primary defendant. Richardson v. Ramirez, 418 U.S. 24, 37–38 (1974).

14. Alan Flurry, "Study Estimates U.S. Population with Felony Convictions," *UGA Today*, Oct. 1, 2017, https://news.uga.edu/total-us-population-with-felony -convictions.

15. Wendy Sawyer and Peter Wagner, *Mass Incarceration: The Whole Pie 2023*, Prison Policy Initiative, Mar. 14, 2023, https://www.prisonpolicy.org/reports /pie2023.html.

16. Jeff Manza and Christopher Uggen, *Locked Out: Felon Disenfranchisement and American Democracy* (Oxford: Oxford University Press, 2006), 23.

17. Kentucky Constitution, Article VIII, Section 2 (1792), https://images .procon.org/wp-content/uploads/sites/48/1792_ky_constitution.pdf.

18. Alexander Hamilton, "The Federalist Papers: No. 65, The Powers of the Senate Continued," available at https://avalon.law.yale.edu/18th_century/fed65.asp.

19. Franita Tolson, "'In Whom Is the Right of Suffrage?': The Reconstruction Acts as Sources of Constitutional Meaning," 169 *Penn Law Review Online* 211, 226 (2021) (internal citation omitted).

20. Id. at 227 (internal citation omitted).

21. Id. at 228.

22. Chris Uggen, Ryan Larson, Sarah Shannon, and Arleth Pulido-Nava, *Locked Out 2020: Estimates of People Denied Voting Rights Due to a Felony Conviction*, report prepared for the Sentencing Project, Oct. 30, 2020, https://www.sentencing project.org/publications/locked-out-2020-estimates-of-people-denied-voting-rights -due-to-a-felony-conviction.

23. Uggen et al., *Locked Out 2020*.

24. Uggen et al., *Locked Out 2020*.

25. Uggen et al., *Locked Out 2020*.

26. Sam Levine, "The Racist 1890 Law That's Still Blocking Thousands of Black Americans from Voting," *Guardian*, Jan. 8, 2022, https://www.theguardian .com/us-news/2022/jan/08/us-1890-law-black-americans-voting.

27. Levine, "The Racist 1890 Law."

28. Hopkins v. Hosemann, No. 19-60662 (5th Cir. 2023).

29. Otsuka v. Hite, 414 P.2d 412, 417 (Cal. 1966) (internal citation omitted).

30. Id. (internal citation omitted).

31. Id. (quoting Washington v. State, 75 Ala. 582, 585 (1884)).

32. *Ramirez*, 507 P.2d at 1350.

33. Kramer v. Union Free School Dist., 395 U.S. 621 (1969).

34. Id.

35. *Ramirez*, 507 P.2d at 1357.

36. Id. at 1355.

37. *See* Reynolds v. Sims, 377 U.S. 533 (1964); Harper v. Virginia State Bd. of Elections, 383 U.S. 663 (1966); *Kramer*, 395 U.S. at 621.

38. U.S. Constitution, Fourteenth Amendment, Section 2.

39. Richardson v. Ramirez, 418 U.S. 24, 74 (1974) (Marshall, J., dissenting).

40. "Richardson v. Ramirez, Oral Argument—January 15, 1974," Richardson v. Ramirez, 418 U.S. 24 (1974) (No. 72-1589), Oyez, https://www.oyez.org/cases /1973/72-1589, at 16:58.

41. Id. at 36:22.

42. Id. at 42:14.

43. Handwritten Notes of Justice Lewis F. Powell (1974), case file 615, page 5, Lewis F. Powell Jr. Papers, Washington and Lee University Law Library, https://scholarlycommons.law.wlu.edu/casefiles/615.

44. *Richardson*, 418 U.S. at 49.

45. Id.

46. Tolson, "'In Whom Is the Right of Suffrage?,'" 225.

47. *Richardson*, 418 U.S. at 74 (Marshall, J., dissenting).

48. Id. at 54.

49. "California Proposition 10, Voting Rights Restoration Amendment (1974)," *Ballotpedia*, https://ballotpedia.org/California_Proposition_10,_Voting_Rights_Restoration_Amendment_(1974).

50. Christopher Uggen and Jeff Manza, "Democratic Contraction? Political Consequences of Felon Disenfranchisement in the United States," 67 *American Sociological Review* 777, 792 (2002).

51. Uggen and Manza, "Democratic Contraction?"

52. Patricia Mazzei and Michael Wines, "How Republicans Undermined Ex-Felon Voting Rights in Florida," *New York Times*, Sept. 17, 2020, https://www.nytimes.com/2020/09/17/us/florida-felons-voting.html.

53. Mazzei and Wines, "How Republicans Undermined Ex-Felon Voting Rights."

54. Damon Winter and Jesse Wegman, "When It Costs $53,000 to Vote," *New York Times*, Oct. 10, 2021, https://www.nytimes.com/2021/10/07/opinion/election-voting-fine-felony-florida.html.

55. Jones v. DeSantis, 462 F.Supp.3d 1196 (N.D. Fla. May 24, 2020).

56. Jones v. Governor of Florida, 975 F.3d 1016 (11th Cir. 2020).

57. Id. at 1030.

58. Id. at 1053 (Lagoa, J., concurring).

59. Id. at 1059 (Martin, J., dissenting).

60. Hayden v. Pataki, 449 F.3d 305 (2d Cir. 2006) (en banc); Simmons v. Galvin, 575 F.3d 24 (1st Cir. 2009); Farrakhan v. Gregoire, 623 F.3d 990 (9th Cir. 2010) (en banc).

61. Perhaps most notably, Justice Sonia Sotomayor, then a judge on the Second Circuit Court of Appeals, dissented from the majority's decision and explained, "It is plain to anyone reading the Voting Rights Act that it applies to all 'voting qualification[s].' And it is equally plain that [New York's law] disqualifies a group of people from voting. These two propositions should constitute the entirety of our analysis." *Hayden*, 449 F.3d at 367–68 (Sotomayor, J., dissenting).

62. Kristen Bialik, "How Americans View Some of the Voting Policies Approved at the Ballot Box," Pew Research Center, Nov. 15, 2018, https://www.pewresearch.org/fact-tank/2018/11/15/how-americans-view-some-of-the-voting-policies-approved-at-the-ballot-box.

63. Matt Vasilogambros, "More States Expand the Ballot to Previously Incarcerated," *PEW Stateline*, June 1, 2021, https://www.pewtrusts.org/en/research-and-analysis/blogs/stateline/2021/06/01/more-states-expand-the-ballot-to-previously-incarcerated.

64. Vasilogambros, "More States Expand the Ballot to Previously Incarcerated."

CHAPTER 5: MONEY TALKS

1. Murray Hill, Inc., "Murray Hill Incorporated Ran for Congress," http://murrayhillincforcongress.com, last visited Apr. 8, 2022.

2. Eric Hensal (partner, Progressive Way LLC), author interview, Jan. 22, 2022.

3. Eric Hensal and William Klein, "Next Step After 'Citizens United': Corporate Candidates," *Politico*, Oct. 29, 2010, https://www.politico.com/story/2010/10/next-step-after-citizens-united-corporate-candidates-044388.

4. Murray Hill, Inc., "Voter Registration Appeal Release," http://murrayhillincforcongress.blogspot.com/2010/03/voter-registration-appeal-release.html.

5. Federal Election Commission, "Contribution Limits for 2023–2024," Feb. 2, 2023, https://www.fec.gov/updates/contribution-limits-for-2023-2024.

6. Heather K. Gerken and Erica J. Newland, "The Citizens United Trilogy: The Myth, the True Tale, and the Story Still to Come," in *Election Law Stories*, ed. Joshua A. Douglas and Eugene D. Mazo (St. Paul, MN: Foundation Press, 2016), 364–65, citing 77 *Texas Law Review* 1705, 1711 (1999).

7. Buckley v. Valeo, 424 U.S. 1, 11 (1976).

8. Randall v. Sorrell, 548 U.S. 230 (2006).

9. Scott Lemieux, "The Five Worst Roberts Court Rulings," *American Prospect*, Aug. 1, 2016, https://prospect.org/justice/five-worst-roberts-court-rulings.

10. Gerken and Newland, "The Citizens United Trilogy," 388.

11. Sean Cockerham, "The Man Behind Willie Horton Ads Has New Target: Hillary Clinton," *McClatchy*, July 14, 2007, https://www.mcclatchydc.com/news/politics-government/article24466504.html.

12. Matthew S. Petersen, FEC chair, letter to Theodore B. Olson, Esq., June 11, 2010, https://saos.fec.gov/aodocs/AO%202010-08.pdf.

13. Citizens United, *Hillary The Movie Trailer*, https://www.youtube.com/watch?v=BOYcM1z5fTs.

14. Jeffrey Toobin, "Money Unlimited," *New Yorker*, May 21, 2012, https://www.newyorker.com/magazine/2012/05/21/money-unlimited.

15. "Citizens United v. Federal Election Commission, Oral Argument—March 24, 2009," Citizens United v. Federal Election Commission, 558 U.S. 310 (2010) (No. 08-205), Oyez, https://www.oyez.org/cases/2008/08-205, at 32:22.

16. Toobin, "Money Unlimited."

17. Toobin, "Money Unlimited."

18. McConnell v. Federal Election Commission, 540 U.S. 93 (2003).

19. Nina Totenberg, "Seen as Rising Star, Kagan Has Limited Paper Trail," NPR, May 9, 2010, https://www.npr.org/templates/story/story.php?storyId=126611113.

20. "Citizens United v. Federal Election Commission, Oral Argument—March 24, 2009," at 1:11:18.

21. Ashley Parker, "'Corporations Are People,' Romney Tells Iowa Hecklers Angry over His Tax Policy," *New York Times*, Aug. 11, 2011, https://www.nytimes.com/2011/08/12/us/politics/12romney.html.

22. Adam Winkler, *We the Corporations: How American Businesses Won Their Civil Rights* (New York: Liveright, 2018), 400.

23. Trustees of Dartmouth College v. Woodward, 17 U.S. 518 (1819); Winkler, *We the Corporations*, 400.

24. International Shoe Co. v. Washington, 326 U.S. 310 (1945).

25. Citizens United v. Federal Election Commission, 558 U.S. 310, 342 (2010).

26. Notably, the Supreme Court abandoned this "means-end" analysis for the Second Amendment right to bear arms, instead focusing solely on an analysis of whether a gun regulation is consistent with history and tradition. New York State Rifle & Pistol Association, Inc. v. Bruen, 142 S.Ct. 2111 (2022).

27. Austin v. Michigan Chamber of Commerce, 494 U.S. 652 (1990); McConnell v. FEC, 540 U.S. 93 (2003).

28. *McConnell*, 540 U.S. at 150.

29. *Citizens United*, 558 U.S. at 359.

30. Nick Corasaniti, "Watchdog Says Buttigieg Campaign Exploited Super PAC Loophole," *New York Times*, Feb. 18, 2020, https://www.nytimes.com/2020 /02/18/us/politics/buttigieg-votevets-super-pac.html.

31. Gerken and Newland, "The Citizens United Trilogy," 393.

32. Amy White, "Trevor Potter and the Magic Briefcase," *Super Lawyers*, Apr. 30, 2015, https://www.superlawyers.com/washington-dc/article/trevor-potter-and -the-magic-briefcase/9f530f9e-d2bc-479e-919a-95f461be8336.html; *The Colbert Report*, "Colbert Super PAC—Trevor Potter & Stephen's Shell Corporation," Comedy Central, Sept. 29, 2011, https://www.cc.com/video/3yzu4u/the-colbert-report -colbert-super-pac-trevor-potter-stephen-s-shell-corporation.

33. Melissa Yaeger, "It's Been 4 Years Since Stephen Colbert Created a Super PAC—Where Did All That Money Go?," Sunlight Foundation, Sept. 30, 2015, https://sunlightfoundation.com/2015/09/30/its-been-four-years-since-stephen -colbert-created-a-super-pac-where-did-all-that-money-go.

34. Karl Evers-Hillstrom, "More Money, Less Transparency: A Decade Under Citizens United," OpenSecrets, Jan. 14, 2020, https://www.opensecrets.org/news /reports/a-decade-under-citizens-united.

35. Anna Massoglia and Karl Evers-Hillstrom, "'Dark Money' Topped $1 Billion in 2020, Largely Boosting Democrats," OpenSecrets, Mar. 17, 2021, https:// www.opensecrets.org/news/2021/03/one-billion-dark-money-2020-electioncycle.

36. Kenneth P. Vogel and Shane Goldmacher, "Democrats Decried Dark Money. Then They Won with It in 2020," *New York Times*, Jan. 29, 2022, https:// www.nytimes.com/2022/01/29/us/politics/democrats-dark-money-donors.html.

37. Evers-Hillstrom, "More Money, Less Transparency."

38. Evers-Hillstrom, "More Money, Less Transparency."

39. Gerken and Newland, "The Citizens United Trilogy," 393.

40. Joseph Fishkin and Heather K. Gerken, "The Party's Over: McCutcheon, Shadow Parties, and the Future of the Party System," 2014 *Supreme Court Review* 175, 203 (2014).

41. Joseph Biden and Michael Carpenter, "Foreign Dark Money Is Threatening American Democracy," *Politico*, Nov. 27, 2018, https://www.politico.com /magazine/story/2018/11/27/foreign-dark-money-joe-biden-222690.

42. Evers-Hillstrom, "More Money, Less Transparency."

43. Jeffrey Rosen, "Ruth Bader Ginsburg Is an American Hero," *New Republic*, Sept. 28, 2014, https://newrepublic.com/article/119578/ruth-bader-ginsburg -interview-retirement-feminists-jazzercise.

44. Brian Boyle, "An Amendment to Center 'We the People' in Our Constitution," American Promise, Feb. 25, 2021, https://americanpromise.net/2021/02/brian

-boyle-an-amendment-to-center-we-the-people-in-our-constitution; Brian Boyle, "A Constitutional Amendment to Revive the Sovereignty of the American People," *American Constitution Society*, Jan. 2021, https://www.acslaw.org/wp-content/uploads /2021/02/Revive-the-Sovereignty-of-the-American-People.pdf.

45. Jeff Clements (president, American Promise), author interview, Jan. 28, 2022.

46. Spencer Overton, "The Participation Interest," 100 *Georgetown Law Journal* 1259, 1274 (2012).

47. Erin Chlopak (senior director, Campaign Legal Center), author interview, Jan. 28, 2022.

48. Adam Bozzi (communications director, End Citizens United), author interview, Jan. 28, 2022.

49. john a. powell, "Campaign Finance Reform Is a Voting Rights Issue: The Campaign Finance System as the Latest Incarnation of the Politics of Exclusion," 5 *African-American Law & Policy Report* 1, 5 (2002).

50. "Shifting Gears—How Women Navigate the Road to Higher Office," *Political Parity* 24, https://www.politicalparity.org/wp-content/uploads/2017/10/Shifting -Gears-Report.pdf#page=24; Jena McGregor, "Why More Women Don't Run for Office," *Washington Post*, May 21, 2014, https://www.washingtonpost.com/news /on-leadership/wp/2014/05/21/why-more-women-dont-run-for-office.

51. Barbara Lee Family Foundation, "Keys to Elected Office—The Essential Guide for Women," http://oe9e345wags3x5qikp6dgo12.wpengine.netdna-cdn.com /wp-content/uploads/KeysReportfinal.pdf; Jennifer Steinhauer, "As Fund-Raisers in Congress, Women Break the Cash Ceiling," *New York Times*, Nov. 29, 2013, https:// www.nytimes.com/2013/11/30/us/politics/as-women-build-political-power-a -fund-raising-tide-turns.html.

CHAPTER 6: AN "EMBARRASSING JUDICIAL FART"

1. Vikram David Amar and Ahkil Reed Amar, "Eradicating Bush-League Arguments Root and Branch: The Article II Independent-State-Legislature Notion and Related Rubbish," 2021 *Supreme Court Review* 1 (2022). The Court cited the case in 2023 in Moore v. Harper, 600 U.S. 1 (2023). See chapter 10.

2. Florida Statutes, Chapter 101.5614(5) (2000); Gore v. Harris, 772 So.2d 1243, 1257 (Fla. 2000).

3. Edward B. Foley, "Bush v. Gore: The Court Stops the Recount," in *Election Law Stories*, ed. Joshua A. Douglas and Eugene D. Mazo (St. Paul, MN: Foundation Press, 2016), 544.

4. *Gore*, 772 So.2d at 1257.

5. Foley, "Bush v. Gore," 562.

6. Bush v. Gore, 531 U.S. 1046 (2000).

7. Id. at 1047 (Scalia, J., concurring).

8. "Bush v. Gore, Oral Argument—December 11, 2000," Bush v. Gore, 531 U.S. 1046 (2000) (No. 00-949), Oyez, https://www.oyez.org/cases/2000/00-949, at 00:26.

9. Jeffrey Toobin, *The Nine: Inside the Secret World of the Supreme Court* (New York: Anchor, 2008), 171–72.

10. *Bush*, 531 U.S. at 104.

11. Foley, "Bush v. Gore," 560.

12. *Bush*, 531 U.S. at 110.

13. Id. at 109.

14. Justice Thomas mentioned *Bush v. Gore* once in a footnote in a dissent, and Justices Thomas and Kavanaugh both cited Chief Justice Rehnquist's separate opinion in *Bush v. Gore* when discussing the role of state legislatures during the 2020 election litigation. Arizona v. Inter Tribal Council of Arizona, Inc., 570 U.S. 1, 35 n.2 (2013) (Thomas, J., dissenting); Democratic National Committee v. Wisconsin State Legislature, 141 S. Ct. 28, 34 n.1 (2020) (Kavanaugh, J., concurring); Republican Party of Pennsylvania v. Degraffenreid, 141 S. Ct. 732, 733 (2021). In addition, the Court cited *Bush v. Gore* in *Moore v. Harper*, 600 U.S. 1 (2023), discussed in chapter 10.

15. *Bush*, 531 U.S. at 128–29.

16. "Al Gore, 2000 Presidential Concession Speech," Dec. 13, 2000, https://www.americanrhetoric.com/speeches/algore2000concessionspeech.html.

17. Ford Fessenden and John M. Broder, "Examining the Vote: The Overview; Study of Disputed Florida Ballots Finds Justices Did Not Cast the Deciding Vote," *New York Times*, Nov. 12, 2001, https://www.nytimes.com/2001/11/12/us/examining-vote-overview-study-disputed-florida-ballots-finds-justices-did-not.html; "Media Recount: Bush Won the 2000 Election," *PBS News Hour*, Apr. 3, 2001, https://www.pbs.org/newshour/nation/media-jan-june01-recount_04-03.

18. Debra Cassens Weiss, "Scalia on Bush v. Gore: 'Get Over It,'" *ABA Journal*, Mar. 10, 2008, https://www.abajournal.com/news/article/scalia_on_bush_v_gore_get_over_it.

19. Edward Foley, *Ballot Battles: The History of Disputed Elections in the United States* (New York: Oxford University Press, 2016), 23, 224–28, 345.

20. Richard L. Hasen, "Research Note: Record Election Litigation Rates in the 2020 Election: An Aberration or a Sign of Things to Come?" *Election Law Journal* at 3 (2022).

21. Hasen, "Research Note."

22. Michael J. Pitts, "Heads or Tails? A Modest Proposal for Deciding Close Elections," 39 *Connecticut Law Review* 752–53 (2006).

23. Gregory Roberts, "Judge Upholds Gregoire's Election; Rossi Won't Appeal," *Seattle PI*, June 5, 2005, https://www.seattlepi.com/local/article/Judge-upholds-Gregoire-s-election-Rossi-won-t-1175262.php.

24. Roberts, "Judge Upholds Gregoire's Election"; "Borders et al. v. King County et al., transcript of the decision by Chelan County Superior Court Judge John Bridges, June 6, 2005, Court's Oral Decision, No. 05-2-00027-3," *Seattle Weekly*, Oct. 9, 2006, https://www.seattleweekly.com/news/borders-et-al-v-king-county-et-al.

25. Jay Weiner, *This Is Not Florida: How Al Franken Won the Minnesota Senate Recount* (Minneapolis: University of Minnesota Press, 2010); In re Contest of General Election Held on November 4, 2008, for Purpose of Electing a U.S. Senator from State of Minnesota, 767 N.W.2d 453 (Minn. 2009).

26. Miller v. Treadwell, 245 P.3d 867, 877–78 (Alaska 2010); William Yardley, "Murkowski Wins Alaska Senate Race," *New York Times*, Nov. 17, 2010, https://www.nytimes.com/2010/11/18/us/politics/18alaska.html.

27. Kevin Robillard, "Allen West Demands Recount," *Politico*, Nov. 7, 2012, https://www.politico.com/story/2012/11/rep-wests-race-still-undecided-083476; Matt Sedensky, "Rep. Allen West Concedes After Fla. Recount Fight," *Daytona Beach News-Journal*, Nov. 20, 2012, https://news-journalonline.com/story/news /2012/11/20/rep-allen-west-concedes-after/30602947007.

28. Stein v. Cortes, No. 2:16-cv-06287 (E.D. Pa. Dec. 12, 2016), https://www .courthousenews.com/wp-content/uploads/2016/12/Stein2.pdf; Steve Eder, "Stein Ends Recount Bid, But Says It Revealed Flaws in Voting System," *New York Times*, Dec. 13, 2016, https://www.nytimes.com/2016/12/13/us/stein-ends-recount-bid -but-says-it-revealed-flaws-in-voting-system.html.

29. Eder, "Stein Ends Recount Bid"; Laura Wagner, "Clinton Campaign Says It Will Participate in Recount Efforts," *The Two-Way*, NPR, Nov. 26, 2016, https:// www.npr.org/sections/thetwo-way/2016/11/26/503432822/clinton-campaign -supports-recount-efforts-in-battleground-states.

30. Adam Gabbatt, "Stacey Abrams Condemns Brian Kemp After He Accuses Democrats of Voter 'Hack,'" *Guardian*, Nov. 5, 2018, https://www.theguardian .com/us-news/2018/nov/05/stacey-abrams-brian-kemp-georgia-race-democrat -voter-hack-claim; Khushbu Shah, "'Textbook Voter Suppression': Georgia's Bitter Election a Battle Years in the Making," *Guardian*, Nov. 10, 2018, https:// www.theguardian.com/us-news/2018/nov/10/georgia-election-recount-stacey -abrams-brian-kemp; Joshua Douglas, "Brian Kemp, If You're Running in an Election, You Shouldn't Be Running the Election," CNN, Nov. 5, 2018, https:// www.cnn.com/2018/11/05/opinions/partisan-elections-futility-josh-douglas -opinion/index.html; Joshua Douglas, "What Stacey Abrams Should Say About Brian Kemp's Victory," CNN, Nov. 19, 2018, https://www.cnn.com/2018/11/19 /opinions/stacey-abrams-should-accept-brian-kemp-win-as-legitimate-douglas /index.html.

31. Trump for President v. Boockvar, No. 602 M.D. 2020 (Pa. Commw. Ct. 2020), https://www.courthousenews.com/wp-content/uploads/2020/11/pa -commonwealth-court.pdf; William Cummings, Joey Garrison, and Jim Sergent, "By the Numbers: President Donald Trump's Failed Efforts to Overturn the Election," *USA Today*, Jan. 6, 2021, https://www.usatoday.com/in-depth/news /politics/elections/2021/01/06/trumps-failed-efforts-overturn-election-numbers /4130307001.

32. Jacob Kovacs-Goodman, "Post-Election Litigation Analysis and Summaries," Stanford-MIT Healthy Elections Project (2021), https://papers.ssrn.com/sol3 /papers.cfm?abstract_id=3978063.

33. King v. Whitmer, 505 F.Supp.3d 720 (E.D. Mich. 2020), First Amended Complaint for Declaratory, Emergency, and Permanent Injunctive Relief, at 2–3.

34. O'Rourke v. Dominion Voting Systems Inc., 552 F.Supp.3d 1168, 1178 (D. Colo. 2021).

35. Joshua Douglas, "Disbar Trump's Lawyers Who Tried to Steal the Election," *Washington Monthly*, Aug. 31, 2021, https://washingtonmonthly.com/2021 /08/31/disbar-trumps-lawyers-who-tried-to-steal-the-election.

36. Texas v. Pennsylvania, 141 S. Ct. 1230 (2020).

37. Kovacs-Goodman, "Post-Election Litigation Analysis and Summaries," 3.

38. Shane Goldmacher, "Trump Lost the 2020 Election. He Has Raised $207.5 Million Since," *New York Times*, Dec. 3, 2020, https://www.nytimes.com/2020/12/03 /us/politics/trump-campaign-money.html.

39. Madison Czopek, "Courts Did Review Trump Campaign 'Evidence' of Election Fraud. Claims That Say Otherwise Are Wrong," *PolitiFact*, Oct. 28, 2022, https://www.politifact.com/factchecks/2022/oct/28/instagram-posts/trump -campaigns-evidence-of-fraud-was-reviewed-bef.

40. Richard A. Posner, *Breaking the Deadlock: The 2000 Election, the Constitution, and the Courts* (Princeton, NJ: Princeton University Press, 2001).

CHAPTER 7: THROWING AWAY YOUR UMBRELLA DURING A RAINSTORM

1. Shelby County v. Holder, 570 U.S. 529, 548 (2013).

2. Stephen Dawkins, "Profile: Kenneth Dukes: Rock of Hope," *Shelby County Reporter*, Feb. 26, 2019, https://www.shelbycountyreporter.com/2019/02/26/profile -kenneth-dukes-rock-of-hope.

3. Scott Mims, "Voting Protections Rally Held for 8th Year," *Shelby County Reporter*, June 27, 2021, https://www.shelbycountyreporter.com/2021/06/27/voting -protections-rally-held-for-8th-year.

4. Ari Berman, *Give Us the Ballot: The Modern Struggle for Voting Rights in America* (New York: Farrar, Straus and Giroux, 2015), 5.

5. Berman, *Give Us the Ballot*.

6. Rebecca Onion, "Take the Impossible 'Literacy' Test Louisiana Gave Black Voters in the 1960s," *Slate*, June 28, 2013, https://slate.com/human-interest/2013 /06/voting-rights-and-the-supreme-court-the-impossible-literacy-test-louisiana -used-to-give-black-voters.html.

7. "Transcript of the Johnson Address on Voting Rights to Joint Session of Congress," Mar. 15, 1965, https://archive.nytimes.com/www.nytimes.com/books/98 /04/12/specials/johnson-rightsadd.html.

8. Berman, *Give Us the Ballot*, 6.

9. U.S. Department of Justice, "Section 4 of the Voting Rights Act," https:// www.justice.gov/crt/section-4-voting-rights-act, last updated May 5, 2020.

10. Act of July 27, 2006, Pub. L. No. 109-246, 120 Stat. 577, https://www .congress.gov/bill/109th-congress/house-bill/9/actions.

11. South Carolina v. Katzenbach, 383 U.S. 301, 335 (1966).

12. Id.

13. Id.

14. Georgia v. United States, 411 U.S. 526 (1973); City of Rome v. United States, 446 U.S. 156 (1980); Lopez v. Monterey County, 525 U.S. 266 (1999).

15. Sergio Munoz, "The White Nationalist Ties of the Next Big Civil Rights Case," Media Matters for America, Dec. 21, 2020, https://www.mediamatters.org /justice-civil-liberties/white-nationalist-ties-next-big-civil-rights-case.

16. Anemona Hartocollis, "He Took On the Voting Rights Act and Won. Now He's Taking On Harvard," *New York Times*, Nov. 19, 2017, https://www.nytimes .com/2017/11/19/us/affirmative-action-lawsuits.html.

17. Bush v. Vera, 517 U.S. 952 (1996).

18. Edward Blum, author interview, May 2, 2022.

19. Hartocollis, "He Took On the Voting Rights Act and Won."

20. Ellen D. Katz, "The Shelby County Problem," in *Election Law Stories*, ed. Joshua A. Douglas and Eugene D. Mazo (St. Paul, MN: Foundation Press, 2016), 521.

21. Northwest Austin Municipal Util. Dist. No. One v. Holder, 557 U.S. 193, 206 (2009).

22. Id. at 203.

23. Elizabeth Chuck, "Meet the Supreme Court Matchmaker: Edward Blum," NBC News, June 11, 2013, https://www.nbcnews.com/news/us-news/meet-supreme -court-matchmaker-edward-blum-flna6c10272394.

24. Blum interview.

25. Hartocollis, "He Took On the Voting Rights Act and Won."

26. Legal Defense Fund, "Shelby First Anniversary Countdown: Day 19," https://www.naacpldf.org/shelby-first-anniversary-countdown/shelby-first -anniversary-countdown-day-19.

27. "Debo Adegbile—Civil Rights Champion and Former 'Sesame Street' Star," *Chambers Associate*, https://www.chambers-associate.com/the-big-interview /debo-adegbile-civil-rights-champion-and-former-sesame-street-star, accessed Sept. 14, 2023; Associated Press, "Attorney for Shelby County Residents Is Only Black Lawyer Supreme Court Justices See This Term," AL.com, May 12, 2013, https://www.al.com/wire/2013/05/attorney_for_shelby_county_res.html.

28. "Shelby County v. Holder, Oral Argument—February 27, 2000," Shelby County v. Holder, 570 U.S. 529 (2013) (No. 12-96), Oyez, https://www.oyez.org /cases/2012/12-96, at 51:49.

29. "Northwest Austin Municipal Util. Dist. No. One v. Holder, Oral Argument—April 29, 2009," Northwest Austin Municipal Util. Dist. No. One v. Holder, 557 U.S. 193 (2009) (No. 08-322), Oyez, https://www.oyez.org/cases/2008/08-322, at 55:55.

30. U.S. Senate, "Supreme Court Nominations (1789–Present)," https://www .senate.gov/legislative/nominations/SupremeCourtNominations1789present.htm.

31. *Shelby County*, 570 U.S. at 540.

32. Coyle v. Smith, 221 U.S. 559 (1911).

33. South Carolina v. Katzenbach, 383 U.S. 301, 329 (1966).

34. *Shelby County*, 570 U.S. at 544.

35. Leah M. Litman, "Inventing Equal Sovereignty," 114 *Michigan Law Review* 1207 (2016).

36. *Shelby County*, 570 U.S. at 547.

37. Id. at 542, quoting Northwest Austin Municipal Util. Dist. No. One v. Holder, 557 U.S. 193, 203 (2009).

38. Id. at 544.

39. "Shelby County v. Holder, Opinion Announcement—June 25, 2013 (Part 2)," Shelby County v. Holder, 570 U.S. 529 (2013) (No. 12-96), https://lawaspect.com /case-shelby-county-v-holder, at 9:48.

40. *Shelby County*, 570 U.S. at 560 (Ginsburg, J., dissenting).

41. Id. at 559 (Ginsburg, J., dissenting).

42. House of Representatives Report No. 109-478, (2006), prepared by Committee on the Judiciary, 6.

43. Katz, "The Shelby County Problem," 519.

44. *Shelby County*, 570 U.S. at 590 (Ginsburg, J., dissenting).

45. Texas v. Holder, Civ. Action No. 12-cv-128 (DST, RMC, RLW) (2012), https://ecf.dcd.uscourts.gov/cgi-bin/show_public_doc?2012cv0128-340.

46. Brennan Center for Justice, "The Effects of Shelby County v. Holder," Aug. 6, 2018, https://www.brennancenter.org/our-work/policy-solutions/effects-shelby -county-v-holder.

47. Greg Abbott, "Statement by Texas Attorney General Greg Abbott," press release, June 25, 2013, https://perma.cc/SL53-AFSG.

48. State of Texas, "Texas Redistricting: 2010s Timeline," https://redistricting .capitol.texas.gov/docs/history/2010s.pdf.

49. Brennan Center for Justice, "Texas NAACP v. Steen (Consolidated with Veasey v. Abbott)," Sept. 21, 2018, https://www.brennancenter.org/our-work/court -cases/texas-naacp-v-steen-consolidated-veasey-v-abbott; State of Texas, "Redis- tricting Lawsuit Activity—Texas," https://redistricting.capitol.texas.gov/pdf/Redist _Timeline/Lawsuits.pdf.

50. Brennan Center for Justice, "The Effects of Shelby County v. Holder."

51. N.C. State Conference of the NAACP v. McCrory, 831 F.3d 204, 226 (4th Cir. 2016).

52. Id.

53. Thomas E. Perez, assistant attorney general, U.S. Department of Justice, letter to Dennis R. Dunn, deputy attorney general, State of Georgia, Dec. 21, 2012, https://www.justice.gov/crt/voting-determination-letter-57.

54. Harry Baumgarten, "Shelby County v. Holder's Biggest and Most Harmful Impact May Be on Our Nation's Smallest Towns," Campaign Legal Center, June 20, 2016, https://campaignlegal.org/update/shelby-county-v-holders-biggest-and -most-harmful-impact-may-be-our-nations-smallest-towns.

CHAPTER 8: AN ACTIVIST COURT

1. Greg Stanton (mayor of Phoenix), letter to Attorney General Loretta Lynch, Mar. 23, 2016, https://www.phoenix.gov/mayorsite/Documents/Mayor%20Greg %20Stanton%20Letter%20to%20DOJ.pdf.

2. Mary Jo Pitzl, Anne Roman, and Rob O'Dell, "Long Lines, Too Few Polling Places Frustrate Metro Phoenix Primary Voters," *Arizona Republic*, Mar. 22, 2016, https://www.azcentral.com/story/news/politics/elections/2016/03/22/arizona -primary-voter-turnout-long-lines/82125816.

3. Ray Stern, "Democratic Party Sues Arizona, County, Declaring That Botched Election Violated Federal Law," *Phoenix New Times*, Apr. 15, 2016, https:// www.phoenixnewtimes.com/news/democratic-party-sues-arizona-county-declaring -that-botched-election-violated-federal-law-8222819.

4. Mary Jo Pitzl and Yvonne Wingett Sanchez, "'Nuts, Nuts, Nuts': Anger in Arizona Builds over Long Voter Waits," *Arizona Republic*, Mar. 23, 2016, https:// www.azcentral.com/story/news/politics/elections/2016/03/23/ducey-rips-long -voter-lines-calls-them-unacceptable/82160766.

5. Pitzl and Sanchez, "'Nuts, Nuts, Nuts.'"

6. Stern, "Democratic Party Sues Arizona, County."

7. Rebekah L. Sanders, "Helen Purcell, Maricopa County's Elections Umpire, Calls Her Last Game and Leaves Lasting Legacy," *Arizona Republic*, Nov. 14, 2016,

https://www.azcentral.com/story/news/politics/elections/2016/11/14/helen-purcell
-maricopa-county-recorder-leaves-lasting-legacy/93650076.

8. Brnovich v. Democratic National Committee, 141 S. Ct. 2321, 2366–67 (2021) (Kagan, J., dissenting).

9. Id.

10. 52 U.S.C. § 10301 (U.S. code section on voting and elections).

11. Bruce Spiva, author interview, July 6, 2022.

12. Democratic National Committee v. Reagan, 329 F. Supp. 3d 824, 843 (D. Ariz. 2018) (citing Burdick v. Takushi, 504 U.S. 428, 433 (1992)).

13. Id. at 845 n8.

14. Id. at 852.

15. Id. at 871.

16. Id. at 878.

17. Rick Hasen, "Marc Elias Is Sometimes Counterproductive When It Comes to Protecting Voting Rights, Election Integrity, and the Interests of the Democratic Party," *Election Law Blog*, Jan. 30, 2022, https://electionlawblog.org/?p=127270.

18. See Democratic National Committee v. Reagan, 904 F.3d 686 (9th Cir. 2018).

19. Democratic National Committee v. Hobbs, No. 18-15845 (9th Cir. 2018), https://www.courtlistener.com/docket/7488003/dnc-v-katie-hobbs.

20. Democratic National Committee v. Hobbs, 948 F.3d 989, 998 (9th Cir. 2020).

21. Jessica Amunson (partner, Jenner & Block LLP), author interview, June 24, 2022.

22. "Brnovich v. Democratic National Committee, Oral Argument—March 02, 2021," Brnovich v. Democratic National Committee, 141 S. Ct. 2321 (2021) (No. 19-1257), Oyez, https://www.oyez.org/cases/2020/19-1257, at 1:10:21.

23. Id. at 1:10:30

24. Adam Liptak, "Supreme Court Upholds Arizona Voting Restrictions," *New York Times*, July 1, 2021, https://www.nytimes.com/2021/07/01/us/politics/supreme
-court-arizona-voting-restrictions.html.

25. League of Women Voters, "Brnovich: A Significant Blow to Our Freedom to Vote," https://www.lwv.org/blog/brnovich-significant-blow-our-freedom-vote, last updated Sept. 2, 2021.

26. Guy-Uriel E. Charles and Luis E. Fuentes-Rohwer, "The Court's Voting-Rights Decision Was Worse Than People Think," *Atlantic*, July 8, 2021, https://
www.theatlantic.com/ideas/archive/2021/07/brnovich-vra-scotus-decision-arizona
-voting-right/619330.

27. Charles and Fuentes-Rohwer, "The Court's Voting-Rights Decision."

28. *Brnovich*, 141 S. Ct. at 2338–40.

29. Id. at 2351 (Kagan, J., dissenting).

30. Ian Millhiser, "How America Lost Its Commitment to the Right to Vote," *Vox*, July 21, 2021, https://www.vox.com/22575435/voting-rights-supreme-court
-john-roberts-shelby-county-constitution-brnovich-elena-kagan.

31. Allen v. Milligan, No. 21–1086 (2023).

32. Id. (Kavanaugh, J., concurring; noting that "the authority to conduct race-based redistricting cannot extend indefinitely into the future").

33. Mark Brnovich (Arizona attorney general), author interview, Aug. 17, 2022.

34. Yvonne Wingett Sanchez, "Arizona Activists Want a Vote on Expanding Access to Voting," *Washington Post*, July 7, 2022, https://www.washingtonpost.com /politics/2022/07/07/arizona-voting-ballot-initiative.

35. Rick Hasen, "Breaking and Analysis: Supreme Court on 6–3 Vote Rejects Voting Rights Act Section 2 Case in Brnovich Case—A Significant Weakening of Section 2," *Election Law Blog*, July 1, 2021, https://electionlawblog.org/?p=123065.

CHAPTER 9: POLITICIANS GONE WILD

1. Columbia Law School, "Keeping Democracy Within the Lines," Jan. 30, 2020, https://www.law.columbia.edu/news/archive/keeping-democracy-within -lines; *Last Week Tonight*, "Gerrymandering: Last Week Tonight with John Oliver (HBO)," YouTube, Apr. 10, 2017, https://www.youtube.com/watch?v=A-4dIImaod Q&t=833s.

2. Lafair Family Games, "Mapmaker: The Gerrymandering Game," Kickstarter, https://www.kickstarter.com/projects/1639370584/mapmaker-the-gerry mandering-game, last updated Nov. 26, 2020; "About Us," Mapmaker: The Gerrymandering Game, https://gerrymanderinggame.com/index.php/about, accessed Oct. 5, 2022; Louis Lafair, "Designer Diary: Mapmaker: The Gerrymandering Game Takes on the Supreme Court," *BoardGameGeek*, Dec. 22, 2020, https:// boardgamegeek.com/blogpost/111646/designer-diary-mapmaker-gerrymandering -game-takes.

3. David Daley, *Ratf**ked: The True Story Behind the Secret Plan to Steal America's Democracy* (New York: Liveright, 2016); "'Gerrymandering on Steroids': How Republicans Stacked the Nation's Statehouses," *Here & Now*, WBUR, July 19, 2016, https://www.wbur.org/hereandnow/2016/07/19/gerrymandering-republicans -redmap.

4. LWV Guest, "The Woman Who Argued 'Rucho v. Common Cause' Looks Back," *LWV* (League of Women Voters blog), https://www.lwv.org/blog/woman -who-argued-v-common-cause-looks-back, last updated Mar. 25, 2022.

5. Davis v. Bandemer, 478 U.S. 109, 132 (1986).

6. Id. at 132–33.

7. Veith v. Jubelirer, 541 U.S. 267, 272 (2004).

8. Baker v. Carr, 369 U.S. 186 (1962); Reynolds v. Sims, 377 U.S. 533 (1964); Wesberry v. Sanders, 376 U.S. 1 (1964).

9. *Veith*, 541 U.S. at 312 (Kennedy, J., concurring in the judgment).

10. League of United Latin American Citizens v. Perry, 548 U.S. 399, 420, 466, 483 (2006).

11. Nicholas Stephanopoulos and Eric McGhee, "Partisan Gerrymandering and the Efficiency Gap," 82 *University of Chicago Law Review* 381 (2014).

12. Whitford v. Gill, 218 F. Supp. 3d 837 (W.D. Wis. 2016).

13. Gill v. Whitford, 138 S. Ct. 1916, 1930 (2018).

14. Id. at 1940–41 (Kagan, J., concurring) (cleaned up).

15. We might learn more about Justice Kennedy's privately expressed views on this case, if any, once the papers from his time on the Court are released to the public.

16. Rucho v. Common Cause, 139 S. Ct. 2484, 2491 (2019).

17. Id.

18. Dianne Gallagher and Giovanna Van Leeuwen, "North Carolina State Rep. David Lewis Resigns After Pleading Guilty to Two Federal Charges," CNN, Aug. 20, 2020, https://www.cnn.com/2020/08/20/politics/north-carolina-david-lewis -federal-charges-resign/index.html.

19. Anita Earls (associate justice, Supreme Court of North Carolina), author interview, Sept. 7, 2022.

20. Nick Stephanopoulos (professor of law, Harvard Law School), author interview, Aug. 9, 2022.

21. Ruth Greenwood (visiting assistant clinical professor of law, Harvard Law School), author interview, Aug. 15, 2022.

22. Mark Sherman, "Supreme Court Says Federal Courts Have No Role in Policing Partisan Gerrymandering," *PBS News Hour*, June 27, 2019, https://www .pbs.org/newshour/nation/supreme-court-says-federal-courts-have-no-role-in -policing-partisan-gerrymandering.

23. *Rucho*, 139 S. Ct. at 2509 (Kagan, J., dissenting).

24. Johnny Kauffman, "55 Years Later, Lawyer Will Again Argue over Redistricting Before Supreme Court," NPR, Mar. 24, 2019, https://www.npr.org/2019 /03/24/705472431/55-years-later-lawyer-will-again-argue-over-redistricting-before -supreme-court.

25. Emmet Bondurant (partner, Bondurant Mixson & Elmore LLP), author interview, Aug. 17, 2022.

26. League of Women Voters of North Carolina Trial Ex. 4003 at 5, Common Cause v. Rucho, 318 F. Supp. 3d 777 (M.D.N.C. 2018).

27. *Rucho*, 139 S. Ct. at 2497 (internal citation omitted).

28. Id. (internal citation omitted).

29. Id. at 2502 (internal citation omitted).

30. Id. at 2520 (Kagan, J., dissenting).

31. Id. at 2507 (internal citation omitted).

32. *Gill*, 138 S. Ct. at 1929.

33. Emmet J. Bondurant, "Rucho v. Common Cause—A Critique," 70 *Emory Law Journal* 1049, 1053 (2021).

34. Guy-Uriel E. Charles and Luis E. Fuentes-Rohwer, "Dirty Thinking About Law and Democracy in Rucho v. Common Cause," 2018–19 *American Constitution Society Supreme Court Review* 293, 293–94 (2019).

35. *Rucho*, 139 S. Ct. at 2507.

36. H.R.1—For the People Act of 2021; H.R.1—For the People Act of 2019.

37. *Rucho*, 139 S. Ct. at 2509 (Kagan, J., dissenting).

38. *Veith*, 541 U.S. at 312 (Kennedy, J., concurring in the judgment).

39. Earls interview.

40. "What Redistricting Looks Like in Every State," *FiveThirtyEight*, https:// projects.fivethirtyeight.com/redistricting-2022-maps, last updated July 19, 2022; Nathaniel Rakich, "How This Redistricting Cycle Failed to Increase Representation for People of Color—and Could Even Set It Back," *FiveThirtyEight*, Mar. 17, 2022, https://fivethirtyeight.com/features/how-this-redistricting-cycle-failed-to -increase-representation-for-people-of-color-and-could-even-set-it-back; Chris-

topher T. Kenny, Cory McCartan, Tyler Simko, Shiro Kuriwaki, and Kosuke Imai, "Widespread Partisan Gerrymandering Mostly Cancels Nationally, but Reduces Electoral Competition," arXiv, Aug. 15, 2022, https://arxiv.org/abs/2208.06968.

41. "Score Electoral District Maps," *PlanScore*, https://planscore.campaign legal.org/#!2020-ushouse, accessed Oct. 5, 2022.

CHAPTER 10: THE NEXT LOOMING CASE

1. Henry Grabar, "An Interview with the College Senior Behind the Iconic Photo of Wisconsin's Pandemic Election," *Slate*, Apr. 7, 2020, https://slate.com /news-and-politics/2020/04/this-is-ridiculous-wisconsin-election-photo-interview .html.

2. Wisconsin Legislature v. Evers, No. 2020AP608-OA (Wis. Apr. 6, 2020).

3. Republican National Committee v. Democratic National Committee, 140 S. Ct. 1205, 1207 (2020).

4. Chavez v. Brewer, 214 P.3d 397, 408 (Ariz. Ct. App. 2009).

5. Joshua A. Douglas, "The Right to Vote Under State Constitutions," 67 *Vanderbilt Law Review* 89, 91–92 (2014).

6. See, for example, League of Women Voters v. Commonwealth, 178 A.3d 737, 801–02 (Pa. 2018); Harper v. Hall, 868 S.E.2d 499 (N.C. 2022); Weinschenk v. State, 203 S.W.3d 201 (Mo. 2006).

7. U.S. Constitution, Article I, Section 4.

8. U.S. Constitution, Article II, Section 1, Clause 2.

9. Smiley v. Holm, 285 U.S. 355, 369 (1932).

10. Anthony J. Gaughan, "The Influence of Partisanship on Supreme Court Election Law Rulings," 36 *Notre Dame Journal of Law, Ethics & Public Policy* 553, 577, 592–93 (2022).

11. Bush v. Gore, 531 U.S. 98, 113 (2000) (Rehnquist, J., concurring).

12. Arizona State Legislature v. Arizona Independent Redistricting Commission, 576 U.S. 787, 792 (2015).

13. Id. at 792–93.

14. Arizona Constitution, Article XXII, Section 14.

15. *Arizona State Legislature*, 576 U.S. at 817–18.

16. Id. at 825–26 (Roberts, C.J., dissenting).

17. Id. at 825 (Roberts, C.J., dissenting).

18. Rucho v. Common Cause, 139 S. Ct. 2484, 2507 (2019).

19. Democratic National Committee v. Bostelmann, 977 F.3d 639, 655 (7th Cir. 2020) (Rovner, J., dissenting).

20. Id. at 656 (Rovner, J., dissenting).

21. Democratic National Committee v. Wisconsin State Legislature, 141 S. Ct. 28, 29 (2020) (Gorsuch, J., concurring).

22. Moore v. Circosta, 141 S. Ct. 46, 47 (2020) (Gorsuch, J., dissenting).

23. Republican Party of Pennsylvania v. Boockvar, 141 S. Ct. 1, 2 (2020) (statement of Alito, J.).

24. *Harper*, 868 S.E.2d at 508.

25. Id. at 508–09.

26. North Carolina Constitution, Article I, Sections 10, 12, 14, and 19.

27. *Harper*, 868 S.E.2d at 551.

28. Vikram David Amar and Akhil Reed Amar, "Eradicating Bush-League Arguments Root and Branch: The Article II Independent-State-Legislature Notion and Related Rubbish," 2021 *Supreme Court Review* 1, 1–2 (2022).

29. Hannah Schoenbaum, "Republicans Retake Control of North Carolina Supreme Court," Associated Press, Nov. 9, 2022, https://apnews.com/article/north -carolina-state-courts-supreme-court-government-and-politics-17651 7442f012865f93d56e9c2827755.

30. Harper v. Hall, No. 413PA21 (N.C. Feb. 3, 2023).

31. *Harper*, No. 413PA21 (N.C. Feb. 3, 2023) (Earls, J., dissenting).

32. *Harper*, No. 413PA21-2 (N.C. Apr. 28, 2023).

33. *Harper*, No. 413PA21-2 (Earls, J., dissenting).

34. Moore v. Harper, 600 U.S. 1 (2023).

35. Id.

36. Id.

37. Id. (Kavanaugh, J., concurring).

38. Richard. H. Pildes, "The Supreme Court Rejected a Dangerous Elections Theory. But It's Not All Good News," *New York Times*, June 28, 2023, https://www .nytimes.com/2023/06/28/opinion/supreme-court-independent-state-legislature -theory.html.

CONCLUSION

1. Senator Mitch McConnell, "The American People Should Have a Voice in the Selection of the Next Supreme Court Justice," press release, Feb. 22, 2016, https://www.mcconnell.senate.gov/public/index.cfm/pressreleases?ID=A3B740CE -F80C-4842-B656-11A1154B55D0.

2. For an earlier scholarly look at this idea, see Steven G. Calabresi and James Lindgren, "Term Limits for the Supreme Court: Life Tenure Reconsidered," 29 *Harvard Journal of Law & Public Policy* 769 (2006). For a more recent take, see Adam Chilton, Daniel Epps, Kyle Rozemar, and Maya Sen, "Designing Supreme Court Term Limits," 95 S. *California Law Review* 1 (2021).

3. Seth Musket, "Why Political Science Doesn't Like Term Limits," Mischiefs of Faction, Jan. 10, 2021, https://www.mischiefsoffaction.com/post/political -science-term-limits.

4. "Length of Terms of State Supreme Court Justices," Ballotpedia, https:// ballotpedia.org/Length_of_terms_of_state_supreme_court_justices.

5. House of Representatives 8424, 116th Congress (2020), "Supreme Court Term Limits and Regular Appointments Act of 2020"; "Proposals to Modify Supreme Court Justices' Tenure: Legal Considerations," Congressional Research Service, Mar. 24, 2021, https://crsreports.congress.gov/product/pdf/R/R46731.

6. Ganesh Sitaraman and Daniel Epps, "How to Save the Supreme Court," 129 *Yale Law Journal* 148, 174 (2019).

7. Chilton et al., "Designing Supreme Court Term Limits."

8. Tracey E. George and Chris Guthrie, "Remaking the United States Supreme Court in the Courts' of Appeals Image," 58 *Duke Law Journal* 1439, 1468 (2009) (cleaned up).

9. See Sitaraman and Epps, "How to Save the Supreme Court," 181–82.

10. Sitaraman and Epps, "How to Save the Supreme Court," 193.

11. Alexander Hamilton, The Federalist Papers: No. 78, "The Judiciary Department," https://avalon.law.yale.edu/18th_century/fed78.asp.

12. Julie Miller, "'A Republic If You Can Keep It': Elizabeth Willing Powel, Benjamin Franklin, and the James McHenry Journal," *Unfolding History: Manuscripts at the Library of Congress* (blog), Jan. 6, 2022, https://blogs.loc.gov/manuscripts/2022/01/a-republic-if-you-can-keep-it-elizabeth-willing-powel-benjamin-franklin-and-the-james-mchenry-journal.

INDEX

ABOUT THE AUTHOR

Professor Joshua A. Douglas of the University of Kentucky J. David Rosenberg College of Law spends most of his time working with law students, thinking about voting rights, and eating tacos. You can find him attending his daughter's drama performances and Irish dance shows and coaching his son's baseball team. In his "spare" time, he hangs out with his amazing wife, Bari, going to ball games, concerts, and shows and spending time outdoors hiking, kayaking, or skiing. He's the author of *Vote for US: How to Take Back Our Elections and Change the Future of Voting*, which provides hope and inspiration for a positive path forward on voting rights.